Transgressing the Modern

Transgressing the Modern

Explorations in the Western Experience of Otherness

John Jervis

 BLACKWELL *Publishers*

The right of John Jervis to be identified as the author of this work has been asserted in accordance with the Copyright, Designs and Patents Act 1988.

First published 1999

2 4 6 8 10 9 7 5 3 1

Blackwell Publishers Ltd
108 Cowley Road
Oxford OX4 1JF
UK

Blackwell Publishers Inc.
350 Main Street
Malden, Massachusetts 02148
USA

British Library Cataloguing in Publication Data

A CIP catalogue record for this book is available from the British Library.

Library of Congress Cataloging-in-Publication Data

Jervis, John.
   Transgressing the modern : explorations in the western experience of otherness / John Jervis.
      p.   cm.
   Includes index.
   ISBN 0-631-21109-8 (hdbk : alk. paper)
   ISBN 0-631-21110-1 (pbk.)
   1. Clivilization, Western—20th century. 2. Civilization, Western—19th century. 3. Civilization, Modern—20th century. 4. Civilization, Modern—19th century. 5. Difference (Philosophy) 6. Difference (Psychology) 7. Modernism (Art) 8. Modernism (Literature) 9. Modernism (Aesthetics) I. Title.
   CB245.J48 1999
   909′.0981208—dc21   99-22429
                                                                              CIP

Typeset in 10½ on 12½ pt Ehrhardt
by Best-set Typesetter Ltd., Hong Kong
Printed in Great Britain by TJ International, Padstow, Cornwall

This book is printed on acid-free paper.

Contents

Plates

Acknowledgements

I have had help from many sources, but would particularly like to thank Roger Cardinal (for advice on modernism in art), Christine Eagle (for saving me from states of technological distress – and discussing films), Mary Evans (for friendly interest and advice), Jacqui Halson (for support in difficult times), Nicola Kerry (for combining cheerfulness and efficiency) and Claire Norris (for reading most chapters, making invaluable comments – and for tremendous encouragement over a long period). Most of all, I thank Naoko (for being patient, practical and delightful), and the goldfish (for swimming placidly round and round).

Introduction

Aims and General Approach

The evolution of modernity has always involved strategies of exclusion: a lot of the dynamism of modernity, its drive as a form of life, has derived from the ability to image and denigrate what is set up as contrast, even as this contrast is thereby constituted as *internal* to modernity itself, as an image of its own unacceptable face. In this sense, an understanding of modernity is inseparable from an understanding of its 'other side', what is expelled as unacceptable or unthinkable, or reduced to inferior status. The central theme of the book, then, is the relationship of modernity to the exclusions and repressions that thereby become central to the modern sense of identity, even though misrecognized or disavowed, hence producing an 'other' as carrier of pollution, irrationality and danger.

After discussing modernity as a cultural and political project associated with notions of 'progress' and the shaping of body experiences through the 'civilizing' of behaviour, the book seeks to go behind the conventional – and characteristically male-oriented – pieties of the 'rational' technological orientation of modernity to uncover these dimensions of the repressed, distorted and tabooed. And these dimensions – the carnivalesque, the 'primitive', madness, nature, sexuality, aspects of the feminine – are shown to hold a powerful fascination for the modern imagination, and to provide potent resources for transgression, conflict and nostalgia.

The other, then, retains the capacity not just to inspire fear, but to tempt and fascinate. Disgust and desire can be very close. A second theme, therefore, is the emergence of transgression as central to the modern experience of otherness. Transgression entails the exploration of the exclusions and disavowals, the taboos, that both surround and define the modern identity; above all, the experience of the crossing, the violation, of these boundaries. Crucial here is the reality/fantasy boundary, given the essential role it plays in constituting the modern self and its desires. Fantasy is an important mode through which those other possibilities that are disavowed and excluded in the modern project can nevertheless remain important as a source of meaning and experience, and it is through transgression that this otherness can be vicariously explored. This can be seen in the direct products of the imagination itself, enacted – and defined – as art, and through the theatrical dimension of everyday life, in which role-play is incorporated as a strategy of selfhood whereby 'otherness' can be rehearsed as a mode of the self in its encounter with the 'other' strangers encountered in the modern city. These explorations of otherness are in varying degrees transgressive, though their status as vicarious means they occupy an ambivalent relation to social and cultural orthodoxy. Overall, then, the transgression of the precarious boundaries that define the modern identity, the exploration of the taboos that separate 'us' and 'them', the 'normal' and the 'pathological', are revealed to be as central to the modern experience of otherness as the endless attempts to shore up and defend these boundaries.

This initial statement of the aims and themes of the book should also clarify its self-imposed limitations. Not only is the concern exclusively with the modern West – how it has constructed images and stereotypes of otherness, and the cultural practices of incorporation, rejection and transgression, in which these are embedded – but, in addition, no attempt is made to look at these themes from 'other' points of view, or to consider whether, when and how 'the other fights back'. This is a crucial area, but would need another book. Some issues related to this are, however, touched on in the last couple of chapters, in conjunction with discussing contemporary changes, and the possible breakdown of the boundaries that have hitherto been constitutive of the modern project.

This book, then, seeks to uncover these peculiarities of the modern experience in a historically informed way, but is not itself history; the emphasis is on modernity as a 'form of life', on the past as source of the present, the roots of contemporary experience. I have tried to write in a lively and approachable way, but without shirking difficult theoretical issues. Hopefully the book may therefore have some appeal not just to the student or researcher in these fields, but to the adventurous, inquisitive general reader who wants to gain a sense of the connections between what can appear to be confusingly disparate aspects of modern cultural and social life. The aim is to be thought-provoking and thematic, not comprehensive; rather than propose a thorough survey of its subject matter, each chapter highlights certain issues and themes that are particularly central.

The book could be seen as a study in applied cultural theory: its subject matter is social life as culture, as cultural practices. It contains essays on 'modernity in its cultural aspect' rather than 'modernity as product of socio-economic change'. The aim is not to make empirical generalizations, or causal claims, or to write narrative history; rather, it is to explore the range of possibilities opened up by the modern imagination, the patterns that constitute the framework of experience and culture in the modern West. However, it is also important to point out that the book is not about ideas, values and representations in themselves, in their self-sufficiency; it is not intended as an 'idealist' reaction to 'materialism'. It considers such values and representations through their embeddedness in cultural practices.

There is another implication. 'Patterns' are not just matters of conventional or 'official' stereotypes: what we should do, how we should think. As hinted at above, the tabooed and the unstated are as significant as the approved and explicit, the prohibited as much as the prescribed. Indeed, the untypical, the obscure, or the extreme can be just as illuminating as the ordinary, since it is here that the latent possibilities of the everyday world become manifest, thus clarifying the 'normal'. It is as though the normal ultimately becomes a subset of the abnormal, and continuous with it. And we find that, in practice, the patterns can have contradictory implications, manifest in strains and tensions. Abnormalities, extremes, contradictions, tensions: there is indeed a sense in which I want to rescue these, bring them into the open, since not only are they important and significant, but they tend to subvert the rather smug complacency of the 'official' ideologies of modernity, the narratives of progress and rationality.

This book is one of a pair, both originally conceived as a single project, a study of the sociocultural dimensions and dynamics of modernity. The more substantial volume has already been published, as *Exploring the Modern: Patterns of Western Culture and Civilization.* This discusses city life, consumerism, fashion, technology, surveillance and social control, popular culture and the media, and the significance of 'modernism' in culture and the arts, in order to draw out the tensions in our experience and images of 'the modern' that underlie – and frequently undermine – the rational pretensions of the modern ethos and modern self-identity. Both books aim to explore the interrelated dimensions of modernity as project, as experience and as representation – distinctions that are elaborated briefly in the glossary at the end of this volume – in order to contribute to the development of a distinctive approach to the study of these sociocultural aspects of modernity, as suggested above. The books stand on their own, but naturally make reference to each other at times. This book's themes do, after all, inevitably surface in the longer volume. In particular, the reader is referred to chapter 10 of *Exploring the Modern* for a discussion of modernism in the arts that foregrounds a sense of modernism's dual and contradictory engagement with 'otherness': firstly, as a vicarious exploration of 'other' themes suppressed in the wider culture (for example, the Djuna Barnes novel, *Nightwood,* is presented as an essay in the carnivalesque); and, secondly, as a cultural-political programme that engenders its own 'others', thereby limiting its own transgressive pretensions. Also, chapter 7, discussing religion and the sublime, raises further issues connected with the relation between the sacred, taboo and transgression that are discussed in this volume, also in chapter 7. And the conclusion to the former book inevitably draws on themes that have run through both volumes.

Elaboration of Central Themes

Transgressing the modern: to 'transgress', in its origin, is to 'step across', traverse; but of course its key sense is closer to 'trespass', to go beyond prescribed limits, thereby breaking some 'law'. Yet it is central to the argument of this book that a consideration of the patterns and dynamics of Western culture and civilization in recent centuries forces us to be aware of this other aspect of the term: what breaks the law and goes beyond the limits, also runs across, through, within, that which is thereby being limited. The trouble is inside, as much as outside; its existence implicitly questions whether there can be an 'outside'. The transgressive is reflexive, questioning both its own role and that of the culture that has defined it in its otherness. It is not simply a reversal, a mechanical inversion of an existing order it opposes. Transgression, unlike opposition or reversal, involves hybridization, the mixing of categories and the questioning of the boundaries that separate categories. It is not, in itself, subversion; it is not an overt and deliberate challenge to the status quo.[1] What it does do, though, is implicitly interrogate the law, pointing not just to the specific, and frequently arbitrary, mechanisms of power on which it rests – despite its universalizing pretensions – but also to its complicity, its involvement in what it prohibits.

Transgressing the *modern*: to be modern in attitude is to be up to date, contemporary, and this includes an awareness of continuous change and a willingness to undergo it, or adapt to it. One aspect of this is surely a readiness to 'break the law', at least in a broad sense, in which 'the law' defines the established, the conventionally prescribed – precisely what, at any given time, is least 'modern'. And indeed, there is a link here with modern ideologies of individualism, as though self-realization needs transgression to shore up its own self-confidence: how can I be sure of my distinctiveness, with a sense of myself as *different*, unless I affirm this through elements of deviance from the norm? This has contributed to the invention of 'youth' as a period almost of 'licensed' transgression, in which 'getting one's kicks' comes to exist on a knife-edge between the permitted and the proscribed. This self-realization calls on the experience of the limit, demands limits in order to overthrow them, or at least engage in a vicarious experience of them. More generally, a sense in which the modern calls upon the transgressive has been significant both in the attitudes of those who see themselves as most defiantly modern and in those who have theorized about this condition, from Sade through Baudelaire, to Wilde and Nietzsche, and on to Bataille and Foucault. And if the modern is *already* transgressive, how can one 'transgress the modern'?

Clearly the word 'modern', which is inherently problematical, needs more attention here. It is important to realize that in addition to the emphasis on the contemporary, the experience of change in the here and now, there is another, powerful sense of the term. After all, historians may refer to the whole period since the Renaissance as 'the modern age'; and whatever the temporal boundaries of the term, this usage clearly points to the emergence of a distinctive culture and society with a particular orientation to the world. And in this sense, modernity can indeed be seen as a consciousness and way of life that are implicitly (and at times explicitly) set against an unacceptable 'other', thereby unwittingly providing the resources for transgression – for 'transgressing the modern' – that lead us back to the 'other' sense of the modern.

In elaborating this, one can begin by suggesting that the period to concentrate on is surely that from around the mid-eighteenth century, when modern notions of selfhood had become widely established, along with the matrix of 'civil society', and on into the nineteenth century and beyond, with the explosive implications of the technological, industrial and political transformations of the world. Modernity is, after all, 'modern civilization': it presupposes the idea of a 'civilizing process', even though this has not been emphasized in recent debates on modernity as such. Being aware of the link is useful in various ways. It reminds us of the formative significance of what historians call the 'Early Modern', when the folk culture of everyday life was transformed and disciplined, and new body-focused norms of behaviour and taboo evolved, since these provide the raw material out of which modern structures of self and other are constituted, along with the memories, fantasies and cultural forms that would constitute key resources for transgression and would leave their legacy in debates on 'popular culture' even in our own time. The link also serves to focus attention on the way cultural and personal identity involve a necessary emphasis on *embodiment*: the body is a cultural signifier, a potent resource for cultural imagery and social regulation, and modernity has, after all, entailed a distinctive regime of body management.[2] What we encounter, then, is the modern experience of selfhood, self as identity, self as project: the bounded, rational self, 'inside' the body – mysteriously – and somehow both governing it, and threatened by it.

The dimensions of 'purposive' control and 'rationality' in this modern orientation are also important here, reminding us of the significance of the development of the instrumental attitude towards a world seen as essentially predictable and intelligible, an attitude central to the scientific and technological appropriation of the world as 'natural', captured in the idea of a 'project' of modernity. Hence the self, defined through its 'rationality', both as the instrument of its own submission to reason, to 'natural order', and as the means of its transformation of this order, through knowledge, so as to 're-order' it in the light of human aspirations, is threatened by the non-reason of its own impenetrability to its own self-examination, its own inadequacy to its rationalist aspirations, and by its subordination to bodily needs and urges. Thus is constituted the fantasy structure inseparable from the emergence of a bounded self able to imagine difference and otherness, yet only able to explore them legitimately in constrained and limited ways: the space of rational selfhood and the space of its transgressive possibilities, the boundaries that engender self as continuity against the flux of otherness, and also posit, through desire, the irreducible presence of the latter *in* selfhood itself, with all the possibilities this opens up for conflict and contradiction. Otherness is internalized in self-identity *and* projected outwards on to 'others', through disavowal.

It is with the Enlightenment that this structure becomes clearly visible. In effect, Enlightenment transforms 'civilizing' into a project; it is developed as an explicit aim of policy among intellectuals, and thereby comes to have a political dimension, influencing state policy. With it come ideological conflicts over the interpretation of the goals, and an embeddedness of Enlightenment programmes in the political dynamics of state and class power. One can point to the fateful link between rationalism and imperialism here: if I am enlightened, it is my *duty* to enlighten you; Enlightenment becomes a mission, necessarily intolerant of otherness. The characteristic Enlightenment emphasis on universality turns out to be problematic here. However apparently progressive the notion may be, Dorinda Outram points to the issue that this raises: 'As the Enlightenment increasingly grounded "rights" in the possession of humanity, it also became increasingly important to define who and what were human.'[3] Mary Wollstonecraft protested at the time that although reason and virtue were supposed to be universal, the former was denied in its application to women, and the latter was given a loaded, discriminatory interpretation that reduced women's capacity for independent agency.[4] Outram adds that 'Colonialism, the exotic and the exploitation of nature were inextricably linked in the eighteenth century', hence confirming that 'Enlightenment and the control of nature were parts of the same project.'[5]

What we see emerging here is the deep structure of the characteristic modern experience of otherness, in which notions of gender, nature and reason are superimposed and interlocked in powerful ways, via binary distinctions. Thus Val Plumwood points out that 'The civilised/primitive contrast maps all the human/animal, mind/body, reason/nature, freedom/necessity and subject/object contrasts', adding that 'A gendered reason/nature contrast appears as the overarching, most general, basic and connecting form of these dualisms.'[6] The role of nature is intriguing here: an object to dominate and transform, but also a bedrock, a final court of appeal. The powerful endorsement of change by the Enlightenment goes hand in hand with the construction of a notion of 'human nature' as timeless and absolute. Nature is the past, but also the future; something to be used, controlled, but also a potential to be realized. 'The primitive' offers a challenge to be overcome, but also a hope of escape from the artificial and the over-civilized. And women, closer to nature, hence credulous, emotional, could also be 'moral exemplars', carriers of an ethic of family life that could create a society that would be 'natural, polite and modern', as Outram puts it.[7]

We can see here how historicity comes into focus as a key implication of Enlightenment. Romanticism, with its emphasis on the 'alter ego', a hidden or 'unconscious' self, linked to nature and the primitive, contributes powerfully to these post-Enlightenment strands. As rationality, science and 'civilization' came to constitute the legitimizing framework of modern Western values, so ideas of evolution could serve to locate the 'primitive' as the other that is past, yet ever-present, as threat of regression, temptation to nostalgic longings, trigger for disparagement or envy, or resource for critique of the pretensions of the present, yet a critique that presupposes the very terms of its own rebuttal. If the primitive can stand as a reproach to the civilized, the modern, it denounces the latter from the very place to which the latter has consigned it. It denounces in the very language, the vestments, of its oppressor.

Overall, then, the Enlightenment drive to universality both presupposes and generates an 'other', even as the latter is rendered mute or incoherent. Thus Young can argue that 'for two hundred years culture has carried within it an antagonism between culture as a universal and as cultural difference, forming a resistance to Western culture within Western culture itself';[8] it is not, after all, just women who can be defined as the 'other within'. Modern culture thereby acts out tensions that it is itself instrumental in producing. Latour adds that we encounter here a tension between modernity as purification, and modernity as the production of mixtures, hybrids, one tendency feeding endlessly off the other.[9] Change itself involves hybridity, after all, as we have seen, and modern 'progress' can be said to entail a dependence on diffusion and mixing, even as this in turn provokes the homogenizing, purifying drive of the modern project. Possible dynamics of this are pointed to by Stallybrass and White, writing within a framework that emphasizes a 'cultural unconscious', in arguing that 'The very drive to achieve a singularity of collective identity is simultaneously productive of unconscious heterogeneity, with its variety of hybrid figures, competing sovereignties, and exorbitant demands.'[10]

The formal characteristics of otherness ascription can now be given more explicit attention. Most apparent, perhaps, is the fact of dualism itself. In her useful discussion, Plumwood points out that dualism is more than dichotomy, difference or non-identity; it results from 'a certain kind of denied dependency on a subordinated other'. It can be defined as 'a relation of separation and domination inscribed and naturalised in culture and characterised by radical exclusion, distancing and opposition between orders construed as systematically higher and lower', hence presented as timeless and unchangeable. It therefore involves 'a maximisation of non-shared characteristics, whereas to establish ordinary difference or non-identity we require only that a single characteristic be different'.[11] This bears a certain similarity to Derrida's deconstructive critique of the categorial oppositions of Western thought, in which one side emerges as ostensibly original, the other as derivative, deficient.[12] We see, then, that a neutralization or denial of the threat posed by difference to the self-sufficiency and coherence of Western identity results in the transformation of difference into otherness.

There are, in effect, two dimensions or mechanisms of this othering. One is exclusionary, involving distancing: it denies continuities and similarities by postulating an otherness that is as 'other' as possible. A second is incorporative: it colonizes, uses the other, assimilates it, denying it any independent validity, its own voice. These can operate together; indeed, characteristically do so.[13] This, in turn, has consequences for the object of these othering strategies. For a start, there is a process of marginalization: what could be, or had been, central, is shifted to the periphery. Then, we encounter a dualistic splitting, a moral doubling, in effect a division into 'good' and 'bad' objects (noble/ignoble savages; madonna/whore); and in this dualism, observes Hall, 'fear and desire double for one another and play across the structures of otherness, complicating its politics'.[14] From this doubling there results the further possibility of fragmentation: both 'good' and 'bad' aspects can be broken down for ease of rejection or assimilation (as in the case of carnival, discussed in the first chapter). And finally, we encounter the objectification and homogenization of the other, processes that are intimately involved in one of the best-known features of othering discourses, namely the production of stereotypes. These simultaneously generalize, exaggerate and fix certain features of particular individual instances of a category, thereby rendering them necessary, universal and immutable features of the category in question.[15] Consequently, the stereotype 'gives knowledge of difference and simultaneously disavows or masks it', in Bhabha's words.[16] Overall, then, we can say that 'otherness' is the object of power/knowledge/desire as produced through stereotypes, an object that is unified only through the repetition of contradictory attributes and an attitude of ambivalence. It is a fantasy constructed out of difference, where difference becomes absolute and the possibility of dialogue is denied. So the drive to homogenization and control constantly recreates otherness out of difference, the other that must be produced only to be reduced, seduced or destroyed.

Methodologically, it is of course important to bring out the way different forms and contexts of otherness have their own distinctive features. The different chapters aim to show this. The discussion of madness raises the issue of reason and its relation to the irrational and the non-rational; can reason have boundaries? The chapter on other cultures pursues the themes of civilization and origins; the discussion of 'woman' and stereotypes of the feminine asks about the politics of the nature/culture boundary, in its links with gender, and, in particular, the implications of situating the feminine as inside/outside; and the discussion of nature presents it as the 'natural', the (frequently disavowed) ground of culture, providing a powerful resource for ideologies of the social order (and challenges to it). These are, then, variations on a theme, rather than manifestations of a shared essence – the latter would be to unwittingly reproduce the modern way with otherness, not analyse it.

This, indeed, is a constant problem. If, as Levinas claims, the West has always manifested an 'imperialism of the same',[17] how can we avoid perpetuating it even as we seek to understand it? One must remember that the misrecognitions and disavowals affect a culture's self-image, which cannot be taken at face value; Bhabha reminds us that 'Cultures are never unitary in themselves, nor simply dualistic in the relation of Self to Other.'[18] We are constantly forced into a self-questioning, reflexive mode of engagement with this material: can we write *about* – yet, in a sense, *within* – these stereotypes, without perpetuating their hold? On the one hand, discussing them can subtly elide the complexity of the lives, experiences and representations in which they are embedded and over which they exercise their suzereignty, thus inadvertently reinforcing them; yet criticizing them for their 'essentialism' can lead to the other extreme, a multiplicity of images or identities, implicitly denying *any* common features, the fact that the power of the stereotype can be real enough in its effects. For example, it is indeed true that 'woman', as a category of analysis, is very crude, and risks eliding crucial differences of class, gender and race; however, merely *replacing* 'woman' with 'femininities', in the current fashion, isn't the answer. To redeploy the terms, so that 'woman' becomes the 'difference' of femininities, is more promising. One approaches such a term deconstructively, aware of its power, but interrogating its apparent coherence, bringing out its own otherness to itself, transgressing its homogeneity. . . .

Similarly, one must be aware of the dangers of the rationalizing ideologies of modernity at the more programmatic, methodological level; for this reason, among others, I try to avoid what have been influential frameworks in this area, namely functionalism and psychoanalysis, both of which are arguably too uncritically embedded in the ethos of modernity to be adequate for analysing it. Of course, this is not to deny specific insights of these approaches, particularly Lacanian psychoanalysis, and I draw on these where appropriate. In particular, the concept of disavowal, with its source in Freud, proves capable of application beyond its discourse of origin; it serves to capture very well the paradoxical way in which otherness is simultaneously seen and not seen, rejected and yet everpresent. As Hall puts it, 'Disavowal is the strategy by means of which a powerful fascination or desire is both *indulged* and at the same time *denied*. It is where what has been tabooed nevertheless manages to find a displaced form of representation.'[19] It both provides, and is, a kind of shifting, permanent alibi, the everdenied, ever-present other at the heart of the same.

Notes

1   See G. Marcus, *Lipstick Traces: A Secret History of the Twentieth Century* (Secker and Warburg, 1989), for a stimulating essay on the subversion strand.
2   See B. S. Turner, *The Body and Society* (Blackwell, 1984).
3   D. Outram, *The Enlightenment* (Cambridge University Press, 1995), p. 74. See also Z. Bauman, *Legislators and Interpreters* (Polity, 1989), chs. 4–6, 7, for a critique of the Enlightenment; K. Malik, *The Meaning of Race: Race, History and Culture in Western Society* (Macmillan, 1996), ch. 8, for a defence; and my *Exploring the Modern: Patterns of Western Culture and Civilization* (Blackwell, 1998), chs. 2, 9.
4   M. Wollstonecraft, *A Vindication of the Rights of Women* (1792).
5   Outram, *Enlightenment*, p. 63.
6   V. Plumwood, *Feminism and the Mastery of Nature* (Routledge, 1993), pp. 45, 44.
7   Outram, *Enlightenment*, pp. 50, 84.
8   R. J. C. Young, *Colonial Desire: Hybridity in Theory, Culture and Race* (Routledge, 1995), p. 54.
9   B. Latour, *We Have Never Been Modern* (Harvester Wheatsheaf, 1993), especially pp. 10, 11.
10   P. Stallybrass and A. White, *The Politics and Poetics of Transgression* (Methuen, 1986), p. 194.
11   Plumwood, *Feminism*, pp. 41, 47, 59.
12   For a useful overview, see R. Boyne, *Foucault and Derrida: The Other Side of Reason* (Unwin Hyman, 1990).
13   Plumwood, *Feminism*, pp. 48–55, 66.
14   S. Hall, 'The New Ethnicities', in J. Donald and A. Rattansi (eds.) *'Race', Culture and Difference* (Sage, 1992), p. 256.
15   On stereotypes, see S. Hall, 'The Spectacle of the "Other"', in S. Hall (ed.) *Representation: Cultural Representations and Signifying Practices* (Sage, 1997); S. Gilman, *Difference and Pathology: Stereotypes of Sexuality, Race and Madness* (Cornell

University Press, 1985), Introduction; and J. N. Pieterse, *White on Black* (Yale University Press, 1992), ch. 15.

16   H. Bhabha, *The Location of Culture* (Routledge, 1994), p. 78.
17   Cited in Malik, *Meaning of Race*, p. 235.
18   Bhabha, *Location*, pp. 35–6.
19   Hall, 'Spectacle', p. 267.

Part I
The Civilizing Imperative

1 Carnival Pleasures and the Spectre of Misrule

In the foreground of Bruegel's picture (see plate 1), the jolly, rumbustious, corpulent figure of Carnival advances menacingly, astride his wine-barrel horse, to do battle with emaciated Lent. He has saucepans as stirrups, a chicken pie for a hat, and a spit loaded with pork as his lance; a dagger is positioned rather suggestively next to his protuberant genitals. In his person, he already embodies the three great excesses of carnival: food (and drink), sex and violence. He is indulgence personified; the everyday taken to extremes. Yet he also embodies reversals that parody the everyday: one does not get far riding on a wine barrel, after all, nor do saucepans make very good stirrups. Clearly Carnival is also Folly, therefore. In Carnival's procession, and in his half of the picture, everyone is enjoying material pleasures – drinking, dancing, playing music, throwing dice, breaking pots – and nearly everyone is masked, with one or two wearing kitchen utensils as hats. In the centre of the picture, a couple are led into the scene by a fool; the woman's unlit lamp contrasts with the fool's lighted taper, as the couple entrust themselves to the enlightenment of Folly. On the left, in front of the inn, and further back, in front of the corner house, popular masques are being performed; the costumes do not differ significantly from those of the other carnival participants, so one has a sense that these are very much plays within the play, continuous with the other inversions and transformations elsewhere in the tableau.

From this picture, we can certainly see how Burke can define carnival in terms of two key contrasts: with Lent, and with everyday life.[1] Lent herself is attired as a nun, and is thin, severe, censorious. She wards off Carnival's attacks with a frying pan on which two rather miserly herrings are displayed; herrings, along with cod, being particularly humble fish, the appropriate food for Lent. If Carnival represents indulgence, Lent represents abstinence. Lent's entourage behave and dress in a sober manner; people give alms and go to church, and the clergy are conspicuous among them. By the time of the painting – 1559 – the clergy would indeed have been in the forefront of campaigns against carnival, so their strong presence is not surprising. The painter himself, however, does not appear to intervene in favour of one side or the other; it is not a morality tale. He might have agreed with Bristol's view that 'The battle is between two equally "full" and complete images of material life. Communal well-being depends on observing the rhythm of alternation.'[2] Indeed, in the light of this, the clergy's efforts to suppress the folly of carnival could be said to be a manifestation of folly in itself. Life after the Fall, in the interregnum before the Second Coming, is inherently foolish, and the folly of carnival simply highlights this, reminding us of the absurdity of human pretensions. Folly must have its place, and the attempts to suppress it force religion into the absurdities of narrow-minded intolerance. But by Goya's time – his painting (see plate 2) dates from about 1815 – this more repressive attitude has largely won out, at least among the educated classes, and the old pattern has unravelled. . . .

The painting depicts the concluding part of the Madrid carnival celebrations, when a sardine, embodying the spirit of carnival, is buried with full honours; it purports to be both a jest at the expense of death, mocked from behind the safety of the masks and disguises, yet also represents the traditional carnival theme of giving death its due and presenting it as regenerative, another side of life. But something fundamental has changed. This is no sunny scene of innocent merry-making. The sky is largely blue, but darkness pervades the festivities. The two dancers, in their virginal white, are outnumbered by more macabre figures. The painted mask on the black banner presides sardonically, threateningly; death, it seems, has the last laugh. The gestures and dances of the participants seem stilted; they have become puppets. Demonic forces are at large. On the bottom left, one of the masks is that of a dark, ferocious beast; and the figure in black domino, dancing at centre-left, may be indeterminate as to gender and status, but clearly wears a devil's horns, and his mask – with its pointed teeth – is a savage death mask. Indeed, the masks contribute to the vague aura of threat, for the eye sockets are very black, very empty; it is as though the dreadful possibility is being suggested that there might be a void behind, a nothingness.

As usual, Goya tells us more than he knows. He paints as a product of the Enlightenment, dedicated to reform and the destruction of ignorance, tyranny and fear; yet the Enlightenment has come to Spain through foreign conquest, pillage and murder. He defends the *pueblo*, the ordinary people, against the obscenities of Church and State; yet that very *pueblo* persists in its folly, remains wedded to its witchcraft, its obscurantist clericalism, its rejection of Enlightenment.[3] Goya's attitude to the *pueblo*, and to carnival, has therefore become deeply ambivalent; something of the old attraction remains, but tinged with fear, even loathing. The Enlightenment war on folly and the irrationalities of carnival here comes full circle, as the anti-clerical reformers take over the anti-carnival role of the clergy. As 'folly' is sundered from 'real life', being reduced either to the fun and games of children, or to the meaningless negativity of insanity, so life has become separated from the springs of creativity; the *pueblo* now embodies darkness as well as life; with folly and death exiled or repressed, life becomes insane, death triumphs. . . .

We can now see what Bakhtin means when he contrasts the 'folk grotesque' of early modern carnival with the 'romantic grotesque' of eighteenth- and early nineteenth-century attitudes to carnival. Let us first take the mask itself:

> The mask is connected with the joy of change and reincarnation, with gay relativity and with the merry negation of uniformity and similarity. . . . In its Romantic form the mask is torn away from the oneness of the folk carnival concept . . . now the mask hides something, keeps a secret, deceives. . . . The Romantic mask loses almost entirely its regenerating and renewing element and acquires a somber hue. A terrible vacuum, a nothingness lurks behind it.

And more generally, 'All that is ordinary, commonplace, belonging to everyday life, and recognized by all suddenly becomes meaningless, dubious and hostile. Our own world becomes an alien world. Something frightening is revealed in that which was habitual and secure.'[4] The significance of this transition – in attitude and experience – will now have to be explored further.

Carnival and the Carnivalesque

Carnival itself was normally celebrated in the period preceding Lent, and was most widespread in southern Europe. It was frequently inaugurated by ringing the bells at the wrong time, or changing the hands of the clock. It seems to have had a new lease of life in the early modern period, from the fourteenth to the early seventeenth centuries, and much of our information dates from this time. It is important to add that, in addition to carnival itself, the whole of the period between the fixed dates of the Christmas festivities and the movable date of Easter held a range of saints' days, rituals, feasts and celebrations, many of which had markedly carnivalesque aspects. In the British context, Phythian-Adams has suggested that the period between Christmas and midsummer can be seen as the 'ritual' half of the year, contrasting with the priorities given to the economic necessities of life in the other half.[5]

This oscillation, this dualism of everyday life versus ritual, is significant for what it tells us about the central significance given to the cyclical, repetitive structure of time, contrasting as it does with the modern priority of linear time. Or else we can say that carnival was in a real sense an anti-time, outside time, when inversion and paradox held sway, when identical past and future were lived in a present which was thereby alien to itself. When carnival was presented as Cockaigne, a land of everlasting plenty, flowing with milk and honey, where food comes effortlessly, and roast pigs run around with knives stuck conveniently in their backs, these images do not serve as a stimulus to some utopian political goal in the future, nor are they nostalgia for a past forever lost. Rather, they reflect a reality which is cyclical in its very essence, oscillating between presents that are ever-recurrent. Peacock writes that this world-view 'nourishes and is nourished by symbols of reversal; the instrumental world view, which emphasizes the sequential harnessing of means to an end, threatens and is threatened by such symbols'.[6]

In being opposed to the everyday, routine world, carnival involved celebrations of communality in which people participated as equals. The normal hierarchical and social divisions were suspended; the exotic dress, outrageous behaviour, masks and acting all served to mark the contrast. We must remember here that carnival and the carnivalesque must be distinguished from the feasts and ritual processions that served to manifest this everyday social order. As Bristol puts it, 'Social structure is made visible by allegorical representation', and in the medieval cosmos,

> The social structure is itself a kind of allegory, in that its order is also a sign of other, larger orders that form a chain of significance leading to that which does not signify – the divine Logos. The majesty of the prince, his or her appearance in ceremonial processions, discloses a hidden coordination and sympathy between the temporal order maintained by constituted authority and the providentially ordered domains of nature and history.[7]

This living allegory was powerfully displayed, for example, in the Corpus Christi procession in early modern Coventry: when the masters and journeymen annually processed in their respective companies at Corpus Christi-tide and on the eves of Midsummer and St Peter, 'the community in its entirety was literally defining itself for all to see'.[8] And such a procession might well have culminated in the kind of 'official' feast that Bakhtin describes, celebrating the existing hierarchy.

Much of the raw material for the carnivalesque imagination was provided by such allegories of the social, for the symbols embodied therein are endlessly available for reinterpretation, ridicule and parody. Any saucepan can now be a crown, and a crown is now revealed to be merely a funny hat. In place of a king, we find the so-called Lord or Abbot of Misrule, the leader of what were frequently youth groups who were important in organizing processions, competitions, and so on. Misrule himself might be a clown, or accompanied by jesters; in short, he was 'immersed in the folly he undertakes to regulate', as Bristol puts it. Through ridiculing and relativizing the symbols of power, Misrule thereby revealed that 'folly and transgression are the covert reality of rational government'.[9] Similarly with carnival feasting:

> As opposed to the official feast, one might say that carnival celebrated temporary liberation from the prevailing truth and the established order: it marked the suspension of all hierarchical rank, privileges, norms and prohibitions. Carnival was the true feast of time, the feast of becoming, change and renewal.[10]

Other examples of the carnivalesque help to reveal the presence of systematic inversions of the social order. This is the theme of the 'world turned upside down', or world reversal. A carnival procession might include people standing on their heads, a horse going backwards with its rider facing the tail, men dressed as women, and women dressed as men. Pictures and banners might depict the fish eating the fisherman, the son beating his father, the husband serving as house-maid to his wife, the laity preaching to the clergy. The Festivals of Fools exemplified many such inversions, as can be seen in an account of one such fes-tival, the Feast of the Circumcision, where 'the churchmen appeared at mass, some in female attire, some dressed as clowns or street performers, others with their capes and cassocks inside out, and almost all wearing grotesque false faces'.[11] After engaging in dice playing and singing wanton songs, they proceeded to ride around town in a dungcart, scattering dung over the passers-by. . . . And at the Feast of the Ass – which purported to mark the flight of Mary and Joseph to Egypt on an ass – the mock cleric would conduct the service by braying all the time, and the congregation would reply in kind, when responses were called for, duly finding themselves cursed instead of blessed at the end of the service. Thus was folly revealed at the very heart of religion.

Not surprisingly, elements of anti-clericalism can easily be present on such occasions; gender inversions and parody have also been hinted at. Stallybrass points out that both elements can be found in the older Robin Hood tales.[12] Not only does Robin consort with Friar Tuck, a typical corpulent carnival cleric, but Maid Marian herself is a typical May Day heroine who – before being made respectable in later versions – is presented as a buxom, earthy wench, exchang-ing lewd jokes with the aforementioned friar. Traditionally, May was thought to be the month when women were particularly powerful, getting a bit above their proper station: a May wife would rule over her husband. On Hock Tuesday, a widespread custom was for women to tie up their menfolk and only release them for a ransom; a practice much attacked by the Church, who saw it as leading to vice. A bishop of Reading condemned 'bindings and, alas, even more wicked doings' by those 'pretending the profit of the church, but getting themselves only damnation'. It is also intriguing that men engaging in deviant *political* activities might dress up as women; there are many examples of riots being led by men thus attired, such as the Skimmington riots in 1641, led by 'Lady Skimmington', and, in the early nineteenth century, the Luddite riots against the use of new technol-ogy, led by 'General Ludd's wives'.[13] Clearly the symbolism of reversal has wide-spread ramifications.

The element of humour in all this is worth further comment. Humour exposes the pomposity, the pretensions, the arbitrary nature of the given order; it involves unexpected juxtapositions and category transgressions; it makes adaptability and creativity possible; it is parodic and reflexive. But while it manifests all these aspects, humour in its carnivalesque mode is above all collective and affirmative, celebratory. Bakhtin goes so far as to suggest that laughter is the sole force that cannot be fully incorporated and controlled. Certainly there is a long tradition of dislike of humour within Christianity; one church father is quoted as saying that laughter is a gift not from God, but from the devil. The Russian critic Herzen writes:

Laughter contains something revolutionary. . . . Laughter is no joking matter, and we shall not give up our right to it. . . . *Only equals may laugh*. If inferiors are permitted to laugh in front of their superiors . . . this would mean farewell to respect.[14]

In subverting seriousness, laughter is a serious business; and this is because of the element of ridicule, with its potentially subversive dimension. Those with status and self-importance are most open to ridicule. Nevertheless, we must avoid an easy romanticism here: difference, as such, also opens us to ridicule; victims of carnivalesque humour were not only the powerful, but outsiders and 'deviants' as well, although this was more likely to occur in rituals and festivals other than carnival itself.

Overall, then, the carnivalesque is a central strand of peasant culture, or a kind of parallel culture, which contrasts both with ordinary everyday culture, and with the 'high' culture of the literate and ruling classes. Bakhtin summarizes this aptly:

A boundless world of humorous forms and manifestations opposed the official and serious tone of medieval ecclesiastical and feudal culture. In spite of their variety, folk festivities of the carnival type, the comic rites and cults, the clowns and fools, giants, dwarfs and jugglers, the vast and manifold literature of parody – all of these forms have one style in common: they belong to one culture of folk carnival humour.[15]

The 'Grotesque Body'

During Kett's Rebellion, in 1549, the sources inform us that the city of Norwich fell to the rebels because the defending archers were put out by the antics and obscene gestures of 'vagabond boyes', who 'bear arssyde came emong the thickett of the arrows . . . and did therewith most shamefully turne up theyr bare tayles agenst those which did shoote, which soe dysmayd the archers that it tooke theyr hart from them'.[16] This display of bare behinds subordinated top to bottom, respect to rudeness, age to youth, decorum to dirt, all in a context of political insurrection. An apparently similar episode from more recent times is described by Ruthven. In 1984, during the campaign by the women encamped at Greenham Common in protest against the US Air Force base and the nuclear weapons stationed there, soldiers leaving the base in a coach exposed their backsides to the women 'in a gesture that had clearly been rehearsed with parade-ground precision'.[17] In a sense, this is an inversion of the previous episode, since here we have the powerful gesturing at the powerless; nevertheless, what both episodes clearly show is the symbolic significance of the lower half of the body, and this is a crucial theme in carnival and the carnivalesque.

When Camporesi describes early modern popular culture as a 'corporeal culture',[18] it is not difficult to see what he means. A central strand in carnivalesque imagery and activity seems to have been the celebration of the body in all its messy materiality: eating, drinking, copulating, defecating, procreating, dying. . . . Normally, such activities are surrounded by restrictions and taboos, but in carnival these are swept away, not only in the language and imagery, with its rich vein of obscenity and verbal abuse, but often in behaviour as well, with 'gargantuan' feasting, and sexual licence. This is what Bakhtin calls the 'grotesque realism' of carnival. The body comes to be the central carnival image; it is a symbol of 'the people', i.e. of the *social* body. Hence the physical body is characterized as huge, ever-growing, ever-renewed, just like society itself. Thus Bakhtin writes:

> In grotesque realism, therefore, the bodily element is deeply positive. It is presented not in a private, egotistic form, severed from the other spheres of life, but as something universal, representing all the people . . . the material bodily principle is contained not in the biological individual, not in the bourgeois ego, but in the people, a people who are continually growing and renewed.[19]

So this is not the privatized, individual body, but the 'grotesque' body, simultaneously communal and material, representing the base, physical reality of life, death and renewal. It is not separate from the rest of the world, but part of it. The grotesque body transgresses its own limits, is excessive in its very nature: it is dirty, uncontrolled, extended, protruding, incomplete, ugly; its apertures are open, and become points of disorder and interchange, so that its bodily secretions link it to other bodies and to the physical processes of decline and rebirth; it is regenerative, but also devouring, destructive. It is therefore opposed to what has been called the 'classical' body, the body of modernity: static, closed, sleek, well-bounded, individual, decorous, attempting to approach ideals of beauty.

Here again we encounter the satirical element; for the grotesque body and its earthy doings are set up in contrast to the spirituality, prudishness and conservatism of 'high' culture. Hence the latter is *degraded*. But this term can be seen to have a more precise meaning now. To 'degrade' high culture is to 'bring it down to earth', into contact with the *real* source of power and fertility: the body, in all its gross physicality. All that is high has to be brought low; life has to become death; but this, argues Bakhtin, is all part of the cycle of renewal:

> Degradation here means coming down to earth, the contact with earth as an element that swallows up and gives birth at the same time. To degrade is to bury, to sow, and to kill simultaneously, in order to bring forth something more and better. To degrade also means to concern oneself with the lower stratum of the body, the life of the belly and the reproductive organs; it therefore relates to acts of defecation and copulation, conception, pregnancy and birth. Degradation digs a bodily grave for a new birth.[20]

This link between birth and death is very significant; in the carnivalesque, these are not separated in space and time, essentially unconnected. Rather, they are aspects of the body itself, inseparable dimensions of existence. Bakhtin refers to terracotta figurines of laughing old hags, who represent 'pregnant death, a death that gives birth'. Sexuality, fertility and birth are not opposed to decay and death, but rely on them; again we see the cyclical model of cosmic process, in which death is simultaneously rebirth. Later, with the modern specialized body, regeneration will become childbirth and death will become finality, extinction; the links will be sundered. 'Death is only death, it never coincides with birth.'[21]

Since the grotesque includes the excessive, the ever-growing, it clearly includes the gigantic. Giant figures seem to have been frequent participants in carnival processions and feasts, and myths about giants are common. Stewart suggests that 'The gigantic appeared as a symbol of surplus and licentiousness, of overabundance and unlimited consumption', and she adds that 'Fantasy in the gigantic exteriorizes and communalizes.'[22] The giant is not only a figure on the boundary between the human and the natural, having something of the monstrous about him, but also brings this sense of natural plenitude, disproportion and uncontrollable vastness into the very centre of human culture, the town or city. Thus we find giants in nature (the Giant's Causeway), but also giants as points of origin, founders of human communities (Gog, Magog and the City of London).

Here we can introduce François Rabelais (1495–1553), whose *Gargantua and Pantagruel*, a sprawling tale of giants, is widely regarded as the greatest bawdy novel of all, and is used extensively in Bakhtin's fascinating book as a source of carnivalesque themes and imagery, particularly in its emphasis on the grossness of the body. The giant Gargantua is, it seems, the founder of Paris: he drowns most of the inhabitants of the preceding settlement in urine, and the survivors, exclaiming that they have been drenched '*par ris*' ('in a jest'), thus rename the rebuilt city. . . . Gargantua himself had been born at a feast held to consume an overabundance of tripe. Tripe – the stomach lining of a cow – is itself the means of consumption, and its becoming the object of consumption makes it an appropriate symbol of carnival's self-consuming self-sufficiency, its embodiment of a consumption that is simultaneously its own death and reproduction. It is appropriate that in this case the process leads to the birth of the ultimate symbol of excess and consumption, a giant. Gargantua's mother, Pantagruel, eats so much tripe that her 'fundament' falls out; a midwife stops up her bottom, and Gargantua triumphantly arrives through his mother's ear, crying 'drink, drink'. The ear, it should be noted, was discussed in medieval theological circles as a possible site through which the Virgin Mary might have been impregnated; so we find here a sort of monstrous parody of the Virgin Birth. . . .

Folk culture, then, uses laughter, earthy humour, and the language of the grotesque body to ridicule and devour the aspirations of 'high' culture and absorb it into its own powerful, regenerative sense of growth and boundless renewal.

The 'Battle for Popular Culture'

There is considerable evidence that carnival and similar festivals were regarded differently by the ruling classes and the general populace; the former saw a danger of subversion, the latter saw a welcome relief from the normal restrictions of everyday life and social hierarchy. If ruling groups saw any virtue in carnival, it was as a warning of the impossibility of any fundamental change in the social order: the *symbolic* inversion revealed the absurdity of a *real* one. As such, carnival could be a safety valve; and Burke quotes clerics defending a Feast of Fools in the fifteenth century on precisely these grounds.[23] One problem with this approach – whether adopted by fifteenth-century clerics or twentieth-century anthropologists – is that carnival seems, not infrequently, to have been both more actively unruly than the approach would imply, and less likely to be readily tolerated by ruling groups.

Overall, then, carnival seems to have had an uncertain status: halfway between licensed and unlicensed licence, poised uneasily between celebration and subversion. Kett's Rebellion, mentioned above, seems to have originated in festivities that went too far; 'too far' from the point of view of the authorities, that is. Carnival elements seem to have been present throughout. A well-documented case is that of an episode in a French town, Romans, in 1579–80. Carnival preparations took place against a background of peasant insurrection in the countryside. The usual processions, feasts, and so on, enabled the artisans to 'act out their revolt in the streets of the city', as the historian of these events, Le Roy Ladurie, puts it, with deliberate ambiguity. But there was nothing ambiguous about the response: after a masked ball, a secretly gathered army of the local notables turned on the artisan and peasant quarters and massacred the leaders and many of the followers. Le Roy Ladurie comments: 'Everything was set right side up again; the dominant classes, for a moment topsy-turvy, landed back on their feet.' The *fear* of subversion, by those who have most to lose, is always there, and can be used to justify repression; and it is certainly true that genuinely *popular* movements often have carnivalesque aspects to them. There are many later examples, up to and including the events in Paris in May 1968, and in Prague in November 1989.[24]

This, then, is the background to the so-called 'battle for popular culture'. In 1500, as Burke observes, it would still be true to say that rulers and ruled shared many elements of the same culture, even though they might react to these elements differently, as illustrated above. By 1800, that was no longer true: the clergy, nobility, and professional and business classes had withdrawn from 'popular culture' and had abandoned it to the lower classes, when they hadn't tried to suppress it altogether.[25] The very term 'the people' had come to mean 'the common people', with connotations of backwardness, and a hint of danger. This transition did not come about in any simple, linear way, and gives interesting clues to the significance of carnival.

Initially, carnival seems both to have been given a fillip by the Reformation, and to have played an active role in spreading it. The episode in 1520 when Luther burnt the papal bull excommunicating him – an episode often taken to mark the real beginning of the Reformation – was followed by an impromptu carnival procession through the streets, with an imitation pope, who was mocked and ridiculed by everyone.[26] The fact remains that Protestantism would soon turn against carnival. The Protestant onslaught against ritual – as in the abolition of Lent itself – would ultimately herald the end of carnival as a significant social form;

Protestantism entailed an austere ethic and practice of daily life that made carnival seem unruly, blasphemous, gross and indecorous.

A similar process can be traced in the decline of clowns, fools and jesters. For a while, they enjoyed a new lease of life; in mocking outdated feudal orthodoxies, they could act as heralds of the new order. But then, increasingly, they were swept away; their disruptive ridicule no longer suited the more sober climate of religious reform and earnest acquisitiveness. Overall, then, we find that under the pretext of 'reforming' popular culture, the authorities moved increasingly to proscribe, suppress and regulate it. However, there could also be elements of appropriation. An example would be May Day and village sports, which were separated from their more unruly elements and made 'respectable'. This process of incorporation was simultaneously one of fragmentation and marginalization, therefore.

We can also see these processes at work in the case of giants. Stewart suggests that while giants as exemplifications of the 'grotesque body' became increasingly unacceptable, violating the new norms of physical restraint and decorum, giants retained a role in processions, as the latter became rationalized into 'parades', manifestations of civic pride and political order.[27] Later, in the eighteenth century, a positive residue of the old sense of the gigantic had been developed into the Romantic notion of the sublime: nature as an awesome presence, gigantic in its transcendence and spiritual power. Conversely, the negative image of the giant – the giant as grotesque – is already present in *Gulliver's Travels*, where Swift presents giants as horrifying and disgusting. By the nineteenth century, we find the construction of the giant as 'freak', along with other manifestations of physical 'imperfection', reaching its culmination in Victorian freak shows and the public exhibition of the so-called 'Elephant Man'. No longer a resource for celebration, the 'grotesque body' has been reconstructed as merely an object of ridicule, though an ambivalent fascination characteristically remains. This is illustrated in Fiske's portrayal of wrestling and the physique of wrestlers as the 'grotesque realism of the ugly body',[28] and Schulze's suggestion that the image of female bodybuilders as intriguing but repulsive testifies to the way 'The deliberately muscular woman disturbs dominant notions of sex, gender, and sexuality.'[29]

These processes of repression and appropriation do not occur uniformly, however. As late as the 1830s and 1840s, many carnivals had escaped the earlier waves of bans and proscriptions. Green makes it clear that Parisian carnival in these decades retained many of the old features: 'This was the last, exuberant fling of a pre-industrial theatre of excess.' At Mardi Gras in 1836, half the population of Paris was said to be out dancing at the public and private balls that filled the city, and masked disguises permitted the usual social boundaries to be transgressed. However, the form of 'these promiscuous mixings and reversals – the irresponsibility of aristocrats, the sudden transgressions around femininity – was deeply threatening to the world-view of metropolitanism'.[30] Consequently, it too succumbed to the processes whereby, as Stallybrass and White argue, 'a fundamental ritual order of western culture came under attack – its fasting, violence, drinking, processions, fairs, wakes, rowdy spectacle and outrageous clamour were subject to surveillance and repressive control'.[31] By the 1860s, carnival was largely overthrown; banned or transformed into civic parades or trade fairs, the paraphernalia of spectacle. With the Enlightenment and the 'civilizing process', it had come to be seen as unruly, and incompatible with the norms of civilized behaviour, decency, respectability, and a coherent sense of self-identity. It had, apparently, become little more than a memory – but a deeply troubling one.

In the end, of course, these processes of marginalization, fragmentation and incorporation can result in carnivalesque elements occurring almost anywhere. They can be encountered as liminal zones – places of pleasure, temptation and danger – but always promising more than they can deliver. The holiday itself fits in here, and Shields gives an account of the history of Brighton beach in these terms, as a site of leisure but also of controversy and trouble (dirty weekends, Bank Holiday riots), not to mention displays of the grotesque body (celebrated in the 'saucy postcard').[32] In his discussion, Bennett points out that these beaches miss the crucial 'discrowning' aspect of carnival, the directly subversive celebration of the reversal of political and social power. The pleasure beach remains paradoxical, then: 'a site to be transgressed but one which, to a degree, invites – even incites – its own transgression'.[33] And of course present-day carnivals are generally revivals or recreations, generally having more to do with consumerism, the leisure industry and tourism than anything else.

Featherstone sees the overall significance of these developments as follows:

> The grotesque body and the carnival represent the otherness which is excluded from the process of the formation of middle-class identity and culture. . . . In effect the other which is excluded as part of the identity formation process becomes the object of desire.[34]

So the 'battle for popular culture' becomes a battle for the identity of the modern self, a battle *within* the self. Using Freud's case notes on his patients, treated in the closing years of the nineteenth century, Stallybrass and White observe that 'It is striking how the broken fragments of carnival, terrifying and disconnected, glide through the discourse of the hysteric', so it can be said that 'Hysterics privately enact the battle between Carnival and Lent.'[35] One aspect of this is elaborated by Wills as follows:

> Just as the hysteric seems to 'store' the misplaced carnival content, representing the past in the present, so . . . this cyclical return to the past mirrors the relation to the past which Bakhtin takes as the mark of carnival: in opposition to the 'official' time, which presents a linear and hierarchical teleology of events, carnivalesque time is aware of 'timeliness' and crisis in the version of history which it presents.[36]

Hysterical symptoms are a kind of eternal return of the repressed, but in ever-renewed and shifting form. So although, on the face of it, the hysteric is at the mercy of these 'symptoms' – they are individual and pathological, rather than collective and celebratory – they could also be seen as a disguised commentary on conventional stereotypes, even embodying resistance. Thus Heath suggests that

> hysteria is a disorder which proves the law of sexual identity, the given order; hysteria is a protest against the oppression of that law of sexual identity, that given order, painfully envisaging in its disorder . . . a quite different representation of men and women and the sexual.

Hence the hysteric is 'entering a protest, but unheard',[37] a view expressed more lyrically by Helene Cixous, when she praises those 'wonderful hysterics' who bombarded Freud with their 'carnal passionate body-words', haunting him with their 'inaudible thundering denunciations'.[38]

The work of Cixous is itself an interesting example of a recent appropriation of carnival by some strands of feminist thought. If hysteria is a disguised protest against the conditions that make it possible, taking the feminine stereotypes to the point where they become parody, then feminist appropriations of hysteria enter a protest against its very control and assimilation by the forces of order, and feminism itself becomes an attempt to 'speak' the language of the hysteric in the public sphere; if hysteria is a kind of desperate, privatized carnivalesque, its recuperation within feminism is an attempt to carnivalize the public spaces of politics, gender discourse and writing. This strategy remembers the explorations by Davis of the significance of gender inversion and images of the 'unruly woman' in early modern carnival, and her claim that 'the image of the disorderly woman did not always function to keep women in their place', as it could 'sanction riot and political disobedience for both men and women'.[39] And the *écriture féminine* of Cixous herself appears as a transgressive disruption of received stereotypes of the independence of 'writing', the separation of discourse from body. 'Woman must write her body, become the unimpeded tongue that bursts partitions, classes and rhetorics, orders and codes':[40] a return of the overflowing, unbounded 'grotesque body'?

This raises issues about carnival and representation that require further discussion; but enough has been said to suggest that however thorough the suppression and incorporation of carnival, ideas of the carnivalesque retain a power to fascinate and disturb.

Carnival, Representation, Spectacle

As carnival withdraws from the world of social life, it enters the cultural world of the imagination, becoming significant in narrative and fantasy, in theatre and novel, and the arts generally. As Barbara Babcock puts it, 'what is socially peripheral is often symbolically central'.[41] Within the social world, the domesticated remnants of it also become a resource for the consumer spectacle, and these twin differentiations – into representation and spectacle – are hardly unconnected. In order to explore this, it is useful to start from that intriguing phenomenon of eighteenth-century London life, the masquerade, or masked ball.

At these balls, which were very popular between the 1720s and the 1780s, the usual carnivalesque elements would be found: eating, drinking, dancing, gaming, all to excess, along with frequently spectacular costumes that might well involve cross-dressing. There was a conspicuous mixing of the classes, men and women of all ranks, since although tickets had to be bought, they seem to have been both cheap and widely available. The general significance of the 'whirling, saturnalian scene' at these masquerades is conveyed by Castle:

> It served as a kind of exemplary disorder. Its hallucinatory reversals were both a voluptuous release from ordinary cultural prescriptions and a stylized comment upon them. . . . On the individual level the conventional alienation between self and other was phantasmagorically overcome. Masquerade disguise affirmed the appropriability of the shape, the very body, of the other: biological separateness itself was ritually revoked . . . counterposed institutions everywhere collapsed into one another, as did ideological categories: masculinity into femininity, 'Englishness' into exoticism, humanity into bestiality.[42]

As with carnival itself, all this was seen as controversial; masquerade may at times have been very fashionable, but it was always being denounced. The masquerade masqueraded, it was said; it purported to be about innocent pleasure, but was really about vice, and was a danger to decency. We are told of an unfortunate gentleman who 'debauch'd his own Daughter' by mistake, and died of shame as a result. The mixing of categories was unacceptably 'promiscuous', and would lead to promiscuity itself, thus being doubly dangerous. Castle writes:

> That world view typical of the anti-masquerade authors, characterized everywhere by a fear of ontological promiscuity and a desire for firm conceptual boundaries, was itself distinctly modern, and becoming increasingly pervasive in the eighteenth century. In effect, the anti-masquerade writers celebrated a world made up of discrete forms, of rigid categories and hygienically polarized opposites. They celebrated, in a word, the world of rationalism.

Indeed, 'The masquerade seemed the triumph of unreason itself.'[43]

Although masquerade was carnivalesque, it is important to point out that it was *not* carnival. Bakhtin claims that carnival does not acknowledge any distinction between actors and spectators: 'Carnival is not a spectacle seen by the people; they live in it. . . . While carnival lasts, there is no other life outside it.'[44] A spectacle, then, implies a distinction between participant and audience; and it is clear that masquerade was a spectacle that people could and did watch. It was well on the way to becoming a category of entertainment, pointing forward to a culture of mass leisure; although the full development of the spectacle awaits the construction of the mass 'public' in the second half of the nineteenth century, the germs are there.

This very distance established by the spectacle – between observing and participating – is significant for the cultural fate of carnival, its possibilities as representation. Castle points out that masquerade becomes an event in the novels of the period; heroes and heroines in Fielding, Defoe and Richardson frequently pass through a masquerade episode, and although masquerade is ostensibly presented in an unfavourable light, actually it has a beneficial impact on those who experience it. Hence 'The pleasurable consequences of masquerade negate its superficial textual inscription as an emblem of vice', as Castle concludes.[45] The didactic, allegorical structure of the novels is disrupted by the masquerade scenes, which thereby question the clarity of the categories of social and moral identity.

Yet perhaps it is the very fact of authorship that needs elaboration here. Carnival, unlike the novel, has no author; nor does 'folk' culture generally, which is fundamentally anonymous. 'Authorship', after all, rests on the notion of the named, separate individual as a creative force, rather than the regenerative power of the 'social body', celebrated in carnival; authorship, then, becomes possible only as carnival and popular culture are marginalized and fragmented. Jefferson outlines the view that 'authoring is by its very nature a decarnivalising activity', since 'the authorial perspective and the demarcations between observer and participants are against the whole spirit of carnival'.[46]

Nevertheless, there is an element of continuity. If there is a sense in which carnival – and carnivalesque figures such as fools and clowns – can be said to 'stand outside' everyday life, offering a frequently ironic commentary on it, so, to an extent, does the novelist. Hence LaCapra's suggestion that 'The clown, the rogue and the fool are the envoys of carnival in everyday life, and the novelist dons their masks in modern society.'[47] The novelist wears a mask to view life, and thereby makes it 'public'. Masks, after all, destabilize fixed identities: for Bakhtin, masks reveal 'noncoincidence with themselves and with any given situation' and show how a person has 'the right not to be taken literally, not to "be himself"'.[48] The novelistic mask therefore permits different identities to be revealed, explored and given voice; and this seems close to Salman Rushdie's view that the novel has always been about 'the way in which different languages, values and narratives quarrel, and about the shifting relations between them', and is the one place where 'we can hear voices talking about everything in every possible way'.[49]

Yet, the distance remains, the sense in which novelistic and authorial *appropriations* of carnival and carnival roles are not themselves *instances* of carnival. Carnival thereby disappears into representation. The distance, the gap, is usefully defined by Kinser: ' "High" art . . . breaks the circuit between living and thinking, experiencing and reflecting, presenting and representing. "Low" art maintains the continuity.'[50]

Carnival itself makes modern representation possible: in breaking the hold of allegory, revealing the symbol as arbitrary sign, carnival frees objects from the power of a hidden meaning, and makes them available as resources for art and literature. A crown is but a hat, and can be painted or described in its very objecthood, without symbolic load, without mystique. A world no longer allegorical is available for representation. Yet in making representation possible, carnival does not permit of its own representation; the banners and displays, the masques and plays, are not so much representations *of* it as acts that take place *within* it. As a depiction of carnival, Bruegel's painting already testifies to a distance being established – the gap that makes representation possible. 'Carnival is a process, representation makes a product', as Jefferson remarks.[51] One might say, then, that carnival *as* representation – in film, for example – necessarily promises a transgression it cannot perform.[52] Carnival, as process, subverts the boundary between observer and participant; carnival as representation relies on this boundary. As process, it also, of course, subverts boundaries between bodies; the grotesque body is, among its other characteristics, the body that overflows its boundaries, the body that defies representation. It is the *classical* body that becomes the 'body of representation'. Carnival is too ill-defined, formless, for representation, or is excessive to it, overflowing it; it represents the unthinkable possibility of unrepresentability.

Within art, Goya's painting could itself be said to represent the point where the death of carnival meets the lethal birth of representation. With Goya, the masks of death represent the death that is implicit in representation: the figures transfixed in a frenzied stillness, the object murdered in the image.

The 'Second Life'

What, then, is the overall significance of carnival? Davis claims that 'Misrule always implies the Rule that it parodies.'[53] This is in need of further interpretation. Is carnival a reversal of everyday categories, a mirror-opposite? Inverting the categories of the game does not challenge the game itself. Or is it a reflexive move, a comment on the categories, sliding into parody and ridicule? It would thereby question the game, not be just a move within it. Or is it a state of confusion, where the categories are mixed up, the boundaries blurred, showing how 'contrasts dissolve at the point of origin', as Duerr writes?[54]

Each possibility seems to correspond to a real aspect of carnival. For example, the costumes in masquerade seem to have been of two kinds, corresponding to the first and third of the possibilities raised above: costumes which enabled one to impersonate a being in some sense 'opposite' oneself; and 'domino', a dark, hooded cloak representing an 'enigmatic uniformity', which in turn could be seen to entail both the possibility of taking on *any* form, and 'the erasure or voiding of all form'.[55] In practice, all three aspects are characteristically present; and all operate together to raise the disturbing questions that seem to be inherent in the promise – and the danger – of carnival.

There may be a sense in which it is the third aspect that is most disturbing, pointing as it does to possibilities lying beyond the present order altogether, indeed questioning 'order' itself, and suggesting the creative power of disorder ('dis-order'). It seems to be this that Stallybrass and White refer to as 'hybridization or inmixing, in which self and other become enmeshed in an inclusive, heterogeneous, dangerously unstable zone', and which 'generates the possibility of shifting *the very terms of the system itself*'.[56] And it also seems to correspond to Bristol's use of the term 'travesty':

> In the pageantry of popular festivals, no fixed order may be set forth, because travesty subverts the possibility of orderly setting forth through the monstrous

proliferation of differences and identities. . . . Identity is made questionable by mixing of attributes. . . . Guise, that is, the customary, appropriate garb or social integument, is permitted to mingle with *dis*guise and the will to deception.

To 'travesty' something is therefore to mock it, show it to be other than what it purports to be, or perhaps other *in* what it purports to be, and to suggest 'other' possibilities that move beyond it. Bristol concludes that 'Travesty, the comprehensive transgression of signs and symbols, is a general "refusal of identity"',[57] and this seems to be close to Bakhtin's claim that carnival identities embody 'the right to be "other" in this world, the right not to make common cause with any single one of the existing categories that life makes available'.[58] And it is this very confusion and ambiguity of carnival, its apparent potential for 'chaos', that makes it so incompatible with the tightly ordered and specialized world of the division of labour, the Enlightenment, and modernity as project.

When Bakhtin states that 'Carnival . . . is life itself, but shaped according to a certain pattern of play', and that 'Carnival is the people's second life',[59] we can begin to see what he means. If carnival *is* life, a sort of double or shadow of life, life's 'other side', as it were, then one can hardly treat it as something separate, performing a function *in* life. It mocks the very idea of 'function', the idea that everything in life should have a purpose, the utilitarian rationalism that can so easily mask power and hierarchy. (And it mocks, in advance, theoretical and political interpretations of its 'function'.) If we recall the claim, cited by Burke, that people lived their lives 'in remembrance of one festival and in expectation of the next',[60] we might almost say that everyday life existed to serve carnival, rather than vice versa; but the real point is that carnival has no point beyond itself. It celebrates the self-sufficiency of life in its endless cyclical repetitiveness, its sublime pointlessness, its effervescent inconsequentiality. Hence its exuberance, exoticism and excess: basic parameters of a world beyond necessity, beyond purpose. It is not so much that carnival 'plays a part' in social life; rather, that it throws into question precisely the 'playing of parts' in social life, putting the play before the part, the dis-guise before the guise.

This also throws light on carnival's anti-institutional quality: 'anti-institutional' in an ontological, pre-political sense. The 'second life' can never be represented in an institution; as carnival becomes institutionalized, it becomes a resource for representation and manipulation. In this sense, carnival is subversive of its own incorporation, its own institutionalization, rather than of everyday life itself; hence Fiske's suggestion that carnival *evades* ordinary life, rather than opposes it.[61] At its most fundamental, this 'other side' of life celebrates difference, non-incorporation; it is radically inconsistent with life lived for a goal beyond itself, whether defined in religious or Enlightenment terms, salvation or secular progress. And as it fell victim to the latter, so increasingly the people's 'second life', a dimension of life as fundamental as the first one, became the people's 'secondary life', attenuated and appropriated into spectacle.

And yet. . . . If, as Stallybrass and White suggest, the act of bourgeois disavowal '*made* carnival into the festival of the Other',[62] if there is a sense in which the disappearance of carnival was accompanied by the construction of 'carnival', this does not imply an end to the 'trouble' that both carnival and 'carnival' signify. If the act of bourgeois disavowal is inseparable from the construction of the modern unconscious, we have already seen that this implies a 'return of the repressed', an eternal recurrence of the cyclical in the present, yet a recurrence that is ever shifting in form, contingent, innovating. And in this sense, carnival also recurs as the principle of fashion itself, that product of the project of modernity that is central to its dynamic yet constantly parodies it, questioning the very notion of project, celebrating excess and superfluity, embodying repetitions of the past in the context of constant yet purposeless novelty. Carnival takes its revenge through the very fact that the modern world cannot but reproduce carnival as the other that is present within it, but cannot be recognized as such, or experienced, save vicariously, through spectacle: the mocking yet affirmative laughter from an impossible elsewhere. . . .

One day, in Prussia in the 1440s, a certain stranger arrives at a town where carnival is taking place. Carnival, of course, was a time of confusion and strange events. At the town in question, it was the custom for 'devils' to chase old people and carry them off to hell. Our stranger, needless to say, does not know this. As he approaches the town, he sees a devil chasing an old woman, outside the walls. A brave man, he did not need to think twice: 'Intrepidly, he . . . smote the devil's head with an axe.' When the people of the town went out to collect the corpse, however, they could find nothing but a pile of empty clothes.[63] Undoubtedly the authorities have often, since then, tried to kill the spirit of carnival; but when they go out to collect the corpse, do they ever find more than the pile of empty clothes?

Notes

1   Here, and elsewhere, I draw on P. Burke, *Popular Culture in Early Modern England* (Temple Smith, 1978).
2   M. Bristol, *Carnival and Theater* (Routledge, 1985), p. 78.
3   My account here is influenced by G. Williams, *Goya and the Impossible Revolution* (Peregrine, 1984).
4   M. Bakhtin, *Rabelais and His World* (Indiana University Press, 1984), pp. 39–40, 39.
5   C. Phythian-Adams, 'Ceremony and the Citizen: The Communal Year at Coventry 1450–1550', in P. Clark (ed.) *The Early Modern Town* (Longman, 1976).
6   J. Peacock, 'Symbolic Reversal and Social History', in B. Babcock (ed.) *The Reversible World* (Cornell University Press, 1978), p. 222. See also my *Exploring the Modern: Patterns of Western Culture and Civilization* (Blackwell, 1998), ch. 8, on modern conceptions of time.
7   Bristol, *Carnival and Theater*, pp. 59, 61.
8   Phythian-Adams, 'Ceremony', p. 107.
9   Bristol, *Carnival and Theater*, p. 67.
10 Bakhtin, *Rabelais*, p. 10.
11 A. Zijderveld, *Reality in a Looking Glass* (Routledge, 1982), p. 61.

12   P. Stallybrass, '"Drunk With the Cup of Liberty": Robin Hood, the Carnivalesque, and the Rhetoric of Violence in Early Modern England', *Semiotica* (1985), 54:1/2.

13   See N. Z. Davis, 'Women on Top', in her *Society and Culture in Early Modern France* (Polity, 1987).

14   Cited in Bakhtin, *Rabelais*, p. 92 (original emphasis).

15   Ibid., p. 4. For an overview of Bakhtin on carnival, see also J. Docker, *Postmodernism and Popular Culture* (Cambridge University Press, 1994), chs. 13, 14.

16   Cited in Stallybrass, '"Drunk With the Cup of Liberty"', pp. 121–2.

17   Cited in P. Stallybrass and A. White, *The Politics and Poetics of Transgression* (Methuen, 1986), p. 24. For more bare bottoms, see V. Cameron, 'Political Exposures: Sexuality and Caricature in the French Revolution', in L. Hunt (ed.) *Eroticism and the Body Politic* (Johns Hopkins University Press, 1991).

18   P. Camporesi, *Bread of Dreams* (Polity, 1989), p. 21.

19   Bakhtin, *Rabelais*, p. 19.

20   Ibid., p. 21.

21   Ibid., pp. 25, 321.

22   S. Stewart, *On Longing* (Duke University Press, 1993), pp. 80, 82.

23   Burke, *Popular Culture*, p. 202.

24   E. Le Roy Ladurie, *Carnival in Romans* (Penguin, 1981). For the Prague events, see also the brief comment at the end of ch. 2 of my *Exploring the Modern*.

25   Burke, *Popular Culture*, chs. 8, 9. See also D. Underdown, *Revel, Riot and Rebellion* (Clarendon Press, 1985), chs. 3, 5.

26   B. Scribner, 'Reformation, Carnival and the World Turned Upside Down', *Social History* (1978), 3:3, p. 304.

27   Stewart, *On Longing*, pp. 81–3.

28   J. Fiske, *Understanding Popular Culture* (Unwin Hyman, 1989), p. 100.

29   L. Schulze, 'On the Muscle', in J. Gaines and C. Herzog (eds.) *Fabrications: Costume and the Female Body* (Routledge, 1990), p. 59.

30   N. Green, *The Spectacle of Nature: Landscape and Bourgeois Culture in Nineteenth-century France* (Manchester University Press, 1990), pp. 77, 79.

31   Stallybrass and White, *Politics and Poetics*, p. 176.

32   R. Shields, *Places on the Margin: Alternative Geographies of Modernity* (Routledge, 1991), ch. 2.

33   T. Bennett, *The Birth of the Museum* (Routledge, 1995), p. 245.

34   M. Featherstone, *Consumer Culture and Postmodernism* (Sage, 1991), p. 79.

35   Stallybrass and White, *Politics and Poetics*, pp. 171, 184.

36   C. Wills, 'Upsetting the Public: Carnival, Hysteria and Women's Texts', in K. Hirschkop and D. Shepherd (eds.) *Bakhtin and Cultural Theory* (Manchester University Press, 1989), pp. 130–1. See also M. Russo, 'Female Grotesques: Carnival and Theory', in T. de Lauretis (ed.) *Feminist Studies/Critical Studies* (Macmillan, 1986).

37   S. Heath, *The Sexual Fix* (Macmillan, 1982), pp. 47–8, 49.

38   H. Cixous, 'Sorties', in H. Cixous and C. Clément, *The Newly Born Woman* (Minnesota University Press, 1987), p. 95.

39   Davis, 'Women on Top', p. 131.

40   Cixous, 'Sorties', pp. 94–5.

41   Babcock, *Reversible World*, p. 32.

42   T. Castle, *Masquerade and Civilization: The Carnivalesque in 18th Century English Culture and Fiction* (Methuen, 1986), pp. 6, 76, 78.

43   Ibid., pp. 81, 102, 71.
44   Bakhtin, *Rabelais*, p. 7.
45   T. Castle, 'The Carnivalization of 18th Century Narrative', *Proceedings of the Modern Languages Association* (1984), 99, p. 911.
46   A. Jefferson, 'Bodymatters: Self and Other in Bakhtin, Sartre and Barthes', in Hirschkop and Shepherd, *Bakhtin*, p. 165.
47   D. LaCapra, 'Bakhtin, Marxism and the Carnivalesque', in his *Rethinking Intellectual History* (Cornell University Press, 1983), p. 301.
48   M. Bakhtin, *The Dialogical Imagination* (Texas University Press, 1981), pp. 36, 163. Bakhtin goes rather further than I would in developing this emphasis on the novel as carnivalesque.
49   S. Rushdie, *Is Nothing Sacred?*, The Herbert Read Memorial Lecture (Granta, 1990), pp. 7, 16, reprinted in his *Imaginary Homelands* (Penguin, 1991). See also my *Exploring the Modern*, chs. 1 (on theatricality) and 6 (on the novel).
50   S. Kinser, 'Presentation and Representation: Carnival at Nuremberg, 1450–1550', *Representations* (1986), 13, p. 32. See also R. Lachmann, 'Bakhtin and Carnival', *Cultural Critique* (1988–9), 11.
51   Jefferson, 'Bodymatters', p. 168.
52   See R. Stam, *Subversive Pleasures: Bakhtin, Cultural Criticism, and Film* (Johns Hopkins University Press, 1989) and Docker, *Postmodernism*, ch. 15.
53   N. Z. Davis, 'The Reasons of Misrule', in her *Society and Culture*, p. 100.
54   P. Duerr, *Dreamtime* (Blackwell, 1987), p. 73.
55   Castle, *Masquerade and Civilization*, pp. 59, 77.
56   Stallybrass and White, *Politics and Poetics*, pp. 193, 58 (original emphasis).
57   Bristol, *Carnival and Theater*, pp. 63–5, 69.
58   Bakhtin, *Dialogical Imagination*, p. 159.
59   Bakhtin, *Rabelais*, pp. 7, 8.
60   Burke, *Popular Culture*, p. 179.
61   Fiske, *Understanding Popular Culture*, ch. 3.
62   Stallybrass and White, *Politics and Poetics*, p. 178.
63   Scribner, 'Reformation, Carnival', p. 318.

2 Manners and Morals:

The Civilization of Culture

Eating and Etiquette

The Spanish economic miracle of the 1970s and 1980s led to a proliferation of etiquette schools, particularly in Madrid, as the new middle classes combined their rising prosperity with an interest in acquiring the codes of manners appropriate to their new status. At these etiquette schools, they would have learnt the importance of using their fingers to peel a banana at mealtimes, but a knife and fork for actually eating it; and that other fruit, too, should be eaten on a plate with a knife and fork, although it was permissible, even desirable, to use the fingers for eating asparagus. And again, although toothpicks might be provided, you should never actually use them – that would lead to an immediate fall from social grace – but conversely, if you noticed someone else using them, and commented on it, then this would rebound on you, and you would be the one to suffer the loss of face. And as for soup, the soup spoon should apparently be moved across the surface *towards* you, never away from you. This last example is in complete contradiction to the accepted practice in Britain, at least as I was taught it, at the dinner table long ago: always propel the soup *away* from you. (The parental rationale offered for this was that if any were spilt, from over-enthusiastic propulsion, you wouldn't spill it over yourself; presumably spilling it over the person seated opposite didn't matter.) Trivial examples, no doubt; but enough to show that 'civilized behaviour' is a matter of some trauma, with pitfalls everywhere, any one of which could lead to social disaster, a situation made all the more complex by the fact that being civilized in one place can clearly differ markedly from the equivalent state elsewhere. The weightiness of such trivia, their significance in the 'civilizing process' to which each generation of children is subjected, can be further brought out in memories recalled many years later, as in Kafka's 'Letter to his Father':

> for me as a child everything you shouted at me was positively a heavenly com-
> mandment, I never forgot it. . . . Since as a child I was together with you chiefly at

meals, your teaching was to a large extent about proper behaviour at table. . . . Bones mustn't be cracked with the teeth. . . . Vinegar must not be sipped noisily. . . . The main thing was that the bread should be cut straight. . . . One had to take care that no scraps fell on the floor.[1]

The fact that 'manners', however deeply ingrained, however taken for granted, nevertheless remain in a sense contingent and arbitrary – cultural products that vary between communities and classes – has been commented on from the earliest period of the modern development of 'manners' as an indicator of 'civilization'. Lévi-Strauss quotes a French writer from 1560:

The Germans eat with their mouths closed and think it is unseemly to do otherwise. The French, on the contrary, half open their mouths and find the German practice rather disgusting. The Italians eat delicately, the French more vigorously, so that they find the Italian practice too refined and precious. And so each nation has something peculiar to it and different from others.[2]

Elias argues that it is nevertheless possible to refer to *the* 'civilizing process', so that these diversities emerge as variations on a common theme, though he adds the important reservation that the process is not uniform.[3] I will explore these issues through developing the example of table manners, along with cooking practices and patterns of consumption; and we will see how the emergence of notions of refinement and 'civility' in effect serves to construct a new language for the management and public presentation of the body and its boundaries. And along with the production of the modern body we find the modern self, simultaneously 'embodied' yet curiously distinct, somehow 'in' the body, yet not 'of' it.

Returning to the medieval period, then, we find that it was the custom, in the tavern, or at court, to eat from a common dish. The only utensil available being a knife, guests would readily dip their hands into the dish. The cup, also, would be communal, passed from mouth to mouth. Since there were no handkerchiefs, people would blow their noses directly into their fingers – the same fingers they had just used in helping themselves from the common dish – and would not turn their heads away when sneezing, thus no doubt making the soup all the more flavoursome. There *were* rules, of course, such as 'don't clean your teeth with your knife' and 'don't blow your nose in the tablecloth'; and gradually these rules became more extensive, and were codified in the manners and etiquette books that began to be published in the fifteenth and sixteenth centuries. These became so popular that even authors of the calibre of Erasmus wrote them.

By the mid-sixteenth century, in Germany, it was becoming customary to allow each guest a spoon, and a separate dish. The knife, while remaining essential, was hedged around with new taboos; it was increasingly seen as an unacceptable reminder of the days of armed warriors. Table knives should not be fully sharp, were never to be pointed at fellow guests, and should be passed by the handle. The fork, too, has a history. It arrived in Venice in the eleventh century, brought by a Greek princess, and Elias informs us that 'this novelty was regarded as so excessive a sign of refinement that . . . the ecclesiastics . . . called down divine wrath upon her'.[4] The historian Braudel confirms that the fork did not really catch on until the sixteenth century in France, and did not become general in England before 1750.[5] By then, the idea that codes of manners and etiquette were essential signifiers of one's 'state of civilization' had become well established.

Cooking practices can be seen to make similar statements. Overall, we find that the characteristic medieval cycles of fasting and gluttony, wherein periods of feasting to excess contrast both with real limitations of the food supply and the symbolic limitations of religious abstention, give way to a more moderate and routinized pattern of consumption. The idea of different courses at a meal, taken in a fixed order, begins to spread. The general significance of cooking in what Mennell calls the 'civilising of appetite'[6] is sketched in by Fiddes, who claims that cooking 'transforms meat from a natural substance to a cultural artifact. Thus, the more skilfully its manipulation is effected, the better it expresses the supremacy of human civilisation.'[7] And Mennell adds that 'a growing sense of "delicacy" and "refinement" in regard to food and cooking – as in other fields of behaviour – is quite inseparable from a growing sense of dislike or aversion towards foods and dishes defined as "indelicate" or "unrefined".'[8]

In his book *All Manners of Food*, Mennell offers a perspective on that well-known British propensity for producing soggy, overcooked vegetables. Nineteenth-century cookery books provide evidence of a widespread fear of indigestion; but it is crucial to appreciate that it is not indigestion as a medical, but as a *social* condition that is at issue here. The various 'symptoms', such as the noisy rumblings of the stomach, were associated with the fear of social embarrassment. Furthermore, the famous cookery authority Mrs Beeton wrote that leeks should be 'well-boiled' (i.e. overcooked) 'to prevent them tainting the breath'; and this fear of 'bad breath' doubtless helps account for the problem that the British have had – until recently, at any rate – with garlic. More generally, the cookery writer Jane Grigson reminisced: 'I remember my grandmother's obsession with her digestive system, her purges and peppermint tablets; I remember too, how constipation hung over some families like a mushroom cloud.'[9] Both indigestion and bad breath pose serious problems, then, but both can be countered, in part, by making sure that food is well cooked; any resulting lack of flavour or texture counts for little by comparison with the greater sense of social refinement.

If we consider meat eating, we find that the British and French experiences are rather closer. Until the late nineteenth century, we find that a vegetarian diet was associated with religious asceticism; but since then, it has become much more widespread, along with increased squeamishness about eating meat. After all, those who continue to eat meat do not generally like to be reminded of what killing the animal involves. From once having been justified as necessary to improve the flavour, certain practices are now unacceptably 'cruel'; we can be confident that the eighteenth-century cookbook that began a recipe by instructing the cook to 'Take a red cock that is not too old and beat him to death'[10] has been long out of print. Learning that some Japanese eat 'live' fish in their restaurants – apparently the tail is still liable to thrash around on the plate while the rest of the fish is being sliced by the chef – is liable to be taken as confirmation of the smug Western prejudice that the Japanese, while unquestionably 'modern', are not yet fully 'civilized' (Western customs like plunging live lobsters into boiling water notwithstanding). This gives point to this observation by Elias on the ideological dimensions of 'civilization': 'this concept expresses the self-consciousness of the West. . . . It sums up everything in which Western society of the last two or three centuries believes itself superior to earlier societies or "more primitive" contemporary ones.'[11] Slaughtering itself used to be a wholly public activity, and indeed something to enjoy. When James I had completed a stag hunt, he would personally cut the stag's throat and daub his courtiers' faces with its blood. Nowadays, on the other hand, slaughtering has become private, indeed shamefaced. The very words reveal this: 'slaughterhouse' has given way to the obscure French of *abattoir* or the American euphemism 'meat factory'. And anyway, we do not, of course, eat cows or cattle, we eat 'beef'; not pigs, but 'pork'. Similarly, much disguise has entered cookery. The modern joint is a rather pathetic remnant of the once-proud display of the whole beast, or at least its head, on the dinner table; and it is generally thought that the joint becomes more acceptable the less it resembles the creature it derives from. Perhaps this helps to account for the rise of mince; nearly half of all beef is now consumed in this form. Mince, after all, does not look like beef; it could be anything. In short, one could apply the Elias thesis to these examples, and suggest that they can be seen in the light of changing codes of civility and refinement, what Elias calls the 'advance of the threshold of embarrassment and shame',[12] and the accompanying feelings of disgust and repugnance; and that this may be more central than the moral rationalizations usually offered (e.g. 'cruelty to animals'), although the relationship between these two dimensions is important and will require further discussion.

Civilizing the Body

This process of 'refinement' is not just a matter of behaviour, of self-presentation through manners; it involves a radical reconstruction of the sense of the body and its boundaries, the development of what was described in the previous chapter as the 'classical' body. We need to remember that there is a powerful sense in which our experience of the body is culturally constructed, particularly in the management of body boundaries. Fiske suggests that

> The body is inherently 'dirty': all its orifices produce dirt – that is, matter that transgresses its categorical boundary, that denies the difference between me and not-me and that contaminates the separatedness of the body, and therefore its purity as a category.[13]

I would prefer to say that these phenomena raise questions about where the boundaries actually *are*; and if body emissions raise these questions, so also do clothes, and the physical space around the body. Anyone who has ever been in crowded public areas, such as the London Underground, will be intuitively aware that there are norms that govern appropriate body distances and body gestures in these situations. The private body in public spaces has a private space around it. We can say that the evolution of the modern body is the evolution of the closed, well-defined, well-bounded body, crucially private even in public, and surrounded by taboos the breaking of which produce feelings of shame, guilt or disgust. The contrast with the pre-modern body is brought out by the historian Porter:

> Much peasant lore . . . seems to glory in mud, filth and excrement . . . within their value-system, dirt (itself, of course, a notably relative phenomenon) was commonly regarded as a form of protective armour for the skin. Whereas we associate clean-liness with health, in traditional peasant culture, health, hygiene, and warmth required a sort of dirty living.[14]

'The' body, then – the taken-for-granted 'modern' body – is a product of taboos that define and stabilize body boundaries; and it is the orifices of the body that prove most significant here, since 'these apertures of ingestion and emission work to constitute the notion of the subject, of the individual body and ultimately the self', as Susan Stewart puts it.[15] Gradually, indeed, all the body's products, except tears, become essentially unmentionable in polite society. And in our time, we can see how AIDS becomes *the* modern polluter, implying as it does a permeable body, the exchange of bodily fluids, and a link with homosexuality, itself a form of boundary-crossing frequently denounced as 'both uncivilized and unnatural', as Judith Butler comments.[16]

We can also see how the control of the body, and its separation from con-tamination by 'dirt', has consequences for our understanding of the significance of 'hygiene' as a cultural practice. The everyday view is that the development of table manners, and the campaign against dirt and pollution, are rational responses stimulated by scientific understanding of germs and infection. However, the historical record suggests that it is not so much concern about health, let alone knowledge of the causes of ill health, that has stimulated these developments; rather, they are consequences of the refined, bounded body and its public pre-sentation, which results in acute embarrassment when the required standard is violated. Only afterwards are the new codes justified in terms of hygiene, or else it is simply taken for granted that they are more 'healthy' than whatever was sup-planted. Elias writes:

> It is well to establish once and for all that something which we know to be harmful to health by no means necessarily arouses feelings of distaste or shame. And con-versely, something that arouses these feelings need not be at all detrimental to health.

In short, there is no necessary connection between knowledge of hygiene and changes in manners: ' "rational understanding" is not the motor of the "civiliz-ing" of eating or of other behaviour'. And he adds, more generally,

> Much of what we call 'morality' or 'moral' reasons has the same function as 'hygiene' or 'hygienic' reasons: to condition children to a certain social standard.

Moulding by such means aims at making socially desirable behaviour automatic, a matter of self-control, causing it to appear in the consciousness of the individual as the result of his own free will, and in the interests of his own health or human dignity.[17]

Hence describing something as 'unhygienic' is really a way of constructing the embodied self through rejecting 'dirt', and rationalizing this in the language of modern biomedicine. This is a never-ending task; the body is never free of the danger of 'defilement', and the rejected constituents are ever reproduced as danger and pollution. 'Its closure and purity are quite illusory.' write Stallybrass and White, 'and it will perpetually rediscover in itself, often with a sense of shock or inner revulsion, the grotesque, the protean and the motley.'[18] Butler concludes that 'The boundary of the body as well as the distinction between internal and external is established through the ejection and transvaluation of something originally part of identity into a defiling otherness.'[19]

It is out of this matrix that the modern concern with 'health' will indeed gradually develop; health as a kind of secular salvation, to be attained through purity and 'cleanliness'. Already by the eighteenth century the manners and etiquette books are spawning a genre of booklets giving homely, popular advice on health, and by the nineteenth century this becomes a flood, with science now constituting the language of body management, and literature being aimed directly at a working-class audience. Anderson comments that publications such as the *Penny Magazine* and the *London Journal* found ways to transmit civilizing exhortations with their stories and pictures; there were 'scientific facts on the healthful benefits of mildness of temper; essays on etiquette and politeness, the hallmarks of civilized society'. The overall message was clear enough: 'be civilized according to your station'.[20] For the responsible individual, health became a *duty*, part of what Turner refers to as 'a calling to world mastery and self-control',[21] and Outram suggests that

His only test in the success of this search for health was himself: he was the instrument and subject of his own experiment. Thus the concept of 'health' also entailed a reflexive idea of the individual body: person, body, health and self-management were welded indissolubly together in a way which separated each body from any other body.[22]

The idea of reflexivity will need further exploration; but it is at least clear that through inculcating table manners and norms of 'good behaviour' generally, the courtesy books and behaviour manuals were also teaching a whole new regime of body management. Greenblatt summarizes the overall significance of this:

The acquisition of the prevailing table manners and modes of speech, mark the entrance into civility, an entrance that distinguishes not only the child from the adult, but the members of a privileged group from the vulgar, the upper classes from the lower, the courtly from the rustic, the civilized from the savage.[23]

For Erasmus, in the early sixteenth century, the inability to manage body products in appropriate ways is to sink into a state of animality. In Spencer's *Faerie
Queene*, civility is said to arise from the effort to surmount primitive existence
through the exercise of courtesy; wild men and savages might possess laudable
attributes, but they lacked courtesy and hence were incapable of civil order.[24] The
danger of animality is again referred to at a later stage, in 1700, by one Cotton
Mather, a New England Puritan, but now with the addition of a significant new
feature. He observes, in his diary, that obeying a call of nature makes humans no
different from dogs; hence, he writes

> I resolved that it should be my ordinary practice, whenever I step to answer the one
> or other necessity of nature to make it an opportunity of shaping in my mind some
> holy, noble, divine thought . . . some thoughts of piety wherein I may differ from
> the brutes.[25]

What is new here is that the emphasis has shifted to civility as evidence of an *inner
state*. With Mather, externals only count if they are an adequate reflection of this
inner state. Here, that problematical construct the modern self has clearly put in
an appearance, together with the distinctively spatialized conception of the self
in its relation to the body, the inner/outer distinction.

The term 'civility' has clearly emerged as central to these discussions; the term
itself became widespread in the eighteenth century, and although, as Bryson
remarks, it is hard to define, it always carried with it 'the connotation of order
based on reason, to which was opposed undisciplined animal instinct and a lawless
primitive nature'.[26] One aspect of this has been examined – the presentation of
the body in everyday behaviour, through the 'refinement of manners' and the construction and regulation of body boundaries – and we have seen how this results
in what Elias calls the 'invisible wall of affects which seems now to arise between
one human body and another, repelling and separating'. This in turn entails a
second aspect, the construction and cultivation of interiority through the development of the notion of the self as the rational and moral 'inner controller' of
the body. But before turning to this, it is worth outlining a third aspect. With the
'advance of the threshold of embarrassment, shame and repugnance',[27] whereby
it becomes vulgar and uncouth, and then positively improper, to eat from a
common dish, share a bed with a stranger, or urinate in public, so the new public
presentation of selfhood entails a transformation in the experience of social life,
and new modes of social identity.

The Social Dynamics of Civility

The 'civilizing process' is embedded in mechanisms of 'social closure' whereby
individuals and groups develop and shift their identities. Codes of etiquette and
manners are modes of social differentiation; they make statements about aspirations and affiliations. What was referred to in the previous chapter as the with-

drawal of the upper classes from 'popular culture' could also be seen, more positively, as a process in which more refined, self-conscious styles of behaviour, based on the cultivation of dignity, formality and etiquette, became prevalent. They learned to speak and write 'correctly', avoiding dialect; they withdrew from eating in great halls with their retainers into separate dining rooms and drawing rooms (originally 'withdrawing' rooms); and they developed new, stylized modes of dancing that involved symmetrical patterns and greater self-conscious awareness of one's position relative to other dancers.

Over time, of course, there could be marked changes in what counted as 'civility'. In the early modern period, the notion of 'honour' played an important part, and was associated with the social institution of duelling, and Morgan rightly observes that 'far from being a straightforward expression of aggression', the duel 'represented the suppression or control of the spontaneous or the "natural"'. But gradually – and far from uniformly – the code of honour itself came to be seen increasingly as a 'relic of an earlier barbarism',[28] and the duel, once a symbol of social superiority, became invested with the absurd. Even here, however, caution is required; present-day societies of southern Europe, where 'civility' has been entrenched even longer than in the north, retain a strong attachment to the culture of 'honour and shame'. . . .[29]

In the early modern period, then, the polished manners of the nobility were imitated by officials, merchants, and the intellectual elite. But this leads at once to paradox. An inherent feature of manners, after all, is that they can be copied; if membership of an elite is defined through manners, that elite is always liable to penetration by outsiders. And indeed, Elias suggests that although there are periods of rigidity in the social structure, the declining significance of old feudal ties as the basis for high status meant that the nobility found it difficult to prevent aspiring members of the bourgeoisie from breaking in, and were indeed liable to social decline themselves, given the costliness of elite membership, particularly at court. But there could also be a *willingness* to see one's code of behaviour more widely adopted: if one is 'civilized', what could be more appropriate than that others should be encouraged to attain the same desirable state? This points to the fateful conjunction between the 'civilizing process' and the project of Enlightenment, to be discussed later. There is, then, a constant tension between social exclusiveness and social inclusiveness, or colonization.

At times, a pattern of behaviour that is diffused downwards through the social structure, *from* the elite, then comes to be rejected *by* the elite. To begin with, white bread was regarded as 'refined', and was socially exclusive in medieval times; the further down the social scale, the darker the bread. By the nineteenth century, workers and peasants were demanding white bread; by the 1920s, with everyone eating it, brown bread appeared to be effectively extinct – except that, within a decade or two, it began to reappear, on *upper*-class tables, and has been working its way down ever since. . . .[30] The means whereby groups construct their distinctive identities, their sense of difference, and often of superiority, can result in undermining this very distinctiveness, leading to a drive to further differentiation. Elias suggests that, over time, this produces a pattern in which the 'civilizing process' becomes ever more entrenched, yet so does the production of internal differentiations within this process: 'The contrasts in conduct between the upper and lower groups are reduced with the spread of civilization; the varieties or nuances of civilized conduct are increased.'[31] This could be seen as an attempt to resolve the problem mentioned at the beginning, the relationship between uniformity and diversity: the *overall* diffusion of 'civility' is accompanied by little nuances whereby particular groups are constructed through an emergent sense of their own identity. And here we have a source of the significance of 'fashion' as a modern mode of identity creation. . . .

Two aspects of *how* civility was socially managed are worth further note. Firstly, it was a matter of moderation, of balance, not of extremes; one could be *too* civilized, as it were. James I advised his son to 'eate in a manly, round and honest fashion', avoiding both daintiness and over-refinement, and grossness and vulgarity;[32] and Rosalind Williams comments that 'If barbarism is the enemy without, decadence is the enemy within.'[33] Both extremes can furnish grounds for criticism; and since both can be associated with court life, they can provide fertile soil in which the bourgeois critique of aristocratic pretensions can flourish, as in Voltaire's claim that 'there is always least honour around the king'.

This is also true of the second aspect, the role of reversals. This can be stated in the form of a paradox: if 'civility' is normally necessary for a successful claim to status, then we nevertheless find that the ostentatious *rejection* of 'normal' patterns of civility can, under some circumstances, also work in this way. If the 'civilizing process' turns against meat eating, then the most extreme form of the latter – the consumption of uncooked red meat – could become an appropriate signifier of aggression and extreme ('raw') competitiveness. Thus Fiddes quotes an entrepreneur who claims to eat steak tartare when attempting to browbeat the opposition at a business lunch, and the former boxing champion Lloyd Honeyghan: 'I'm still so hungry for success I've been living on raw steak.' And this does, of course, have implications for the gender dimension, whereby meat consumption can become a sign of masculinity.[34]

Placing this aspect in historical perspective, Bryson writes:

> Status could be associated with deliberate licence, as was most bizarrely illustrated by the fashion among Restoration courtiers for 'streaking' naked through the streets. This kind of joke and the more usual forms of 'gentlemanly' extravagance in conduct, effectively inverted the 'civil' values of hierarchy, locating social superiority in freedom from rules and restraints, and locating inferiority in an obligation to self-control.[35]

It is the *inferior* who needs to obey the rules; the superior can break them. An implication of this is that what are normally mundane, private, even shameful activities, can become transformed by high status, particularly association with the King. Starkey gives the most graphic example, from the period of the Tudor monarchy, when the Groom of the Stool, who attended the King in his 'privy room', became a person of high status and power, able to arrest the highest in the land, even a Cardinal Wolsey. Comparing then and now, Starkey writes:

In the sixteenth century, the Groom of the Stool's highly personal job as the royal lavatory attendant was the foundation for his rise to public power and influence. Now, on the other hand, the monarch's relieving of him or herself is so awesomely private that one of the usual preparations for a royal visit (so it is rumoured) is the construction of a special WC, dedicated to the king or queen's sole use. Thus the symbol . . . is the same, but its meaning in the twentieth century is not merely different from its meaning in the sixteenth century, but, in fact, is its opposite.[36]

This introduces another idea, that the development of notions of 'civility' goes hand in hand with the construction of the modern public/private distinction. We find that 'the distasteful is removed behind the scenes of social life', as Elias puts it.[37] If the public world is the world of civility, then the private world ambiguously comprises both the domestic sphere, of permissible – if limited – relaxations of civility, and the sphere of the distasteful, the tabooed and the transgressive. Civility thereby rests on, and reproduces, its opposite.

As for the public arena, it is the street that had come, by the eighteenth century, to represent the heart of the civil. The street was urban and urbane, the world of public transactions, socializing, 'civil affairs'; above all, the world of the citizen, interacting through the norms of decorum with other citizens on the public stage of politics and social life. This realm contrasts not only with the domestic sphere, but with the countryside, coded as 'wild', as nature rather than culture. The discourse of 'civility' and 'civilization' is still redolent of these dichotomies, as Fiddes points out: 'Thus, in the popular conception of town dwellers, country people – almost by definition – are less civilised since they are more directly associated with those natural processes that urban civilisation has sought to transcend.'[38] And the Corbins point out that during the first wave of mass tourism in Andalusia in the 1960s, tourists were criticized for exposing their bodies in the street; this was seen as 'uncivilized' behaviour, and implied that they were treating town as country, and the locals as barbarians.[39]

One might add, finally, that in the contemporary West, elements of 'decivilized' behaviour have become claims to status more generally: the relatively marginal or dispossessed can thereby assert defiance; and the middle class can imply that to be truly 'civilized' implies less emphasis on 'mere' formality. Once again, it is as though actual class-based contrasts in these aspects of transgressive behaviour become less marked, even as the 'varieties or nuances' increase.

The Self in the Body

Giving advice to a young nobleman in 1607, Cleland writes: 'Many men seeing you passe by them, will conceive presently a good or bad opinion of you. Wherefore yee muste . . . consider with what grace and countenance yee walke'.[40] And La Bruyère, at the court of Louis XIV, adds: 'Let a favourite observe himself very closely, for if he keeps me waiting less than usual in his antechamber, if his face is more open, less frowning . . . I shall think he is beginning to fall, and I shall be right.'[41] Face, gesture, posture, deportment: all become revealing, all can be 'read'.

Calculation, observation of others, and self-consciousness, all become necessary traits in the emerging world of competitive civility. The era of psychological observation – and representation – is born. Elias suggests that

> The new stage of courtesy and its representation, summed up in the concept of *civilité*, is very closely bound up with this manner of seeing. . . . In order to be really 'courteous' by the standards of *civilité*, one is to some extent obliged to observe, to look about oneself and pay attention to people and their motives. . . . People, forced to live with one another in a new way, become more sensitive to the impulses of others.[42]

We are clearly in the presence of the 'rational', instrumental self, albeit constituted through unconscious as well as conscious dimensions: 'beside the individual's conscious self-control, an automated, blindly functioning apparatus of self-control is firmly established'.[43]

'Manners' become fundamental to the representational structure of the modern self. Bryson brings this out effectively, suggesting that we find

> a changing conception of what manners are for or, more precisely, what they 'represent' . . . writings on conduct from the Renaissance onward emphasise another function for the rules of manners: that of presenting or 'representing' personality, rather than simply acknowledging relationship. . . . This representational view of manners implies a sense of the continual interpretative gaze of a social audience, deducing character from external signs.

Since a gentleman's status was increasingly located in his possession of 'inner virtues perfected by education', these posed problems of social representation and visual embodiment.[44] Externals of behaviour and dress were seen as mirrors of the internal reality of self.

A similar representational matrix links the interior and the external worlds through cognition. To know the world is no longer to understand one's place in a divine cosmos; rather, it is to have an accurate representation of things, 'a correct picture within of outer reality', as Taylor puts it. The self as interior subject brings with it a conception of the world as outer object, open to investigation through 'rational' procedures: 'Knowledge comes not from connecting the mind to the order of things we find but in framing a representation of reality according to the right canons.'[45] From this point of view, our own bodies are part of the world, and can be examined mechanistically; and not just our bodies, for with 'self-control' and 'self-consciousness' comes the capacity to objectify and examine our feelings and emotions as well. The world of the Scientific Revolution and the world of modern selfhood come into being together.

This 'radical stance of disengagement', this capacity to objectify not only the outside world but also the 'internal' world of the emotions, is essential for the capacity to develop and alter identity through reshaping the presentation of body and self. This is what Greenblatt refers to as 'self-fashioning', or 'an increased self-consciousness about the fashioning of human identity as a manipulable artful process'.[46] And this disengagement, linked to self-fashioning, is an aspect of what Weber called the 'disenchantment' of the world: the birth of the world of subjects and objects, linked instrumentally, out of the sundering of the links that constituted the pre-modern cosmos. The world becomes a resource for manipulation; *we* can define goals, and realize them through rational strategy. Taylor suggests the momentous scale of the shift:

> The cosmos is no longer seen as the embodiment of meaningful order which can define the good for us. And this move is brought about by our coming to grasp this world as mechanism. . . . We demystify the cosmos as a setter of ends by grasping it mechanistically and functionally as a domain of possible means. Getting insight into the world as mechanism is inseparable from seeing it as a domain of potential instrumental control. . . . Rational control can extend to the re-creation of our habits, and hence of ourselves. . . . To take this stance is to identify oneself with the power to objectify and remake.[47]

This has implications for our sense of the world as a moral order. Morality becomes less a matter of externals of behaviour, judged in the light of fixed duties that are ultimately defined theologically, and more a question of what the externals 'reveal' about the inner self. Moral codes become situationally fluid, both part of what is manipulated *by* the self, and part of the representation of the self, in everyday life. The social structure of 'civility' retains a moral dimension – the self has to 'carry off' a presentation of itself as worthwhile, respectable and reliable, and interprets the behaviour of others in the light of these criteria – but moral questions become shades of grey, embedded in the constant negotiations of everyday problems. Small nuances of behaviour can thereby become all the more significant, setting the 'moral tone' for relationships. We are entering the world that makes the novel possible. . . .

One aspect of this that needs further discussion is the *spatial* sense of self, the idea of the self as interior, as 'inside' the body; and indeed, not just of the self as interior, but as 'having' an interior, recesses that are difficult to penetrate. 'We are creatures with inner depths', as Taylor suggests.[48] This can help clarify our sense of the distinctiveness of the modern self. Benton argues that there was no concept of an interior, unique individual self in the medieval cosmos: the 'persona' was not inside but on the surface, or 'outside', a mask between oneself and the outer world; and 'looking behind the individualized mask eventually brought one closer to the uniqueness, not of self, but of God'.[49] With the early modern shift away from this, we find that thoughts, attitudes and emotions can now be conceptualized as 'psychological', properties of mind; and room is made for 'guilt' and 'shame' as internal psychological mechanisms. What previously existed 'outside', or in the relationship between subject and object, is now firmly reconstructed as an activity or experience of the subject, and the older mode of relating to the world can become difficult for us to grasp today. Taylor cites this passage from *The Merchant of Venice*: 'How many things by season season'd are/To their right praise and true perfection!' He points out that this makes 'praise' as much the property of the 'things' as a result of the activity of the subject, so that 'The significance of being objects of praise inhabits, as it were, praiseworthy things'; it 'emanates' from them. Similarly, 'melancholy', which we now see as clearly 'mental', was seen as somehow residing *in* 'black bile', which we would code as 'physical'.[50] The development of the modern self, then, rested on the insertion of a decisive boundary here, a boundary that nevertheless remains inherently problematical. This boundary-making entailed the destruction of pre-modern notions of 'influence', now denounced as 'magical', since these notions posed a threat to the emergent sense of self-possession and self-control as essential attributes of independent selfhood. The witch-hunts can be seen in this light: the witches symbolized this threat, even as the destruction of the threat would soon make witchcraft itself inconceivable. . . .

Yet, what is this mysterious self of modernity, somehow 'inside' the body, yet also distinct from it, and in a strange relationship with it, tenuous yet intimate? Elias points to the oddity of this conception when he suggests that

> there is no structural feature of man that justifies our calling one thing the core of man and another the shell. . . . On this level, there is nothing that resembles a container, nothing that could justify metaphors like that of the 'inside' of a human being. The intuition of a wall, of something 'inside' man separated from the outside world, however genuine it may be as an intuition, corresponds to nothing in man having the character of a real wall.[51]

Here we encounter the character Elias calls *Homo clausus*, or 'closed man', with a strong sense of boundaries and physical separation; and I refer to 'man' here advisedly, since although of course both sexes are crucially affected by these developments, it is, as we shall see later, particularly 'masculinity' that is in play here. Yet Elias also hints at problems in this character. *Homo clausus* is armoured; the body is like a protective shell that enhances the sense of autonomy from the world. Yet – and this is the central paradox – it is not only true that the self can use the body as its boundary *from* the world, it is also true that the self rejects the body as *itself* being part of the world, the world's boundary against *it*, hence encountering the body, like the rest of the world, as something alien, to be controlled and restrained. The self *uses* the body for protection against the 'outside', yet also needs to protect itself *from* what are now experienced as the threatening drives and needs of the body. On the one hand, the body is exiled, disinherited, traduced as what Barker calls 'a rootless thing of madness and scandal';[52] but simultaneously, it is protection and resource, indeed vital as instrumentality, as labour. The very objecthood of the body, as armour, enables it to protect and define the self, giving it an 'edge', an 'outside'; yet this very fact means that it is *itself* outside, and can never really 'be' the subject or be adequate to allow the latter to recognize itself *in* it or *as* it.

Clearly one cannot presuppose any harmonious body–self relation, therefore. The distinctions between self and other, self and body and inside/outside can easily be superimposed, but are also crucially unstable. In extreme cases, this can have a crippling effect on the self's capacity to function at all; it can become a victim of these splits, fragmented by them. This is what occurs in schizophrenia. In other cases, 'the body' can appear to be an object manipulated from behind the scenes by the self, and this extreme 'separation' from the body may lead the individual to feel invisible to others. In such situations, Giddens suggests, the 'narrative of self-identity' is 'woven in a manner which allows the individual to witness the activities of her body with neutral detachment, cynicism, hatred or ironic amusement'.[53]

So the experience of 'body' and 'self' as 'separate spheres' is itself highly problematical. If the body is something to be controlled, it becomes potentially something that can be experienced as recalcitrant, rebellious. The more one tries to control it, sees this as a test of self, the more one is aware of its intractable resistance. It can be as though life itself becomes that which escapes control, resists it; resistance is created in the very act of suppression, since without the suppression there would be no life at all, only empty form, the inertia of pure self-identity only possible in death; the suppression not only manifests the control, but reproduces its 'necessity', endlessly justifies it. 'Nature', the body, becomes 'disorder', an inarticulate, silent resistance. And inevitably, the resistance will at times win, the body will have its way, so to speak; the rational self will succumb to the temptations it both fears and, through endlessly re-creating them, has come to seek as well. Hence the mechanisms of punishment and revenge, through guilt and shame. Ultimately, mastery of the body can become a kind of search for perfection, resulting in the deadly paradox pointed to by Turner, wherein 'this attempt to control the body results in its dominance'.[54] It is the anorexic body that thereby becomes the ultimate symbol both of the ethos of control and of the body's revenge. The anorexic teenager saying that 'You make of your own body your very own kingdom where you are the tyrant, the absolute dictator' is thereby doomed to become victim of her own tyranny.

But it is also possible to react in the opposite fashion, to *celebrate* 'giving way', derive a vicarious sense of transgressive selfhood from it. 'Logically entailed in any discourse of self-control is its opposite', writes Crawford, hence 'a disciplinary regime in the name of health is opposed by a belief in the salubrious qualities of release'.[55] This is the 'permissive' mode of the cycle of repression and release made possible by the body politics of modernity.

Applied to the self, then, paradoxes are necessarily engendered. 'Self-control' is a very odd notion, after all. The self is both subject and object of control; the omnipotent controller, and the everlasting resistance; split between domination and submission, ever recalcitrant to itself, defined partly through its own escape strategies. Out of this cauldron, psychoanalysis will in due course emerge: the Freudian model will schematize these divisions, and, in its therapeutic mode, try to paper them over, or, more ambitiously, try to 'heal' them, and no doubt in everyday life we live with them, more or less adequately; but such achieved self-identity is always precarious, and the hold of therapeutic strategies in our culture suggests that the work of reconciliation or fusion is indeed interminable.

These issues of self-control have another dimension: if boundary uncertainties can lead to problems, so can the sense of a solid boundary, the body as 'armour'. Doubts can arise about the reality of 'what lies outside', and how to 'know' it. As the environment becomes a realm of objects, related to instrumentally by subjects, so individuals become puzzling to others, and to themselves; to know oneself as object is to become mysterious to oneself. Writing of the consequences of this for individuals in the emerging world of modernity, Theweleit suggests that we encounter

> the development of an armor that made them feel 'separate' from the rest of the world and prevented them from finding convincing arguments to show that what penetrated that armor was not just an illusion, not something invented or added by them, and therefore real.[56]

And this uncertainty about outside 'reality' becomes uncertainty about the self. Can we refer to our own feelings to 'validate' the self, confirm a sense of self-identity? Feelings have an ambiguous status; they are definitely 'inside', but are also part of what the self must control. The self needs both to 'test' their validity, convince itself of their reality and genuineness *as* self, yet also needs to rely on them to validate itself. One cannot be confident of how to recognize feelings, where they come from, who they 'belong' to:

> Here then the notion of 'relying on one's own judgment and feelings' is propagated at a moment in history when . . . the ego is extremely uncertain of the reliability of its own judgment and feelings . . . one should 'have faith in one's own feelings', without knowing how to recognize or understand them, or which feelings belong to whom, or even which feelings one has oneself.[57]

Modern notions of love emerge out of this, with eighteenth-century courtship rituals becoming an endless testing of the masks, interrogation of one's own feelings and those of the other, alternative withdrawal and commitment, with no real certainty; one has to have 'faith' in one's feelings, but one cannot really 'know' them; they have become opaque. A discourse of feelings simultaneously creates them as obscure; they speak, but we cannot understand the language, or whence they come. We construct feelings and emotions in the image of interiority; we experience them as going from the inside out, as needing 'release'; and we identify with them as being somehow the core of our subjectivity, even though they exist in a problematical relation with thought, with rationality. So the 'rational', controlling self also has expressive depths, and this simultaneously 'grounds' the self, gives it meaning, and represents a challenge to it.

How, indeed, can the self become aware of itself, take itself as object? How can it *represent* itself to itself? In returning to problems of representation, we need to confront the significance of reflexivity in the construction of the modern self. Taylor observes that although there may well be self-referential terms in any language, this is not at all the same as making 'self' into a noun, as we do, and one which then becomes crucial to our modern sense of agency. What we find here is what Taylor calls 'radical reflexivity', the drive to 'become aware of our awareness, try to experience our experiencing'; we thereby 'turn inward and become aware of our own activity and of the processes which form us', aspiring to improved self-understanding and control.[58] By the end of the eighteenth century, the term 'self-consciousness' is entering the language, apparently first used by Coleridge.[59] Self-fashioning is therefore self-referential; 'the self becomes a reflexive project', as Giddens puts it, with the body both as the raw material, and the framework through which the project is realized. The etiquette manuals and their successors – the self-help guides, magazines, TV programmes – not only reflect on the self, and 'prescribe' for it, they constitute the sense of self and body in the very act of reflexivity: 'they serve routinely to organise, and alter, the aspects of social life they report on or analyse'.[60] Identity is thus constituted reflexively through the narratives with which we organize ourselves, the stories we tell ourselves about ourselves.

Reflexivity notoriously engenders paradox: the reflexive act requires that I stand outside myself, take myself as 'other', while yet remaining 'within', self-identical. The self thus 'knows' itself through an act of self-consciousness that is inseparable from self-constitution; it finds what it has put there in the finding. . . . No wonder David Hume's celebrated philosophical quest for the self was in vain – there is nothing 'there' to find – yet the very fact of the search indicates precisely the 'space' or 'function' that we designate as 'self', and try to grasp through image and metaphor.

The pursuit of self-understanding is necessarily, therefore, a process of self-construction: 'becoming aware' of the self entails language and imagery through which the self can be grasped, yet it is this very language and imagery that will constitute our sense of what this self is. The self is thus constructed through narrative, in diary or novel or letter, or everyday speech; through drama, as role-playing; and through the imagery of clothes, fashion and art. These metaphors through which we elaborate an ever-elusive sense of self run in endless streams through the culture of modernity.

Yet the drive to rational self-control, central to the project of modernity, does not easily coexist with these images and metaphors. Self-awareness, geared to purposeful change, attempts to gloss over the paradoxes of self and reflexivity through the imposition of a purposeful, future-oriented sense of identity as project, guided by notions of 'rationality' and 'progress'. Contributing to this are tensions in the very notion of 'civility', and to these we now turn.

The Mask and the Face: Civility, Civilization, Enlightenment

When Hamlet tells us that 'I have that within which passes show/These but the trappings and the suits of woe', he is drawing our attention to the possibility that outward form may deceive. Barker elaborates the point as follows:

Hamlet asserts against the devices of the world an essential interiority. If the 'forms, modes, shapes' fail to denote him truly it is because in him a separation has already opened up between the inner reality of the subject, living itself, as 'that within that passes show', and an inauthentic exterior: and in that opening there begins to insist, however prematurely, the figure that is to dominate and organize bourgeois culture.[61]

We can state the problem as follows. If civility requires foresight, the self-conscious presentation of self through manners, so that manners 'represent' the self, then this implies the possibility that civility may be just a veneer, a cover for manipulation and self-interest. Appearance and character may diverge. Elias writes, of the socially competent modern individual,

> Just as he is forced to seek the true motives of others behind their controlled outward behaviour, just as he is lost if he is unable to unmask the affects and interests of his rivals behind their dispassionate façades, he must know his own passions if he is to conceal them effectively.[62]

Since the emergence of this universe of discourse, the problematic nature of the relation between external virtue and possible inner vice, appearance and reality, form and substance, has been central to discussions of the modern self. Thus Finkelstein writes:

> The paradox of manners . . . is that the display of manners is not proof of the virtues they represent despite the commonplace use of them as such . . . on the one hand, manners provide us with mutually understood techniques which prepare us for social engagement and, on the other hand, they are devices through which we have learned to conceal our sentiments and moral positions from the other in the hope that we may gain some purchase on their behaviour.[63]

Civility swings between conformism and manipulation, raising the issues of role-playing and authenticity, hypocrisy and credibility. And the elder Mirabeau's complaint, in the eighteenth century, that all too often we find 'the mask of virtue and not its face', reminds us of the relevance of 'civility' to debates on the very nature of civilization and Enlightenment.

By the 1830s and 1840s, the fact of 'civilization' is no longer in question; it is taken for granted that 'we' are civilized, though 'the other' may have a long way to go. 'Civilization' had come to incorporate the idea of process and development, together with what Raymond Williams calls 'the associated sense of modernity: an achieved condition of refinement and order'.[64] But the results of the process are given conflicting evaluations. For Balzac, it had become a middle-class façade, 'civilized egoism'. For Coleridge and Mill, it had brought physical comforts, improved manners, science, political liberties – but also monotony, the creation of artificial wants, mechanistic rationalism, the loss of spiritual insight. And in effect, this reproduces the structure of debate on civility and civilization as it had developed in the eighteenth century, and which in turn rested on the dialectic of control and interiority, appearance and depth, that has been outlined above.

The core of the debate was over the extent to which 'civility', refinement in manners, could produce moral improvement, *real* 'civilization'. The French eighteenth-century argument focused on the relationship between moral progress and material luxury. Rosalind Williams points out that

> The essential ambiguity of the civilizing ideal is that it inevitably includes a material component; its potential tragedy is that the material forms can survive and even flourish while the vitality of the ideal withers. . . . In the eighteenth century the idea of civilization referred both to a general social and political ideal and, more narrowly, to a comfortable way of life reserved for the upper classes.[65]

On one side of the argument, Voltaire was prepared to defend upper-class luxury as necessary for general social progress; in England, versions of the argument, cast in terms of political economy, were popular in the form given it by Mandeville and Petty. In effect, private vices can produce public benefits. But there is also a more subtle version of the argument, pointed to by Sennett when he suggests that 'civilization' could be said to have 'represented a certain kind of acceptance of difference', through accepting 'the virtues of a certain kind of disguise'; the codes of behaviour set a value on impersonality, and were 'one release from obsessive interiority'.[66] In effect, this raises the issue of the role of theatricality in selfhood, an issue I discuss in the first chapter of *Exploring the Modern*. For Rousseau, both versions of the argument were fatally flawed; the effect was simply that people became puppets. Their newly cultivated vices make them 'love their slavery, and turn them into what is called civilized people'.[67]

The German argument is posed in a confusingly different terminology, but has basically the same structure: Kant and Herder counterposed *Kultur*, with its connotations of inwardness, spirituality and authenticity, against *Zivilisation*, with its over-refinement and superficiality. Nevertheless, Kant himself can be seen as trying to improve the quality of the 'civilizing process' rather than engaging in any thoroughgoing critique of it. 'Civilizing' should not be simply about manners; it required the development of human faculties and the improvement of morals. If civility was concerned with the mask, civilization should be concerned with the face, and the reality underneath: motives, passions and reasons. The tensions between appearance and reality can therefore engender a programme for human betterment: the 'civilizing process' meets the Enlightenment project.[68]

That the culture of 'civility' has political aspects has been noted by various commentators. Civility is significant in the construction of the self as subject to the nation-state: 'becoming civilized' and 'becoming a citizen' go hand in hand. Indeed, the words have the same root. In effect, to 'civilize' someone is to make that person into a citizen. Bauman also points out that, in France, *civiliser* retains links with a term it largely replaced, namely *policer*. A *policé* society is one that is well organized, transparent, ruled by law and order.[69] This is also quite close to the connotations of the expression 'civil society', as it came into use in eighteenth-century British debates. Also pertinent is Turner's observation that 'regimen', meaning 'specialized diet', has the same root as 'regime', meaning 'form of government', and this points very clearly to the political dimension of the out-pouring of etiquette and dietary manuals: 'The solution to social and physiological pathology was to be sought in the government of the body through diet and discipline.'[70] Social control, civilization and education are therefore closely connected, and it is this matrix that characterizes the Enlightenment project.

Bauman writes that Enlightenment thinkers 'saw the world as composed of individuals left to their own resources, needing the light of knowledge to cope with their life tasks, waiting for the wisdom of the state to supply them with the proper conditions and the proper guidance'.[71] Education is therefore of crucial importance; the Enlightenment is above all an educational project. In turn, education was to involve the inculcation not only of manners but of values and knowledge; and education was to be primarily the responsibility of those who were already being called 'ideologists' in some quarters, with ideology being conceived as 'the science of society'. Destutt de Tracy, who introduced the term, argued that 'it will be easy for us to indicate to people the rules (of thought and action) they must follow'. The emphasis on rules, and the authoritarian flavour, are not untypical, and point to a necessary link with state power. Bauman points out that the word 'culture' itself – in widespread use in eighteenth-century discussion – originally had gardening connotations, and these clung to it in its new connection with education. Whereas pre-modern rulers had practised a 'gamekeeper' role, merely keeping out poachers, as it were, philosophers and administrators of the Enlightenment saw society as a 'garden culture', requiring active positive intervention and constant attention, a sense of overall design, careful planning, and the elimination of weeds. . . .[72]

The other essential theme of the Enlightenment is that of 'progress'. The idea that history could be conceived as a process of gradual development in a particular direction, revealing the growing extent, and deepening, of 'civilization', became widely influential. This was linked to the idea of a critique of existing, and 'outdated', social and political institutions; enlightened statecraft should sweep away obstructions to this growth of knowledge and culture. Here, then, is the radical, cutting edge of the Enlightenment. The most optimistic version of this thesis is here stated by the Enlightenment's greatest philosopher, Kant himself:

> I will therefore venture to assume that as the human race is continually advancing in civilization and culture as its natural purpose, so it is continually making progress for the better in relation to the moral end of its existence, and that this progress, although it may be sometimes interrupted, will never be entirely broken off or stopped.[73]

The duty of the state was to promulgate rational laws in the light of human knowledge, so as to encourage the continued betterment of the human condition. According to Lovejoy, this entailed the Enlightenment ideal that 'man should conform as nearly as possible to a standard conceived as universal, uncomplicated, immutable, uniform for every rational being'. The Enlightenment was, in short, 'an age devoted . . . to the simplification and the standardization of thought and life'.[74] But in conclusion, let us remember that the universalizing pretensions of Enlightenment were 'carried' by a very specific figure, a particular historical product: we are, after all, talking first and foremost about *Homo clausus* again, or 'bourgeois man', even though, of course, the influence of these ideas and patterns of behaviour goes well beyond him. Referring to the point reached by the French Revolution, Dorinda Outram summarizes the argument well:

> the public body on which the middle class founded its political legitimation during the Revolution was that of *homo clausus*, the male type validated by . . . body-control leading to an increasingly painful yet necessary sense of separation from other individual human beings. *Homo clausus* legitimated himself by his superiority to the somatic relationships enjoyed by other classes – aristocracy, peasants and workers – and by the other gender . . . display is characterized as aristocratic, emotionality and subjectivity as feminine, physical energy as plebeian.[75]

'Civilization' and 'Enlightenment' therefore exist in dynamic relation to their opposites, continually recreating these as the necessary yet troublesome 'other' to themselves. . . .

Notes

1   F. Kafka, *Wedding Preparations in the Country* (Secker and Warburg, 1954), p. 167.
2   C. Lévi-Strauss, *The Origin of Table Manners* (Cape, 1978), p. 498.
3   N. Elias, *The Civilizing Process*, Vol. I, *The History of Manners* (Blackwell, 1978). See also S. Mennell, *Norbert Elias* (Blackwell, 1992) and J. Fletcher, *Violence and Civilization* (Polity, 1997), which include discussion of possible 'decivilizing' tendencies.
4   Elias, *Civilizing Process*, I, p. 69.
5   F. Braudel, *The Structures of Everyday Life* (Collins, 1981), p. 206.
6   S. Mennell, 'On the Civilizing of Appetite', in M. Featherstone et al., *The Body* (Sage, 1991); and see M. Visser, *The Rituals of Dinner* (Viking, 1992).
7   N. Fiddes, *Meat: A Natural Symbol* (Routledge, 1991), p. 91.
8   S. Mennell, *All Manners of Food* (Blackwell, 1987), p. 291.
9   Ibid., p. 301. See also G. Paster, *The Body Embarrassed* (Cornell University Press, 1993).
10 Cited in Fiddes, *Meat*, p. 66.
11 Elias, *Civilizing Process*, I, p. 3.
12 Ibid., p. 101.
13 J. Fiske, *Understanding Popular Culture* (Unwin Hyman, 1989), p. 99.
14 R. Porter, preface to P. Camporesi, *Bread of Dreams* (Polity, 1989), p. 5.
15 S. Stewart, *On Longing* (Duke University Press, 1993), p. 104.
16 J. Butler, *Gender Trouble* (Routledge, 1990), p. 132.
17 Elias, *Civilizing Process*, I, pp. 158, 116, 150. See also J. Goudsblom, 'Public Health and the Civilizing Process', *Milbank Quarterly* (1986), 64: 2.
18 P. Stallybrass and A. White, *The Politics and Poetics of Transgression* (Methuen, 1986), p. 113.

19   Butler, *Gender Trouble*, p. 132.

20   P. Anderson, *The Printed Image and the Transformation of Popular Culture, 1790–1860* (Clarendon Press, 1991), pp. 120, 124. On gender aspects, see also J. Craik, *The Face of Fashion* (Routledge, 1994), pp. 49–50, and, on cleanliness, A. McClintock, *Imperial Leather: Race, Gender and Sexuality in the Colonial Context* (Routledge, 1995), ch. 5, discussing the cultural politics of soap.

21   B. S. Turner, *The Body and Society* (Blackwell, 1984), p. 78.

22   D. Outram, *The Body in the French Revolution* (Yale University Press, 1989), p. 48.

23   S. Greenblatt, 'Filthy Rites', *Daedalus* (1982), 111: 3, p. 2.

24   Cited in B. Sheehan, *Savagism and Civility* (Cambridge University Press, 1980), p. 76.

25   Cited in K. Thomas, *Man and the Natural World* (Penguin, 1984), p. 38.

26   A. Bryson, 'The Rhetoric of Status: Gesture, Demeanour and the Image of the Gentleman in 16th and 17th Century England', in L. Gent and N. Llewellyn (eds.) *Renaissance Bodies* (Reaktion Books, 1990), p. 149.

27   Elias, *Civilizing Process*, I, pp. 69, 101; see also C. Shilling, *The Body and Social Theory* (Sage, 1993), ch. 7.

28   D. H. J. Morgan, '"No More Heroes?": Masculinity, Violence and the Civilising Process', in L. Jamieson (ed.) *State, Private Life and Political Change* (Macmillan, 1990), pp. 17, 18. Duelling continued later in Germany: see Fletcher, *Violence*, ch. 6.

29   See, for example, J. and M. Corbin, *Urbane Thought: Culture and Class in an Andalusian City* (Gower, 1987).

30   Mennell, *All Manners of Food*, p. 303.

31   N. Elias, *The Civilizing Process*, Vol. II, *State Formation and Civilization* (Blackwell, 1982), p. 255. See also the discussion of consumerism and fashion in my *Exploring the Modern: Patterns of Western Culture and Civilization* (Blackwell, 1998), chs. 4, 5.

32   Bryson, 'Rhetoric of Status', p. 149.

33   R. Williams, *Dream Worlds* (California University Press, 1982), p. 25.

34   Fiddes, *Meat*, pp. 91, 154.

35   Bryson, 'Rhetoric of Status', p. 152.

36   D. Starkey, 'Representation through Intimacy', in I. M. Lewis (ed.) *Symbols and Sentiments* (Academic Press, 1977), p. 221.

37   Elias, *Civilizing Process*, I, p. 121, original emphasis.

38   Fiddes, *Meat*, p. 104. See also R. Sennett, *The Fall of Public Man* (Faber and Faber, 1986), and my *Exploring the Modern*, ch. 1.

39   Corbin, *Urbane Thought*, p. 21.

40   Cited in Bryson, 'Rhetoric of Status', p. 145.

41   N. Elias, *The Court Society* (Blackwell, 1969), p. 104.

42   Elias, *Civilizing Process*, I, pp. 78, 80.

43   Elias, *Civilizing Process*, II, p. 233.

44   Bryson, 'Rhetoric of Status', pp. 143, 144, 145, 146.

45   C. Taylor, *Sources of the Self* (Cambridge University Press, 1989), pp. 144, 197. See also the discussion of science in ch. 6 of the present volume.

46   S. Greenblatt, *Renaissance Self-fashioning: From More to Shakespeare* (Chicago University Press), 1980, p. 2.

47   Taylor, *Sources*, pp. 149, 171.

48   Ibid., p. 111. For the novel, see my *Exploring the Modern*, ch. 6.

49   J. Benton, 'Consciousness of Self and Perception of Individuality', in R. L. Benson and G. Constable (eds.) *Renaissance and Renewal in the Twelfth Century* (Harvard University Press, 1982), p. 285.

50 Taylor, *Sources*, p. 187.

51 Elias, *Civilizing Process*, I, pp. 258–9.

52 F. Barker, *The Tremulous Private Body* (Methuen, 1984), p. 67.

53 A. Giddens, *Modernity and Self-Identity* (Polity, 1991), p. 59. See also ch. 4 of the present volume.

54 Turner, *Body*, p. 184.

55 R. Crawford, 'A Cultural Account of "Health": Control, Release, and the Social Body', in J. B. McKinlay (ed.) *Issues in the Political Economy of Health Care* (Tavistock, 1984), p. 81. See also the discussion of consumerism in my *Exploring the Modern*, ch. 4.

56 K. Theweleit, *Male Fantasies*, Vol. I, *Women, Floods, Bodies, History* (Minnesota University Press, 1987), p. 328.

57 Ibid., p. 330.

58 Taylor, *Sources*, pp. 130, 174.

59 C. Campbell, *The Romantic Ethic and the Spirit of Modern Consumerism* (Blackwell, 1987), p. 73.

60 Giddens, *Modernity*, pp. 32, 14.

61 Barker, *Tremulous Private Body*, p. 35.

62 N. Elias, cited in J. Finkelstein, *Dining Out: A Sociology of Modern Manners* (Polity, 1989), p. 129.

63 Finkelstein, *Dining Out*, pp. 134, 166.

64 R. Williams, *Keywords* (Fontana, 1976), p. 49.

65 Williams, *Dream Worlds*, pp. 25, 38.

66 R. Sennett, *The Conscience of the Eye: The Design and Social Life of Cities* (Faber and Faber, 1991), pp. 79, 81.

67 Cited in Williams, *Dream Worlds*, p. 43.

68 Sennett, *Conscience of the Eye*, pp. 84–6; Elias, *Civilizing Process*, I, pp. 3–10.

69 Z. Bauman, 'On the Origins of Civilisation: A Historical Note', in *Theory, Culture and Society* (1985), 2:3, p. 8.

70 Turner, *Body*, p. 167.

71 Z. Bauman, *Legislators and Interpreters* (Polity, 1989), p. 38.

72 Ibid., ch. 4. For the controversies over the later results of the Enlightenment project, see my *Exploring the Modern*, ch. 9.

73 Cited in R. Nisbet, *Social Change and History* (Oxford University Press, 1969), p. 117.

74 A. Lovejoy, *The Great Chain of Being* (Harvard University Press, 1960), p. 292.

75 Outram, *Body*, p. 73. On political and economic aspects, see also C. B. Macpherson, *The Political Theory of Possessive Individualism* (Clarendon Press, 1962).

Part II
Modernity and Its Others

3 Exotic Encounters:

Savagery, Civilization and the Imperial Other

Bougainville and Cook, the two great explorers of their day, fascinated the Enlightenment reading public with their descriptions of their Pacific expeditions. Approaching Tahiti, during his voyage of 1766–9, Bougainville recounts the approach of canoes, one of them full of women:

> Most of these nymphs were naked. . . . They first made from their canoes provocative gestures in which, in spite of their innocence, one could detect a certain embarrassment, either because nature has everywhere embellished their sex with a naive timidity or because, even in lands where the freedom of the Golden Age still reigns, women appear not to want what they desire the most.

Sexual favours are given freely, he remarks, and adds, not surprisingly: 'I thought I had been transported to the Garden of Eden.'[1] Cook's men had similar experiences. The surgeon's mate, Samwell, wrote that the young women of Hawaii were 'exceedingly beautiful', and when they found the sailors 'were not to be allured by their blandishments, they endeavoured to force them and were so importunate they would absolutely take no denial'. In short, 'there was hardly one of us that may not vie with the grand Turk himself'[2] – which rather suggests that the sailors' resistance may not, perhaps, have been wholehearted.

Leaving aside the Turk for a moment, we can note that here we are witnessing the birth of the myth – or male fantasy – of the idyllic South Sea Islands as blissful paradise, a myth that draws on ideas of the 'noble savage' and will have a long subsequent history, through Melville, Stevenson and Gauguin, to Margaret Mead. It is also clear that, right from the start, the myth tells us more about the myth-makers than it does about the islanders. Bougainville's text, in particular, manifests conspicuous vacillations over how to characterize the 'otherness' of the inhabitants, over nature and culture, 'civilization' and the 'Golden Age'. In the original 'state of nature', equated with the Golden Age, we find an 'innocence' that nevertheless coexists with the 'embarrassment' that is implicitly a product of civilization, and, moreover, an 'innocence' that involves 'provocative gestures'. We even find the irony that one of the hoariest patriarchal myths of the West – that women 'really' want sex even when they appear not to – can be projected back into the state of 'innocence' of the Garden of Eden. One might say that it is the visitors – and their categories – who are embarrassed, not the women; and that the 'provocation' of the gestures is a translation of these gestures into the language of sexual enticement that the sailors are familiar with from their own culture. Indeed, as Sahlins points out, since the sailors 'reified the women's embraces as "services" by the gifts they made in return',[3] they in effect reconstructed the whole scene in the language of prostitute and client. Thus do the women swing between innocence and whoredom, Paradise before and after the Fall.

As for Cook, his death at the hands of these same islanders was, from their point of view, a sacrifice, and served to reinforce his already suspected divinity in their eyes. But Sahlins remarks that it had similar consequences for the *Western* view of Cook. In the published account of the voyage, Lieutenant King tells us that the Hawaiians 'considered him a being of superior nature'; yet a midshipman in Cook's crew describes him in virtually identical terms, as a 'kind of superior being'.[4] By the early nineteenth century, at least four different engravings depicting Cook's ascension into Heaven had been published, with the conventional iconography of angels and trumpets; and the rock at the spot where Cook had met his fate seems to have been regarded as sacred by both sides, so that by the 1840s, after successive waves of Hawaiian and European visitors had furtively helped themselves to its 'power', none of it remained. . . .[5]

Thus does the Age of Reason encounter, in the 'primitive idolatry' of those it locates at the furthest possible extreme from itself, an 'other' oddly similar, while conversely, in the sexual arena, its uncertain universalizing of its own categories threatens to deny otherness altogether. And just as it is not the first time that these responses of disavowal and projection will produce these problems of recognition and misrecognition, nor will it be the last; we find here a logic of distancing and assimilation constantly reproduced in the modern encounter with otherness. If we say that in 1492 America and Christopher Columbus discovered each other, it is also true that they did no such thing: America thought he was some*thing* else (a god, probably), and he thought he was some*where* else (a few miles from the Great Khan's palace in Peking). If Todorov is right, in his claim in *The Conquest of America*, that 1492 can be taken to mark 'the beginning of the modern era',[6] then it would clearly have to be said that this 'modern era' was the offspring of a union of mutual incomprehension; and it could be claimed that incomprehension has characterized the relation between modernity and those characterized as its others ever since.

In exploring these issues, it will become apparent that the imperial adventure has indeed been central to the development of the modern West, which has always sought to validate itself through an encounter with those it can define as 'primitive', thereby confirming the superiority of its essential attributes of 'civilization' and 'rationality'; and has, in turn, often projected unacceptable facets of itself, so that what is not recognized in itself can be denounced in another. Yet this search for validation allows the other an entry, even makes the other necessary, and thus potentially dangerous, as though the other is required to give a paradoxical confirmation of its own inferiority, a confirmation that it could only give if it were 'rational', 'civilized', and no longer itself. . . .

Noble Savages?

Columbus is greatly troubled by the attitude to possessions and money that he encounters in the New World. Never had he met so munificent a people: 'They are to such a degree lacking in artifice and so generous with what they possess, that no man would believe it unless he had seen such a thing!' He adds, in amazement: 'All that they have, they give for any trifle we offer them, so that they take in exchange pieces of crockery and fragments of glass goblets.' Clearly not the sort of 'rational' behaviour expected of modern profit-maximizing individuals. His very first observations generalize this perception: 'These people are very gentle and fearful, naked . . . , without weapons and without laws.' Furthermore, 'They have no religion, nor are they idolators.'[7]

Here we see the emergence of the early modern version of the 'noble savage': primitive, yet gentle and innocent; closer to nature; both human – just about – yet almost superior. The claim that they are without laws and without religion amounts to saying that they lack custom and culture, and this claim is highly significant. For a start, it implies a blindness to the possibility of *other* cultures: either cultures are sufficiently close to us to be versions of us, or they are not cultures at all. There is, in short, no *ethnographic* consciousness in Columbus; no interest in exploring the otherness of other cultures.

In addition, if these 'savages' have no law and no religion, then are they really, or fully, 'human' anyway? Logically, the absence of culture opens up two further sets of possibilities. One poses a dilemma of communication. The general form of this is stated by North: 'The colonial subject is either a part of nature, utterly literal and therefore soothingly simple, or menacingly unreadable, mysterious, and suggestive of some vast unknown.'[8] The other poses a dilemma of existential status. The savage may be qualitatively superior, hence 'noble'; or, conversely, we encounter inferiority, with 'savage' meaning 'sub-human'. What is fascinating in Columbus is the way he swings between these alternative versions of a structure that reappears constantly in modern constructions of the 'primitive'. Thus Columbus exclaims that 'Even bits of broken cask-hoops they took in exchange for whatever they had, like beasts!' The very same behaviour that previously made them noble now makes them animal. He comments on the 'shameless' way they steal everything; from being generous, they have now become thieves. The other swings dramatically from being a 'noble savage' to being a 'dirty dog'. And if they are the latter, all that matters is how they can be *used*. 'They are fit to be ruled',[9] he writes to his sponsors, the Catholic Monarchs, and suggests that they would make industrious slaves, if properly trained. And in practice, both assimilating them to us (as human) and distancing them (as subhuman) can be combined, through seeing them as 'fallen', accursed of God: we are all corrupt, but the Indian is far more so. This becomes the dominant perspective, and illustrates how discovery and dispossession can easily be two sides of the same coin, as will now be shown.

Montrose observes that by the 1570s, allegorical personifications of America as a female nude with a feathered headdress were appearing in engravings, paintings and title-pages throughout Western Europe.[10] America was 'virgin', the settlers representing a latter-day Adam, ready both to name and 'possess' her. Ella Shohat points to the implications of this discourse:

> A 'virgin' land is implicitly available for defloration and fecundation. Implied to lack owners, it therefore becomes the property of its 'discoverers' and cultivators. The 'purity' of the terminology masks the dispossession of the land and its resources. A land already fecund, already producing for the indigenous peoples, and thus a 'mother', is metaphorically projected as 'virgin', 'untouched nature', and therefore as available and awaiting a master.[11]

As Walter Raleigh puts it in 1596, in gleeful anticipation, 'Guiana is a countrey that hath yet her maydenhead.' Thus we find what Hulme calls the 'classical colonial triangle':[12] the settler, the 'virginal' land, and the original possessors who have to be dispossessed. His discussion of Virginia can serve as a typical instance.

Prior to the traumatic events of 1622, the Virginia colony had hardly been a flagship for European superiority. English agriculture and technology proved useless, and the colony became dependent for food on the surrounding Algonkin Indians:

> So not only was the survival of European culture in America in doubt, but the founding values of that culture – stability, organization, civility itself – stared back at it from the supposed chaos of the savage wilderness. In such circumstances the establishment of a colonial presence could only find the necessary support through massive efforts of discursive projection and psychotic disavowal.

Observing that 'successful narratives can only be written backwards', *after* the event, Hulme suggests that the crucial event here was the 'massacre' of 22 March 1622, when the Algonkins finally turned on the English interlopers and nearly wiped them out. Only then could 'history' begin; for in this act the Algonkins could be presented as having committed a primal transgression, the constitutive 'betrayal' that legitimates everything that is to follow. Through spilling their blood, the English settlers become identified with the land of Virginia – it is *they* who become the violated virgins, raped by the treacherous Indians. The original inhabitants are thus expelled from their lands, even *by* their lands: Virginia, rendered properly virgin, can now be wooed by the English, the Algonkin reduced to 'sullen and rejected suitors'.[13] It is as though Virginia has to be raped into virginity; and the act is carried out not by the colonists, but by the Indians themselves. And this scenario will be re-enacted many times in the history of colonialism: the 'Black Hole of Calcutta', for example, will retrospectively provide the 'justification' for the final push to empire in India, the atrocities committed by the British troops in suppressing the 'Mutiny' being written out of the narrative. . . .[14]

Ideologically, the fact of dispossession itself came increasingly to be justified by the 'property is use' argument: the right to property is not untrammelled; property has to be used, worked, not merely 'occupied'. Indians did not 'develop' the land, hence forfeited their rights; and as Brantlinger observes, the task of 'civilizing' them was 'defined in terms of their conversion both to Christianity and to "productive labor" or "industry"'.[15] Much the same argument is used by the future president, Theodore Roosevelt, at the other end of the process, in 1896: 'The settler and the pioneer have at bottom had justice on their side; this great continent could not have been kept as a game preserve for squalid savages.'[16]

The impression remains, then, that the 'nobility' of the 'savage' in the early modern period was alluded to only to be disallowed and disavowed; it is really the Enlightenment period that celebrates this figure. With their interest in 'culture' and 'civilization', Enlightenment authors were fascinated by the possibility of 'cultureless beings', characterized by 'absences and lacks'.[17] Horigan suggests that they implicitly distinguished between 'soft' primitivism, where savages are creatures of leisure, living in harmony with nature, and 'hard' primitivism, involving a spartan existence and a constant war with nature;[18] but in either case, the trappings of 'civilization' are clearly absent, and either could be used as the basis for the elaboration of a critique of the 'artificiality' and 'corruption' of civilization itself. But always we find the ambiguity we have seen in Bougainville's text: behaviour that can be presented as 'innocent' can as easily be seen as 'wanton'. And the paradox: that the nobility of the other is ascribed from a position that necessarily implies a self-refuting superiority; it is only the 'civilized' who can recognize it.

The sentimentalizing of the South Sea Islands does not, moreover, preclude their incorporation into the new commercial trading patterns. A vicarious enjoyment of 'otherness' in no way inhibited its scientific and colonial appropriation; thus Hulme comments that 'sentimental sympathy began to flow along the arteries of European commerce, in search of its victims'.[19] After all, while enjoying the Garden of Eden, Bougainville does not omit one crucial detail. He tells us: 'I buried . . . an act of taking possession inscribed on an oak board', a gesture which, as Porter writes, 'effectively politicized paradise'.[20] Baudet concludes, on the myths of the Golden Age:

> The myths covered the distant earthly paradise with a veil of enchantment through which they were seen as the home of the blessed and the elect, but they formed no hindrance to their intensive and ruthless economic exploitation. . . . There was, on the one hand, the actual physical outside world which could be put to political, economic and strategic use; there was also the outside world onto which all identification and interpretation, all dissatisfaction and desire, all nostalgia and idealism seeking expression could be projected.[21]

Race and Evolution

In moving on to the nineteenth century, we encounter the age when colonialism made its most dramatic impact: Said claims that in the century from 1815 to 1914, the proportion of the land surface of the globe taken over by European powers rose from 35 per cent to 85 per cent.[22] It is Africa and Asia that bear the brunt of imperial expansion, and it is they that come increasingly to hold centre stage in the modern imagination of the other, an imagination now coloured by the fateful intersection of new ideas of race and evolution.

In the main, racism, in the modern sense, was not a feature of early modern attitudes to other cultures.[23] The Spanish conquest of Latin America featured plunder and massacre, but there is little evidence that racism as such was a factor, and interbreeding between the Spaniards and the local inhabitants occurred relatively freely from early on. In the eighteenth century, the general view was still that differences in colour, hair, and so on, were not of great significance, and were merely due to differences of food and environment, and this was linked with a lack of any clear distinctions between physical, psychological and social attributes. Linnaeus proclaimed the unity of one species, 'Homo sapiens', and distinguished six 'varieties', including 'European Man', characterized by 'blue eyes' and being 'governed by law'; 'Asiatic Man', with 'black hair' and 'ruled by opinions'; and 'African Man', with 'frizzled hair', who is 'crafty, indolent, negligent' and 'governed by caprice'.[24]

Implicit in this is the possibility that these 'varieties' *could* be separate species; and this doctrine – polygenism – became quite popular until the late nineteenth century, as it was easy to combine with emergent ideas of history as evolution, safeguarding the position of Europeans as the 'most advanced' species. But the final victory of monogenism, again asserting the oneness of the human species, went hand in hand with a further development of evolutionary and racist ideas. It was now *races*, defined in biological terms, that could be ranked on an evolutionary scale; and physical differences were increasingly seen to underlie cultural ones. The apparently progressive notion of human unity was thus developed in a way that enabled the other to be assimilated but simultaneously reduced in status, becoming an earlier, less developed stage in 'our' history: identity plus inferiority, as it were. Hence the distinctiveness of the nineteenth-century category of the 'primitive', the sense in which explorers of Africa did not *discover* 'primitive peoples', but rather, as McGrane writes, 'It was only through this Eurocentric construction of and commitment to the concept of "progress" . . . that "primitive peoples" came into being.' He concludes: 'Progress produces primitives; primitives do not prove progress.'[25] And when the ruins of Great Zimbabwe were discovered in 1871, they had to be 'explained away' – they were ruins of Phoenician civilization, perhaps, since 'primitive' Africans could never have produced them. . . .[26]

In this perspective, it becomes possible to construct an 'evolutionary ladder'. At the top is the middle-class white man; and at the lowest point, closest to the apes, is the black woman, particularly the stereotype 'grinning Hottentot'. Black skin is the ultimate signifier of primitiveness, and African customs are reconstructed in the light of this; by the 1860s, the model of the 'African as cannibal' was becoming widely influential. In the USA, racist ideas of this kind became even more significant after the abolition of slavery, ensuring a pervasive institutionalization of discriminatory norms that remained largely intact, at least in the South, till well into the 1960s. Typical of this incorporation of racial stereotypes was the California Supreme Court ruling in 1854 that 'No Black, or Mulatto person, or Indian shall be allowed to give evidence in favour of, or against, a White man', since non-whites are 'people whom nature has marked out as inferior, and who are incapable of progress or development beyond a certain point'.[27] At one time, 40 per cent of the US states prohibited interracial marriage; such laws were declared unconstitutional as late as 1967.[28]

It is the 'miscegenation' issue that reveals the implications of this most dramatically.[29] For the racist, interbreeding is the ultimate sin against the natural order. Mapped on to gender stereotypes, racist assumptions characteristically produce the following matrix. Sexual relations between white women and black men must inevitably involve rape (since black men, being 'primitive', are insatiable, whereas white women are refined, restrained, and could not possibly desire black men); sexual relations between white men and black women cannot involve rape (since black women, too, are insatiable); nor can relations between blacks.[30] This intersection of racial and gender stereotypes has not only been central to cultural representations – in novels, films and the media generally – but has had fateful consequences in everyday life. It provides the clue to the lynching of black men for alleged sexual offences against white women; and between 1945 and 1965, seven times more blacks than whites were executed for rape in the southern USA, and it rises to eighteen times more when the victim is white.[31]

In considering the implications of these ideas for colonialism it is useful to consider the work of Darwin himself, since his ideas reveal a tension that is central to the philosophy and practice of imperial intervention. On the one hand, Darwin was totally contemptuous of the 'uncivilized', and looked forward to a time, 'not very distant', when an 'endless number of lower races will have been eliminated by the higher civilized races'. This channels directly into the so-called 'Social Darwinist' strand in late nineteenth-century thought, celebrating the 'survival of the fittest', and implying that the pillage of the world by the white man stood in need of no higher justification. But there is another strand in Darwin. In *The Descent of Man*, Darwin proclaimed that the very hallmark of progress and civilization was 'disinterested love for all living creatures', and that this had to be extended to 'men of all races, to the imbecile, maimed and other useless members of society'.[32] The struggle for existence has itself produced a creature with a 'moral sense', able to question the very process that produced it.

This second strand is important for our understanding of the paternalist, humanitarian rationale that was often invoked for colonialism. Here we have the source of the 'white man's burden', 'civilization' as a moral duty, as embedded in the theory and practice of figures like Livingstone. And ultimately, there was no agreement between these two poles of Victorian imperial ideology: at one extreme, full-blooded racists could argue that savagery was irredeemable; at the other, racism itself could fall into insignificance, and in effect all we are left with is an educational problem. As a rationale for colonialism, a mid-point is clearly most suitable, implying that while 'primitives' are capable of improvement, their condition means that they cannot improve themselves, and require the prolonged tutelage of enlightened colonial rule. And Brantlinger suggests that this became the broad consensus: just as 'the British were inherently, by "blood", a conquering, governing and civilizing "race"', so 'the "dark" races whom they conquered were inherently incapable of governing and civilizing themselves'.[33]

There is also an extension of these ideas and practices *within* the home culture, a kind of 'internal colonialism': Pratt comments that colonialist ventures served as 'models, inspirations and testing grounds' for 'modes of social discipline which, imported back into Europe . . . were adapted to construct the bourgeois order'.[34] Gender, class and race became powerfully superimposed. Thus Anne McClintock points out that 'the agency of women, the colonized and the industrial working class are disavowed and projected onto anachronistic space: prehistoric, atavistic and irrational, inherently out of place in the historical time of modernity'.[35] The working class was frequently portrayed by analogy with the 'uncivilized' of foreign lands. The master contrast of 'light' and 'dark' was much employed; 'darkest Africa' could be found nearer home. Nord suggests that the contrast between the prosperous West End and the working-class East End of London was often drawn in these terms: 'the West represented all that was bright, open, dazzling and enlightened; the East all that was dark, labyrinthine, threatening, and benighted'.[36] General Booth, founder of the Salvation Army, entitled his programme for the alleviation of poverty *In Darkest England*; and Bristow points out that Baden-Powell, in his widely influential *Scouting for Boys* (1908), includes pictures of a 'working-class oaf' and a primitive 'Black man' on either side of a 'bright-eyed public school boy' – the latter, of course, being the ideal scout.[37]

The pervasiveness of this pattern of assumptions can hardly be underestimated. Even the most 'advanced' opinion was affected: John Stuart Mill's argument for liberty was based on a prior division of the world into cultures of 'civilization' and 'barbarism';[38] and Marx provided a conventional evolutionary justification for British rule in India. And today, the Nigerian novelist Chinua Achebe suggests that there is still a tendency for the West to 'set up Africa as a foil to Europe, a place of negations', so that by comparison Europe's own 'state of spiritual grace will be manifest'.[39] In short, modern racism emerges as a distinctive historical product and – through its links with nineteenth-century science – as an unintended heir of the Enlightenment.[40]

The Exotic and the Erotic

The very qualities that are seen as making Africa and the Orient so 'distant' can also render their strangeness fascinating, and it is this that constitutes them as 'exotic', objects that inspire both desire and fear. Elaine Showalter points to the popularity of what she calls the 'male quest romance' in the late nineteenth century, with narratives that involve adventure and danger, a penetration into 'the imagined center of an exotic civilization . . . the heart of darkness which is a blank place on the map, a realm of the unexplored and unknown'. And she adds that this 'free space' is usually Africa.[41]

If Africa is 'dark', the Orient is 'mysterious'. Said refers to a cluster of notions that develop around the idea of the Orient, for instance its 'separateness, its eccentricity, its backwardness, its silent indifference, its feminine penetrability, its supine malleability'.[42] Other ideas that can be incorporated include its love of excess, in which the veneer of civilization barely conceals eroticism and violence, and its unchanging timelessness. The French poet Nerval refers to it as 'the land of dreams and illusion'. Rochegrosse's *Death of Babylon* (see plate 3) portrays the fall of the city of iniquity, with the palace burning, and the death of the naked women of the royal harem clearly imminent, the whole scene conveying images of dramatic excess, voluptuousness and destruction, and exotic decadence. This conjunction of sexuality and death is not unusual in Orientalist depictions and accounts; Porter suggests that Flaubert's journey to the East reveals how the wish to see the other's body is 'joined to the desire to overpower it and despoil it'.[43]

The mystery of the Orient is characteristically presented as 'feminine'. The Orient is frequently *veiled*. As Joanna de Groot puts it,

> In the romantic travel literature it is the sight of veiled women which tells the voyager that he is in the Orient, just as their presence on the eastward voyage poses the first challenge to understanding. They are the image of what the 'Other' actually *is*, their veils and harems the symbol of that 'Other'.[44]

For novelists like Flaubert, the Orient is the scene of escapist sexual fantasy, where harems, princesses, dancing girls, slave girls – and, of course, boys – ensure the endless availability of the illicit. The Orient has connotations of 'not only fecundity but sexual promise (and threat), untiring sensuality, unlimited desire, deep generative energies'.[45] The Orient *itself* seduces. Flaubert writes: 'that's the true Orient, a melancholy effect that makes you feel sleepy; you sense right away something immense and implacable in the midst of which you are lost';[46] a sort of post-coital languor, together with fear of engulfment by the powerful feminine other.

To complicate the picture, it must be added that there has been a significant feminine Orientalist discourse, in both literature and painting. Challenging Said's emphasis on Orientalism as 'a homogeneous discourse enunciated by a colonial subject that is unified, intentional and irredeemably male', Reina Lewis suggests that the female 'Orientalist gaze' was more compromised, less secure, less absolute, more nuanced.[47] Western women, after all, occupied ambiguous positions, 'as both subordinates in colonial hierarchies and as agents of imperial culture in their own right', as Ann Stoler claims.[48] And this is highly relevant to portrayals of the harem.

The word 'harem', in effect, means 'tabooed' (separate and holy), and the taboo clearly works on the Western masculine imagination, with its connotations of attraction and danger. Leila Ahmed notes that Western travellers were both fascinated and threatened by the togetherness of women in the harem, swinging between portraying it as dependence and exploitation, and as dangerous power, manifested in illicit sexual relations between the women themselves.[49] Indeed, these reinterpretations of the harem in contemporary feminist scholarship reveal the way it can be seen as 'simultaneously shoring up and challenging a vision of absolute phallic power', as Lewis puts it.[50] Thus 'Oriental women were painted as erotic victims and scheming witches', writes Rana Kabbani;[51] they were incarnations of the devious Cleopatra, who 'makes hungry where most she satisfies'.

The imagery of veiling is by no means restricted to the Orient; 'darkest Africa' has its erotic charms as well, and veils can play a part in this. Rebecca Stott points to a descriptive passage in Rider Haggard's *King Solomon's Mines* (1886) in which the African scenery is likened to a recumbent woman, 'veiled mysteriously in sleep', and suggests that 'The fantasy is that of a *passive* body, naked beneath the thin veil, and half asleep. Africa invites. Africa is veiled but offers tantalising glimpses of herself. She beckons in her sleep, in her passivity.' Africa also tempts, then; but temptation is dangerous. To penetrate Africa is risky; many do not survive her embraces. 'To be absorbed is to become other, to go native, to regress', writes Stott: 'The frontiers of self, manhood, civilization and progress must be protected.'[52] There is real fear, of 'falling out of the light, down the long coal chute of social and moral regression', in Brantlinger's words. Can the white male explorer or colonialist retain his whiteness and his manhood in the face of barbarism? A missionary suggests that even witnessing heathen customs can corrupt: 'Can a man touch pitch, and not be himself defiled?'[53] The ultimate horror is to 'go native', lose one's sense of difference, superiority.

It is notable that while gender and sexual symbolism is rife in these quest narratives, women as individuals are generally conspicuous by their absence; and any black woman who does have the misfortune to become involved with a white man is invariably doomed. Thus the beautiful black girl who falls for the hero in *King Solomon's Mines* seems to know her own fate in advance when she asks: 'Can the sun mate with the darkness, or the white with the black?' As has been seen, racial interbreeding would threaten the whole precarious sense of difference and superiority that the white man must maintain at any cost. In Kipling's *The Man Who Would Be King* (1888), it is Dan's decision to take a native wife, after becoming the King of 'Kafiristan', that inaugurates the disastrous end to the story.

This all seems to fit a pattern: in effect, we are dealing here with the raw material of a white male initiation rite. Out in the bush, the boy or young man can test himself against trials and temptations; and in the Orient, the writer or artist can discover himself, forge his creative identity; and in each case, this can be done free of the normal restrictions of bourgeois culture. Either way, the experience makes a boy into a man; through exploring the other, he must also resist it, thereby showing the self-mastery required of the white male adult bourgeois. A confrontation with the exotic is therefore a confrontation with the self, a journey into unknown regions that are as much inside as outside. Hence Bristow's claim that 'Darkness was, in many respects, a deepening shadow cast by whiteness. For Victorians, the picture of a miserably unenlightened Africa brought together a number of interrelated European anxieties about religion, sexuality, and history on to this highly physicalized terrain.'[54] And Stott points to the homology of psychological and historical regression: 'To "go native" is to regress, to revert to a savage past, it is to descend the ladder of evolutionary progress, but it is also to release the repressed self.' Hence, to explore Africa is 'to explore oneself, to test the strength of the veneer'.[55] To encounter the 'primitive other' is simultaneously to encounter the past in the self and the self in the past, thereby constructing a present in which the self is forever meeting up with fragments, doubles or repressed portions of itself. This can be further explored by penetrating deeper into the Dark Continent. . . .

Dark Encounters

A picture of David Livingstone in Africa shows him with his bible, bringing enlightenment to the darkness; already halfway between hero and saint, a halo of light is shown surrounding his head. His place in myth was already prepared, therefore, before the famous encounter with Henry Stanley, who found him 'lost' in the heart of the continent. And Stanley was very far from sainthood; a plunderer and adventurer, he will later play a role as an agent of the Belgian ruler Leopold II, whose infamous creation of the Congo Free State as a private fief within which exploitation, slavery and even genocide could be practised on a massive scale became one of the greatest scandals of late nineteenth-century colonialism. Stanley may, indeed, have been a model for the evil Kurtz in Joseph Conrad's *Heart of Darkness* (1898). It is as though Livingstone, a light lost in darkness, encounters a rescuer who represents the darkness of that same light.[56]

However, it is certainly the encounter between Marlow and Kurtz in *Heart of Darkness* that brings out these themes most vividly. Conrad had been in Leopold's Congo for a few months in 1890, and much of the book is autobiography masquerading as fiction; indeed, since an aura of myth has always hung around the Stanley–Livingstone encounter, we could say that Conrad's account of Marlow's meeting with Kurtz is no less 'truth' than Stanley's account of his meeting with Livingstone is 'fiction'. In Conrad's story, Marlow recounts his adventures as a steamer captain in the Congo, agent for a trading company. He hears rumours about another agent, the charismatic Kurtz, and sails into the interior to meet him; discovers that Kurtz has succumbed to 'savagery', living and ruling as a god, encouraging violence and cannibalism, and taking a native mistress; finds Kurtz seriously ill, and stays with him as he dies, impressed by the apparent clarity with which he confronts the horror, at the last; and returns to lie to Kurtz's devoted fiancée (the Intended), in order to salvage his reputation and give her something to live for.

As Marlow sails up the Congo, Africa is revealed as awesome wilderness:

> Going up that river was like travelling back to the earliest beginnings of the world, when vegetation rioted on the earth and the big trees were kings. An empty stream, a great silence, an impenetrable forest. The air was warm, thick, heavy, sluggish. There was no joy in the brilliance of the sunshine. The long stretches of the water-way ran on, deserted, into the gloom of overshadowed distances. . . . It was the stillness of an implacable force brooding over an inscrutable intention. . . . We penetrated deeper and deeper into the heart of darkness.[57]

So Africa is dark even in the sunlight; but the darkness is the darkness of the primeval, not the darkness of evil. And this is also true of its inhabitants. In that environment, they are 'natural' – 'They wanted no excuse for being there' – and such 'pure, uncomplicated savagery' had every right to exist there. But this very fact made them unfathomable:

> The steamer toiled along slowly on the edge of a black and incomprehensible frenzy. The prehistoric man was cursing us, praying to us, welcoming us – who could tell? We were cut off from the comprehension of our surroundings, we glided past like phantoms, wondering and secretly appalled.[58]

And then there is the brief, mysterious encounter with the ultimate human embodiment of this wilderness, the African Other:

> And from right to left along the lighted shore moved a wild and gorgeous appari-tion of a woman. She walked with measured steps, draped in striped and fringed cloths, treading the earth proudly with a slight jingle and flash of barbarous orna-ments. . . . She was savage and superb, wild-eyed and magnificent. . . . And in the hush that had fallen suddenly upon the whole sorrowful land, the immense wilder-ness, the colossal body of the fecund and mysterious life seemed to look at her, pensive, as though it had been looking at the image of its own tenebrous and passionate soul.[59]

A mirror: Africa the immense, prolific, fertile body, reflected in this figure of a woman, handsome, imperious – and voiceless. Like the other 'savages', her unreflective existence stands in no further need of justification. She is beyond (or beneath) good and evil; she just *is*, in all her primitive splendour. She may even have been the instrument of Kurtz's downfall; but his downfall is not to be laid at her door.

It is tempting to contrast her with the other woman in the text, the Intended. The African has speechless integrity; the Intended speaks, but only to be enmeshed in untruth. She can only be maintained in her state of purity, the refined epitome of civilization, through a diet of self-deception and lies fed to her by men. In her, civilization reveals itself as lie. She is, in her own way, as perni-cious an idol as the idol, Kurtz, she joins the 'savages' in worshipping. She and Kurtz constitute the two poles of a 'civilization' that self-consciously raises itself above 'the primitive' only to sink deeper in the mire. . . . And Marlow, in telling her the lie, and keeping Kurtz's secret, thereby reproduces this 'civilization' as a secret knowledge of evil, transmitted by and to men.

And Kurtz? It was as though in falling from a civilized state, he had fallen *below* the 'savages' with whom he was surrounded. He knows the heights of civilized virtue and the depths of its betrayal. His soul had become 'avid of lying fame, of sham distinction, all the appearances of success and power';[60] he had become the incarnation of Rousseau's critique of civilization, corrupted by reflexive self-awareness and comparison with others, seeking competitive acclaim. And Africa had become his stage, the scene of his downfall. Africa is not dark in itself, then, but only in relation to 'us'; the threat, the attraction, of an impossible freedom. And in succumbing, in this scene of otherness, you do not again become 'primitive' – for once lost, that state is never regained – you become truly *savage*. Only those who have known civilization can know true evil.

And how did it happen? Marlow speculates:

> The wilderness had found him out early. . . . I think it had whispered to him things about himself which he did not know, things of which he had no conception till he took counsel with this great solitude – and the whisper had proved irresistibly fascinating. It echoed loudly within him because he was hollow at the core . . . his soul was mad. Being alone in the wilderness, it had looked within itself, and, by Heavens I tell you, it had gone mad.[61]

In this 'solitude', surrounded by wilderness and Africans, Kurtz had looked inwards, into his 'self', and had found nothing. The horror of this had sent him, in desperation, to the other horror, that of unreflective immersion; he would go off hunting for ivory, and would 'forget himself'; but that way, too, lies disaster, madness, the 'return' of a 'primitive' no longer innocent. Hence Conrad's modernism, his sense of the hollowness beneath: the curse of the modern self, that it cannot, must not, 'forget' itself – it is condemned to reflexivity – but neither can it exist in the pure reflexive state, cannot look too hard at itself (its self), for there may be nothing there.

Yet Marlow's ambivalence towards Kurtz is revealing; Kurtz remains – ambiguously – heroic, precisely because he did try to confront fundamentals of self and meaning. In this sense, a confrontation with the 'heart of darkness' is necessary, unavoidable, for only thus could the truth of self be revealed, even if this 'truth' turns out to be incommunicable, or even a lie. And there is a hint here that perhaps the modern self needs its heart of darkness; that the latter turns out to be subtly constitutive of the former. In this light, the 'civilizing mission' looks more and more like a rationalization: 'a desire to rid the world of this heart of darkness rests on a desire for it', suggests Bristow,[62] and imperialism constantly re-creates it, maybe lives it, even in fighting it. If 'fetishism' is created in the nineteenth century as the alleged mode of primitive experience of the world, it simultaneously seems to apply to a world of experience opened up by and for colonialism itself. As Brantlinger puts it: '*all* ideals transform into idols. . . . The natives in their darkness set Kurtz up as an idol; the Europeans worship ivory, money, power, reputation. Kurtz joins the natives . . . worshipping his own unrestrained power and lust.'[63] Again, a world of mirrors: Marlow confronts Kurtz as his alter ego, recognizing yet disavowing. In the depths of otherness, 'there's always an astonished white face staring back'.[64]

Kurtz therefore embodies the paradoxes and problems of modern imperialism in the confrontation with otherness: 'All Europe contributed to the making of Kurtz',[65] and the exploitation of the Congo reveals a 'rapacious and pitiless folly'. And while Conrad's own text manifests its fair share of racist expressions, it also reveals a more sophisticated understanding:

> It was unearthly and the men were. . . . No they were not inhuman. Well, you know that was the worst of it – this suspicion of their not being inhuman. It would come slowly to one. They howled and leaped and spun and made horrid faces, but what thrilled you was just the thought of their humanity – like yours – the thought of your remote kinship with this wild and passionate uproar.

It is this 'claim of distant kinship'[66] that is crucial here. What challenges, what disgusts the racist is not difference as such, but the difference that threatens to become the same, the hint of kinship, of shared identity, beneath the hated signifiers of racial otherness. Racism thus involves, most fundamentally, a disavowal of the threat of community. Perhaps it is not surprising that the most overtly racist passage in the novel is not found in the descriptions of 'primitive' Africans, but in a description of an African who is no longer in that pristine state, one employed on the cruiser, as fireman:

> He was an improved specimen; he could fire up a vertical boiler. He was there below me and . . . to look at him was as edifying as seeing a dog in a parody of breeches and a feather hat walking on his hind legs . . . he was hard at work, a thrall to strange witchcraft, full of improving knowledge. He was useful because he had been instructed; and what he knew was this – that should the water in that transparent thing disappear the evil spirit inside the boiler would get angry through the greatness of his thirst and take a terrible vengeance. So he sweated and fired up and watched the glass fearfully.[67]

There is both contempt and fear in this writing, as though to be 'half'-civilized is to be too close, becomes a form of mimicry, a perverse doubling. A similar unease can be found in the treatment of the 'colonial Indian', notably the figure of the Indian civil servant, in Orientalist memoirs and novels; this 'hybrid' figure becomes all the more problematical, his 'mimicry' all the more convincing, and hence the textual disavowals all the more tortuous. 'Hybridity' is a kind of cultural miscegenation, representing what Bhabha calls 'a disturbing questioning of the images and presences of authority'.[68] And 'disavowal' is not just a simultaneous fascination with, and resistance to, close identification; that resistance is based on a deeper resistance, to an unacceptable, threatening difference, the difference of rival possibilities, the relativity of cultural absolutes, the implicit challenge of being both *other* and *equal*. To reject *this* possibility, the threat of closeness must be decisively closed off, repudiated. Hence Young suggests that 'Colonial dis-course does not merely represent the other' so much as 'simultaneously project and disavow its difference'.[69]

This also gives clues to the 'African' form of the dualism already encountered in the reactions of Columbus; with the disavowals, the stereotype swings between opposed but equally essential poles. Thus Bhabha points to how 'The black is both savage (cannibal) and yet the most obedient and dignified of servants (the bearer of food); he is the embodiment of rampant sexuality and yet innocent as a child'; and finally, 'he is mystical, primitive, simple-minded and yet the most worldly and accomplished liar'.[70] And just as this can pose problems for the victims of these contradictory stereotypes – escaping from one trap may unwittingly entail falling into the other – so the colonialist, also, gets caught in the nets of confusion and deceit.[71]

In telling the African that the boiler works if the spirit is propitiated, Marlow is not only – again – in the realm of lies, but is giving himself the power of ridicule, persuading himself that the African is not only ignorant, but also gullible, easily led. A contemporary of Conrad writes that 'savages' can be ruled by either force or 'humbug';[72] and the humbug certainly seems to have been a frequent accompaniment to the force, ever since Columbus, knowing the time of an immi-nent lunar eclipse, pretended to bring it about himself. And this make-believe technology enables Marlow both to recognize and negate the learning capacity of the African, the implicit threat to Western supremacy presented by the very pos-sibility of educability. In the end, the African can *only* mimic, not understand; enough to keep a boiler going, but no more. But then again, the hint of anxiety, the nervousness: are not the knowledge claims of the 'civilized world' also fragile, not qualitatively so different, really just more 'strange witchcraft'? And is civi-lization worth so much, if it has to be maintained by cheap deceit? Thus do the complexities of 'disavowal' reveal projection, denial and recognition, along with the impulses of fear, fascination, even need; and Laura Chrisman concludes that imperialism can thereby both 'acknowledge and disavow itself'.[73]

Decadence and Splendour

While both Africa and the Orient are 'exotic', they are so in different ways; you never hear of 'darkest Orient', after all. While Africans are seen as unquestion-ably 'primitive', they are not decadent, whereas Orientals are the latter more than the former. 'Decadence' is a tricky notion: it implies 'arrested development', in the sense that a certain very real level of achievement is reached, justifying the use of the word 'civilization', but then a timeless stasis sets in, which implies a certain regression (if you fail to progress, you go backwards . . .). This is clearly an attempt to answer the challenge posed by the Orient to the modern Western understanding: if the Arab world, China and India are indisputably 'civilized', in some sense, what nevertheless gives the West its 'superiority', indeed its right not just to interfere, but even to govern?

Crucial here is the Oriental city, for this is the site both of Oriental civilization and the embodiment of its imperfections. The Oriental city is always characterized, in Orientalist literature, as 'teeming', a chaotic, convoluted, undisciplined mass of people, activities and impressions, its streets winding, crooked, full of noise and odours, with animals and humans all mixed up, and an untidy confusion of buildings. This description, by Naipaul, dates from the 1960s, but could have come from any time in the preceding century:

> It was a town, damp or dusty, of smells: of bodies and picturesque costumes discoloured and acrid with grime, of black, open drains, of exposed fried food and exposed filth; a town of prolific pariah dogs of disregarded beauty below shop platforms, of starved puppies shivering in the damp caked blackness below butchers' stalls hung with bleeding flesh; a town of narrow lanes and dark shops and choked courtyards, of full, ankle-lengthed skirts and the innumerable brittle, scarred legs of boys.[74]

Kabbani adds that the town, 'like the whole of the East, is a jumble of contradictory and disturbing images; filth, food, beauty, blood' – in short, a spectacle far removed from the 'sanitised West'.[75] And it becomes particularly clear, in Orientalist literature, that these streets and towns carry a heavy symbolic load; their teeming chaos is a signifier of those very qualities of the 'Oriental mind' that confirm its inability to develop beyond this early form of civilization. Thus Said quotes that late Victorian proconsul of Empire, Lord Cromer:

> Want of accuracy, which easily degenerates into untruthfulness, is in fact the main characteristic of the Oriental mind. . . . The mind of the Oriental . . . like his picturesque streets, is eminently wanting in symmetry. His reasoning is of the most slipshod description.[76]

One can see the aptness of Haraway's comment that 'Orientalism concerns the Western imagination of the origin of the city.'[77] Indeed, when European colonial administrators wanted to emphasize their own distance from the Orient, they typically did so through adding on, or rebuilding, a section of the city, to be used for European trading and administrative purposes, or building a new city, as the French did at Rabat. The layout of the latter, according to its architect, would represent 'the genius of order, proportion and clear reasoning' of the French.[78] Here we see the truth of Fanon's description of the colonial world as 'a world cut in two',[79] in which the excluded part is nevertheless integral to the West's identity and power.

However, what we find in these Orientalist constructions of the Orient is not just a contrast of Oriental and Western city, but also city versus desert; and the former is always 'civilized', relative to the latter. The desert has a fascination as a place of undifferentiated anomaly, a site of both temptation and danger. Discussing the cinematic fascination with the Orient since the 1920s, Shohat writes:

The Orientalist films tend to begin in the city – where European civilization has already tamed the East – but the real dramatic conflicts take place in the desert where women are defenceless, and White woman could easily become the captive of a romantic sheik or evil Arab.[80]

But it is Chateaubriand who captures the romance of the desert most vividly, in his prose:

> When one travels in Judea. . . . Extraordinary things are disclosed from all parts of an earth worked over by miracles: the burning sun, the impetuous eagle, the sterile fig tree; all of poetry, all the scenes from Scripture are present there. . . . God himself has spoken from these shores: the arid torrents, the riven rocks, the open tombs attest to the prodigy; the desert still seems struck dumb with terror, and one would say that it has still not been able to break the silence since it heard the voice of the eternal.[81]

So again, it is through a Western man that the East can find its voice; the East speaks, but in a language it no longer understands. The East cannot know itself; and it cannot rule itself, either, and this becomes fundamental to the Western image of the Orient.

To say that Orientals are incapable of self-government is to say that they are natural prey to the despot, liable to succumb to tyranny. 'Despotism', as a noun, comes into use in the mid-eighteenth century, and is early attached to the Orient as its best exemplification. 'Oriental despotism' is a regime of blind obedience to one who treats his subjects as slaves; and the despot, in turn, is ruled by desire and caprice. Richon suggests that the despot 'seeks his own pleasure, unlike the magistrate or the king, who represent the common interest of all'. Hence the tyrant 'upsets the regime of representation', and the Orient necessarily 'cannot represent itself'.[82]

'Representation' operates here as a concept both cultural and political: in this perspective, to be 'modern', whether as self or society, is to be capable of self-representation, to recognize oneself in oneself, hence be capable of self-government. The other hence lacks these attributes; and not only must others be represented, but must be tempted – or forced – to self-recognition in the images produced *of* them. Hence Harbsmeier's suggestion that 'Cultural hegemony might be defined as the power to reproduce the temptations for others to recognize themselves in the images and representations which others make of them.'[83] Colonialism thus becomes, crucially, a regime of representation, in which the other acquires a voice not its own, and images imposed on it, images that it has to recognize itself in.

The result can well be that the Orient, for the visitor, becomes a sort of inadequate copy of its own representation. The career of Orientalist painting illustrates this. Painters such as Gros, Bonington and Delacroix constructed an image of the Orient in the studio, before they ever set foot in the East – if they ever did. So when painters *did* actually travel out there, they looked for scenes conforming to their expectations, or painted what they thought 'ought' to be there, 'illustrating once again', suggests Richon, that 'representations refer to other representations and not to the truth of the represented'.[84]

Not surprisingly, such travellers were often disappointed. The Orient might well appear not sufficiently 'Oriental', as it failed to fit the preconceptions; or it might seem *too* Oriental, as it 'exceeded' the stereotypes and thereby became confusing and incomprehensible. Both reactions could be found together. In the first case, Gérard de Nerval complained that 'it is only in Paris that one finds cafés so Oriental'; at least Paris is true to the *idea* of the Oriental café, as it were. But conversely, accompanying a photographer who sought a photograph of a city, he plunged into the labyrinthine streets, but they lost their bearings completely in the profusion of people and noise; to take the photograph, they had to flee outside, and take it from afar. Visitors thus sought to 'plunge' into the Orient, immerse themselves in it, experience it 'for real'; but they could only do this having recognized it *as* the 'Orient', which entailed distance. And when – a third possibility – the 'real' Orient *was* encountered, this meant that it was only ever a reconfirmation of the image one started with: 'The Orient was something one only ever rediscovered',[85] as Mitchell puts it. Thus does the Orient pose a central challenge to the Romantic imagination – and hence the recourse to figurative language, metaphor and reverie, in the desperate attempt to mesh together immersion and distance, novelty and recognition, in the 'capture' of the otherness of the Orient.

Kabbani suggests that the Orient becomes 'a pretext for self-dramatisation and differentness', a 'malleable theatrical space',[86] and Said claims that 'The idea of representation is a theatrical one: the Orient is the stage on which the whole East is confined.'[87] This can be elaborated by seeing theatricality as a response to the representational paradoxes outlined above. The participant–observer is a central actor in the drama of the Orient, so what could be more natural than that the tensions between immersion and distance be worked out through the assumption of *disguise*? Edward Lane, a translator of the *Arabian Nights*, became Mansoor Effendi, living in the Arab section of Cairo, the better to grasp the local mores; and the remarkable Sir Richard Burton, translator, traveller, anthropologist and pornographer, took on many guises, though particularly favoured Mirza Abdallah of Bushire. Kabbani adds that 'The disguise permitted its wearer to move from one racial category to another as if by magic', and this mode of disguise became 'the classic method through which the British related to the Arab world'.[88]

The initiation rite and the pleasures of transgression are never far away; like Africa, the East becomes an escape from bourgeois domestic restrictions. In the main, no doubt, just a game; though Lawrence ('of Arabia') suggests that it could turn out to be a disturbing one:

> In my case, the efforts for these years to live in the dress of Arabs, and imitate their mental foundation, quitted me of my English self. . . . At the same time I could not sincerely take on the Arab skin: it was an affectation only. . . . Sometimes these selves would converse in the void; and then madness was very near, as I believe it

would be near the man who could see things through the veils at once of two customs, two educations, two environments.[89]

The East, distanced as other, is here becoming threateningly close.

Modernism and Primitivism

Orientalist themes and images saturated the cultural milieu from the 1900s to the 1920s, the era of the modernist revolutions in art, thereby becoming a significant presence in – and influence on – modernist works themselves (notably Matisse, with his arabesque motifs and interest in 'the decorative').[90] For all that, Orientalism is very clearly not modernism. In conveying – and creating – a sense of the Orient as exotic, it tames and recuperates this potential challenge within the confines of profoundly conservative representational canons. The combination of exotic themes and accuracy of detail frequently makes these paintings 'taxidermy rather than ethnography', as Linda Nochlin puts it:[91] specimens in cases, part and parcel of the acquisitive consciousness of an age of exhibitions and consumerism. In modernist art, however, 'the primitive' is allowed a more forceful presence – or, perhaps, enforces its presence – and seems to pose a dynamic interrogation at the heart of the project. This presence is deeply troubling – and troubled – and it disrupts both form and content, and the relation between them. Subject and style become mutually interrogatory, harmony and homogeneity are supplanted by fission and dissonance. In *The Rite of Spring*, Stravinsky dramatized the modern *as* primitive, in a dynamism of energy and colour.

The apparent strangeness of this move – why go back to go forward? – reminds us of key dilemmas in representation. As has been seen with carnival and will be seen with pornography, there are problems in the representation of immediacy, presence and involvement, and the drive to be 'modern', to capture experience, the here and now, intensifies them: the present fractures in the intensity of the reflexive gaze, as it seeks the moment of its own experiencing. Modernism can either push forward, disavow the past, press on insistently towards a future it can only celebrate but never realize – broadly, the alternative chosen by Futurism and (Russian) Constructivism[92] – or it can explore the new through the fragments of a past that can only ever be juxtaposed, recombined, with a reflexive awareness that their 'pastness' is indeed forever unattainable, thus feeding into a nostalgia for meaning and origin that appears resolutely 'un-modernist' but has always been there as modernism's shadow. Thus Foster can refer to the way ' "the primitive" is doubled by the machine as the principal object phantasms of high modernism', both being central to its 'fables of identity'.[93]

Modernism could, then, be said to bring to the fore what Miller defines as a central paradox of art itself, its status as 'a fragmented comment upon the nature of fragmentation', including the fragmentation implicit in its own separate existence;[94] and it cannot have recourse to Romantic primitivism *simpliciter*, to the assumption of an original unitary simplicity and totality, even though that may be crucially present *as aspiration*. The tension that results is thus constitutive of modernist primitivism. Modernism is the heir to Romanticism, but can no longer accept it: the search for a founding past is necessary for escape from the representational paradoxes inherent in mapping the present, but could only succeed by reproducing those paradoxes, doubling them. The unity of the origin is no less mythical than the unity of the present; past as origin is necessarily contradictory, neither what it was nor what it is to become – or both together – though this can be papered over in the mystery of charismatic creation, in the power of genius implicit in the creative act, artist become god. 'The primitive' is also the primal, the primordial: the beginning is also the foundation, that which is basic, the creative source. And hence the interest not only in 'primitive cultures' – indeed, as Rhodes points out, the word 'savage' tended to be used more frequently, in this context[95] – but in contemporary 'others', such as children, or 'the mad',[96] who may be in close proximity; for what is basic to all these is that the primordial can thus be 'seized from time', made present, and thereby both charismatic, creative, and simultaneously destructive, tension-laden, bearer of contradiction. Modernism reinforces this elitist mystery of creation even as it remorselessly subverts it, just as it swings between the alternatives of past and future for the materials of its inspiration.

In the tension is the radicalism. Foster points out that identification with 'the primitive', 'however imaged as dark, feminine, and profligate, remained a *dis*identification with white, patriarchal, bourgeois society'. Yet we are also right to distrust this; these 'identifications' could be little more than an artistic version of the tourist spectacle of otherness already pervasive in Western culture. The sophistication of these modernist explorations, their drive to reflexive awareness, will not save them from an implicit or explicit reproduction of some of the constitutive Western assumptions about otherness, as indeed we have seen with Conrad; there are always limitations to the reflexive grasp and the adequacy of its representational correlates. The drive to break down, subvert, the cultural oppositions themselves, in the very enterprise of exploring them, is real enough; but so is a revulsion against crossover, a fear of dissolution and confusion, a contrary drive precisely to shore up these boundaries. As Foster expresses it, 'the primitivist seeks to be both *opened up to difference* (to be made ecstatic, literally taken out of the self sexually, socially, racially) *and* to be *fixed in opposition* to the other (to be established again, secured as a sovereign self)'.[97] It may well be that some of the best-known of these tense encounters with the primitive other – those by Picasso in art[98] and Eliot in poetry[99] – tend particularly to the second of these poles; Gauguin, on the other hand, by no means unequivocally 'modernist' anyway, is more difficult to place, his own conflicts reflected appropriately in disputes between the commentators.[100] These artists, then, stage these 'primal scenes' in 'the melodramatic register of desire and fear'.[101] And not only artists. We are reminded here of Franz Boas, one of the 'founding fathers' of anthropology, eating raw seal meat among the Eskimo, incorporating otherness through literal ingestion in a collective, ritual, sacrificial meal, a primal act of destruction that is also a charismatic creation of the anthropological enterprise.[102] Thus does post-evolutionary anthropology come into being as another instance of the pervasive modernist revolutions of Western culture. Young observes that 'the idea of the culture of a society as an artefact worth studying in itself reflects early twentieth-century modernist aesthetic practices', though he emphasizes the conservative strand here: 'the "primitive" animal vitality and emotionalism of the lower races was reassigned its Romantic role as an object of value to be retrieved for the benefit of a tired, degenerate, vulgarized European civilization'.[103]

If Rhodes is right, then, in claiming that 'Primitivism describes a Western event and does not imply any direct dialogue between the West and its "Others"',[104] it is also true that, as Barkan and Bush put it, 'It is the essence of modernism . . . that it encodes the uncertainties of that dialogism at the heart of procedural self-consciousness.'[105] 'The primitive' may not communicate; but it is silent no longer. Strange questions trouble Western culture; strange voices interpellate themselves into its very core. And in this sense, 'the primitive' retains its capacity to challenge. Exploring northern Italy in pursuit of the 'primitive scratch', early wall paintings and markings, Cardinal expresses this eloquently:

> The authentic apprehension of Otherness is perhaps grounded in some form of self-knowledge; or rather, knowledge of the Other is indissociable from the knowledge we concurrently gain of ourselves. Upon the high granite of the Val Camonica, a minimal sign speaks to me across the dimness of time, and voices a primitive truth, what I and its maker most authentically share: it is only desire, imagination, and fear that hasten understanding.[106]

The aspiration remains powerful, then, even if, as we have seen, the realization of it – whether in terms of art, or more broadly – has proved inseparable from the powerful workings of the stereotypes that have shaped Western consciousness and the canons of representation.

To conclude, by returning to the beginning. It can fairly be said, as Todorov does, that 'Columbus himself is not a modern man';[107] his own attitudes are, in many respects, strikingly medieval. He lives in a world of signs and portents, of pre-given meanings, divine interventions. Barely one generation later, in 1519, Cortés advances into Mexico, and within two years the Aztec Empire has been destroyed. Unlike Columbus, Cortés comes over as a man unequivocally 'modern'. Of what, then, does his 'modernity' consist? For a start, signs and portents have given way to purposeful instrumentalism, improvization, an openness to the world that simultaneously reduces it to the status of an exploitable object. And money comes to prominence in its modern role of universal equivalent, the language in which all value can be expressed. But Cortés is a man with an historical sense, not just a plunderer; in the long term, power and wealth are best secured by conquest and colonization. The cunning and ingenuity of Cortés come over not just as individual character traits but as a distinctive cultural orientation. In addition to all this, though, there is something more. Todorov suggests that Cortés reveals an interest in the other,

> at the cost of a certain empathy or temporary identification. Cortés slips into the other's skin. . . . Thereby he ensures himself an understanding of the other's language and a knowledge of the other's political organization. . . . But in so doing he has never abandoned his feeling of superiority; it is even his very capacity to understand the other that confirms him in that feeling.[108]

From the imaginative ingenuity of Cortés to the theatrical impersonations of Burton, and beyond, is but a short step; both imply a notion of 'understanding' as 'simulated membership', while implying that this capacity to 'understand', and the wish to do so, are the very hallmarks of the superiority of modern civilization. But we have seen deceit at work here, and a sense in which 'understanding' the other has involved disavowal, projection and rationalization, whereby it has frequently served as a cloak for domination, and a prelude to destruction.

Notes

1   D. Porter, *Haunted Journeys: Desire and Transgression in European Travel Writing* (Princeton University Press, 1991), p. 98.

2   M. Sahlins, *Islands of History* (Tavistock, 1987), pp. 2, 3. See also R. Porter, 'The Exotic as Erotic: Captain Cook at Tahiti', in G. S. Rousseau and R. Porter (eds.) *Exoticism in the Enlightenment* (Manchester University Press, 1990).

3   Sahlins, *Islands*, p. 6.

4   M. Sahlins, 'The Apotheosis of Captain Cook', in M. Izard and P. Smith (eds.) *Between Belief and Transgression* (Chicago University Press, 1982), pp. 74, 76.

5   Sahlins, 'Apotheosis', p. 80.

6   T. Todorov, *The Conquest of America* (Harper and Row, 1984), p. 5.

7   Ibid., pp. 39, 38, 35. See also S. Greenblatt, *Marvelous Possessions* (Clarendon Press, 1991), ch. 3.

8   M. North, 'Modernism's African Mask: The Stein–Picasso Collaboration', in E. Barkan and R. Bush (eds.) *Prehistories of the Future: The Primitivist Project and the Culture of Modernism* (Stanford University Press, 1995), p. 276.

9   Todorov, *Conquest*, pp. 38, 46.

10   L. Montrose, 'The Work of Gender in the Discourse of Discovery', *Representations* (1991), 33, p. 3.

11   E. Shohat, 'Gender and the Culture of Empire: Towards a Feminist Ethnography of the Cinema', *Quarterly Review of Film and Video* (1991), 13:1–3, p. 47. See also E. Shohat and R. Stam, *Unthinking Eurocentrism: Multiculturalism and the Media* (Routledge, 1994), on other aspects.

12   P. Hulme, 'Polytropic Man: Tropes of Sexuality and Mobility in Early Colonial Discourse', in F. Barker et al., *Europe and Its Others*, Vol. 2 (University of Essex, 1985), p. 18.

13 Ibid., pp. 26, 24.

14 P. Brantlinger, *Rule of Darkness: British Literature and Imperialism 1830–1914* (Cornell University Press, 1988), ch. 7.

15 Ibid., p. 25.

16 R. Kabbani, *Europe's Myths of Orient* (Macmillan, 1986), p. 4.

17 M. L. Pratt, *Imperial Eyes: Travel Writing and Transculturation* (Routledge, 1992), p. 53. See also S. During, 'Rousseau's Patrimony: Primitivism, Romance, and Becoming Other', in F. Barker et al., *Colonial Discourse/Postcolonial Theory* (Manchester University Press, 1994), on Bougainville and Diderot.

18 S. Horigan, *Nature and Culture in Western Discourses* (Routledge, 1988), p. 52.

19 P. Hulme, *Colonial Encounters: Europe and the Native Caribbean, 1492–1787* (Cambridge University Press, 1987), p. 229.

20 Porter, *Haunted Journeys*, p. 99.

21 H. Baudet, *Paradise on Earth* (Wesleyan University Press, 1988), pp. 54, 55.

22 E. Said, *Orientalism* (Penguin, 1991), p. 41.

23 D. T. Goldberg, *Racist Culture: Philosophy and the Politics of Meaning* (Blackwell, 1993), p. 24.

24 Pratt, *Imperial Eyes*, p. 32.

25 B. McGrane, *Beyond Anthropology* (Columbia University Press, 1989), p. 99. See also P. Bowler, *The Invention of Progress* (Blackwell, 1989).

26 L. Chrisman, 'The Imperial Unconscious? Representations of Imperial Discourse', *Critical Quarterly* (1990), 32:3, pp. 50–1.

27 R. V. Lucas, 'Yellow Peril in the Promised Land', in F. Barker et al., *Europe and Its Others*, Vol. 1 (University of Essex, 1985), p. 43.

28 R. J. C. Young, *Colonial Desire: Hybridity in Theory, Culture and Race* (Routledge, 1995), p. 148.

29 The word itself seems to date from the 1860s: ibid., p. 9.

30 Shohat, 'Gender and the Culture', p. 65.

31 J. N. Pieterse, *White on Black* (Yale University Press, 1992), ch. 12, and Young, *Colonial Desire*, ch. 6. Such laws and practices served also to control white women: see A. L. Stoler, 'Carnal Knowledge and Imperial Power: Gender, Race and Morality in Colonial Asia', in M. di Leonardo (ed.) *Gender at the Crossroads of Knowledge: Feminist Anthropology in the Postmodern Era* (California University Press, 1991), pp. 67–75.

32 B. Easlea, *Science and Sexual Oppression* (Weidenfeld and Nicolson, 1981), pp. 154, 155.

33 Brantlinger, *Rule of Darkness*, p. 21.

34 Pratt, *Imperial Eyes*, p. 36. See also K. Malik, *The Meaning of Race: Race, History and Culture in Western Society* (Macmillan, 1996), p. 81.

35 A. McClintock, *Imperial Leather: Race, Gender and Sexuality in the Colonial Context* (Routledge, 1995), p. 40.

36 D. E. Nord, 'The Social Explorer as Anthropologist', in W. Sharp and L. Wallock (eds.) *Visions of the Modern City* (Johns Hopkins University Press, 1987), p. 123.

37 J. Bristow, *Empire Boys: Adventures in a Man's World* (Harper Collins Academic, 1991), p. 192.

38 Cited in R. Young, *White Mythologies; Writing, History and the West* (Routledge, 1990), p. 124.

39 Cited in P. Brantlinger, 'Victorians and Africans: The Genealogy of the Myths of the Dark Continent', *Critical Inquiry* (1985), 12:1, p. 199.

40   On debates on the Enlightenment, see Introduction to this volume, n. 3; also D. T. Goldberg (ed.) *The Anatomy of Racism* (Minnesota University Press, 1990).

41   E. Showalter, *Sexual Anarchy* (Virago, 1992), p. 81.

42   Said, *Orientalism*, p. 206. On Said, see also the critical appraisal in J. Clifford, *The Predicament of Culture* (Harvard University Press, 1988), ch. 11.

43   Porter, *Haunted Journeys*, p. 167. See also N. Leask, *British Romantic Writers and the East* (Cambridge University Press, 1993).

44   J. de Groot, '"Sex" and "Race": The Construction of Language and Image in the Nineteenth Century', in S. Mendus and J. Rendell (eds.) *Sexuality and Subordination* (Routledge, 1989), p. 105.

45   Said, *Orientalism*, p. 188.

46   Porter, *Haunted Journeys*, p. 181.

47   R. Lewis, *Gendering Orientalism: Race, Femininity and Representation* (Routledge, 1996), pp. 4, 178–9.

48   Stoler, 'Carnal Knowledge', p. 51.

49   L. Ahmed, 'Western Ethnocentrism and Perceptions of the Harem', *Feminist Studies* (1982), 8:3.

50   Lewis, *Gendering Orientalism*, p. 180. See also E. Apter, 'Female Trouble in the Colonial Harem', *Differences* (1992), 4:1.

51   Kabbani, *Europe's Myths*, p. 26.

52   R. Stott, 'The Dark Continent: Africa as Female Body in Haggard's Adventure Fiction', *Feminist Review* (1989), 32, pp. 79, 87.

53   Brantlinger, 'Victorians and Africans', pp. 196, 194.

54   Bristow, *Empire Boys*, p. 131.

55   Stott, 'Dark Continent', p. 77.

56   See discussions in Brantlinger, 'Victorians and Africans', and M. Torgovnick, *Gone Primitive: Savage Intellects, Modern Lives* (Chicago University Press, 1990), pp. 26–33.

57   J. Conrad, *Heart of Darkness* (Penguin, 1985), pp. 66, 66, 68.

58   Ibid., pp. 40, 98, 68–9.

59   Ibid., pp. 100, 101, 101.

60   Ibid., p. 110.

61   Ibid., pp. 97, 97, 108.

62   Bristow, *Empire Boys*, p. 163.

63   Brantlinger, *Rule of Darkness*, p. 262. On fetishism and sexuality in this context, see also McClintock, *Imperial Leather*, chs. 2–4.

64   Brantlinger, 'Victorians and Africans', p. 195.

65   Conrad, *Heart of Darkness*, p. 86.

66   Ibid., pp. 43, 69, 88.

67   Ibid., p. 70.

68   H. Bhabha, 'Signs Taken For Wonders', in Barker, *Europe*, 1, p. 98.

69   Young, *White Mythologies*, p. 143.

70   H. Bhabha, *The Location of Culture* (Routledge, 1994), p. 82.

71   S. Hall, 'The Spectacle of the "Other"', in S. Hall (ed.) *Representation: Cultural Representations and Signifying Practices* (Sage, 1997), p. 263.

72   Cited in B. Street, *The Savage in Literature* (Routledge, 1975), p. 67.

73   Chrisman, 'Imperial Unconscious?', p. 51.

74   V. S. Naipaul, *An Area of Darkness* (André Deutsch, 1964), p. 123.

75   Kabbani, *Europe's Myths*, p. 132.

76 Said, *Orientalism*, p. 38.

77 D. Haraway, *Primate Visions* (Routledge, 1989), pp. 10–11.

78 Cited in T. Mitchell, *Colonising Egypt* (Cambridge University Press, 1988), p. 161.

79 F. Fanon, *The Wretched of the Earth* (Penguin, 1979), p. 29.

80 Shohat, 'Gender and the Culture', p. 75.

81 Said, *Orientalism*, p. 173.

82 O. Richon, 'Representation, the Despot and the Harem', in Barker, *Europe*, 1, p. 9.

83 M. Harmbsmeier, 'Early Travels to Europe', in Barker, *Europe*, 1, p. 86.

84 O. Richon, 'Representation', p. 2.

85 T. Mitchell, 'The World as Exhibition', *Comparative Studies in Society and History* (1989), 31:2, p. 234.

86 Kabbani, *Europe's Myths*, p. 11.

87 Said, *Orientalism*, p. 63.

88 Kabbani, *Europe's Myths*, pp. 89, 91. On disguise and theatricality, see also my *Exploring the Modern: Patterns of Western Culture and Civilization* (Blackwell, 1998), ch. 1.

89 Cited in Kabbani, *Europe's Myths*, p. 92.

90 See P. Wollen, *Raiding the Icebox: Reflections on Twentieth-Century Culture* (Verso, 1993), and my *Exploring the Modern*, ch. 10, for a more thorough treatment of Matisse and modernism generally. C. Butler, *Early Modernism* (Oxford University Press, 1994) is also useful.

91 Cited in C. Rhodes, *Primitivism and Modern Art* (Thames and Hudson, 1994), p. 79.

92 B. Fer, 'The Language of Construction', in B. Fer et al., *Realism, Rationalism, Surrealism* (Yale University Press, 1993).

93 H. Foster, '"Primitive" Scenes', *Critical Inquiry* (1993) 20:1, pp. 75,76.

94 D. Miller, 'Primitive Art and the Necessity of Primitivism to Art', in S. Hiller (ed.) *The Myth of Primitivism* (Routledge, 1991), p. 55.

95 Rhodes, *Primitivism*, p. 21.

96 See L. Sass, *Madness and Modernism* (Basic Books, 1992), especially pp. 28–38, on literary aspects; and D. Maclagan, 'Outsiders or Insiders?', in Hiller, *Myth*, on painting.

97 Foster, '"Primitive" Scenes', pp. 76, 85 (original emphasis). See also his *Compulsive Beauty* (MIT Press, 1993), which brings out the relevance of Surrealism to these themes.

98 See Foster, '"Primitive" Scenes', and M. North, 'Modernism's African Mask: The Picasso–Stein Collaboration', in E. Barkan and R. Bush (eds.) *Prehistories of the Future: The Primitivist Project and the Culture of Modernism* (Stanford University Press, 1995).

99 See S. Smith, *The Origins of Modernism: Eliot, Pound, Yeats and the Rhetorics of Renewal* (Harvester Wheatsheaf, 1994), and M. H. Levenson, *A Genealogy of Modernism: A Study of English Literary Doctrine 1908–22* (Cambridge University Press, 1984).

100 In addition to Foster, '"Primitive" Scenes', see A. Solomon-Godeau, 'Going Native', *Art in America* (1989), 77; P. Brooks, 'Gauguin's Tahitian Body', *Yale Journal of Criticism* (1990), 3:2; and G. Perry, '"Primitivism" and the Modern', in C. Harrison et al., *Primitivism, Cubism, Abstraction* (Yale University Press, 1993), pp. 26–32.

101 Foster, '"Primitive" Scenes', p. 86.

102 Barkan and Bush, 'Introduction' to *Prehistories*, p. 7.

103   Young, *Colonial Desire*, pp. 51, 52.

104   Rhodes, *Primitivism*, p. 8.

105   Barkan and Bush, 'Introduction' to *Prehistories*, p. 18.

106   R. Cardinal, 'The Primitive Scratch', in A. Gilroy and T. Dalley (eds.) *Pictures at an Exhibition: Selected Essays on Art and Art Theory* (Tavistock, 1989), p. 125.

107   Todorov, *Conquest*, p. 12.

108   Ibid., p. 247.

4 The Alienated Mind:

Reason and the Exile of Madness

Writing Madness Lucidly?

In 1868, Hersilie, née Rouy, was released from the last of the several asylums in which she had been forcibly confined for fourteen years. A music teacher, from a comfortable but not affluent background, she had originally been incarcerated at the behest of her half-brother. In 1876 the French National Assembly made financial reparations to her after an official investigation showed that her confinement had been illegal as it had not been motivated by clear evidence of insanity. She was not the first, and was far from being the last, to have been locked up on flimsy evidence and for dubious motives, though most of these unfortunates are lost to history; she, however, wrote it all down, while incarcerated, using any scraps of paper she could find, and these 'journals' were published posthumously, a decade after her release. They provide fascinating evidence: but evidence of what, precisely? Her memoirs join a significant body of writings by former inmates of the asylum, and certainly provide evidence of 'the modern way with madness', of how those viewed as mad are treated by those who come into contact with them. But whether she achieves her own aim – to 'prove her sanity' – is another matter.

I will follow Jann Matlock, who tells her story, in referring to her by her first name, Hersilie, since as will be seen later, the identity of her surname is crucially at issue in her account.[1] But I am also aware that in doing this, I thereby join a tradition. The 'heroines' of Freud's texts are also known by their first names, real or given – Anna O, Dora, etc. – so is Victor Tausk's Natalia, and so on to Julie, the 'ghost in the weed garden' of Laing's *The Divided Self*. It is as though these troublesome women, who disturb the neat contours of masculine reason, and ripple the smooth surfaces of the pages in which they are entombed, have to be rendered safe, almost childlike, by this implicit familiarity, lest their anguish be too unsettling. Yet this strategy of familiarity is itself troublesome: it reminds us that it is indeed the family, the haven of domestic bliss, the private womb of security and affection, that is the site where neurosis and madness classically reveal themselves, where those who are subsequently labelled 'insane' first have their alleged peculiarities 'recognized' as such. Indeed, the idea that the family both transmits and magnifies the stresses of 'modern civilization' – while adding the pressures of its own 'tawdry secrets' – runs like a *leitmotif* through discussions of madness since the eighteenth century.[2]

The family can be a site where overt victimization occurs. Hersilie's text is haunted by an awareness that her family betrayed her, that her half-brother chose to pass her off as mad, and John Perceval's account of his incarceration in the early 1830s is likewise full of a similar sense of betrayal by those who should have known him best, and should have had his interests most at heart.[3] However, this victimization need not be so overt; it can be more a matter of collusion, in which even the victims are implicated, in effect acquiescing in their 'election' to the role. Bateson claims that, in the family, 'the psychotic individual has the functions of a necessary sacrifice', since that individual's behaviour will 'conceal or justify' the actions of the rest of the family that fail to fit the image it presents to the world;[4] and that point, if valid, would fit not just a John Perceval, who, in present-day parlance, probably was psychotic when confined, but also a Hersilie, who probably was not. If the victim cannot recognize the hate as well as the love, the hurt and pain as well as the affection, in the attitudes of others, then the resulting feelings of resentment or anger may well induce guilt, and he or she may come to accept the fate of victim as 'just', hence the collusion. Through sacrifice, the secrets can remain secret. But if, like Hersilie, the victim protests, then it is all the more necessary to resort to repression, and the protests become 'paranoia', part of the symptoms that justify the label of madness in the first place. Madness becomes part of the sacrificial structure of modernity, whereby virtue and rationality can be achieved only through the exile of that – and those – that contradict the official self-image, disturb its clarity, question its necessity.

As a woman, Hersilie was particularly vulnerable. She was incarcerated at an early stage of what could be called the 'century of confinement', the period when the asylum became the dominant institutional focus for the modern politics of madness, the place where it was simultaneously exiled, contained and 'treated'. Already in Hersilie's time it was noticed that there were more women than men in the public asylums; by the 1890s this was true also of the private ones, and it has remained true ever since.[5] In the UK, the 1913 Mental Deficiency Act allowed the detention of unmarried pregnant women in mental hospitals; such women were still being detained there into the 1940s. Dossiers in the famous Parisian asylum, the Salpêtrière, describe cases of wives who were handed over by their husbands for flirting too much, daughters for refusing to marry the men chosen for them, and mothers for 'religious fervour';[6] and Hersilie herself was labelled 'manipulative' and 'sexually provocative', the one being seen as a perversion of the female role, the other an inversion of it.

It became a commonplace of medical opinion in the second half of the nineteenth century that women were inherently more vulnerable to insanity because their reproductive systems rendered them vulnerable to emotional upsets and made self-control difficult. It was as though masculinity provided the standard for normality, and feminine divergence from this always represented the potential for pathology. Much the same was reported as recently as 1970, in a study that claimed that mental health professionals saw 'mental health' in terms that brought it closer to the masculine stereotype than the feminine, with women being seen as 'more excitable', 'less objective', etc.[7] The formidable Henry Maudsley, presiding over Victorian psychiatry, proclaimed that the intellectual training of adolescent girls could produce permanent injury to their reproductive systems and their brains.[8] Elaine Showalter gives a vivid account of how the long-established Ophelia image of the madwoman, with its contradictory fusion of the virginal and the erotic, the innocent and the indecent – readings made possible by Ophelia's ambiguously indecorous appearance and extravagant speech – became differentiated into the Crazy Jane image of the betrayed, deserted victim, devoted to the commemoration of the lost lover, and the vengeful, violent image of Lucy, from Scott's *The Bride of Lammermoor*, forced to marry against her will, mad and murderous in her bridal chamber.[9] And sexuality itself becomes linked with madness; in either sex, self-abuse was thought likely to lead to insanity, and masturbation was in some cases given as grounds for confinement.[10]

And the asylum regime? Certainly it did not require that the patient be listened to. Samuel Tuke, presiding over the relatively enlightened York Retreat at the beginning of the century, had nevertheless argued that it was unwise to allow 'lunatics' to speak: 'No advantage has been found to arise from reasoning with them on their particular hallucinations', and 'In regard to melancholics, conversation on the subject of their despondency is found to be highly injudicious.' And Charcot, the dominant French psychiatrist of later in the century, will echo this opinion; he dismisses the speech of his patients as 'much ado about nothing'. Showalter adds that

> Victorian madwomen were not easily silenced, and one often has the impression that their talkativeness, violation of conventions of feminine speech, and insistence on self-expression was the kind of behavior that had led to their being labeled 'mad' to begin with.[11]

Indeed, Skultans observes that the emphasis on female vulnerability and pathology increased as the demand for emancipation became increasingly articulate towards the end of the century.[12]

Echoing through this modern period then, across the decades, is this silence: this loud, terrified silence of the mad – tormented but unheard – that is also, generally, a silence of women. Speech and writing are denied them. Hersilie is constantly persecuted for her attempts to write: 'Writing in the asylum is always transgressive', always scrutinized and censored, an arena of power struggles. It is no good trying to write to demonstrate one's sanity, for as Matlock suggests, 'writing one's sanity only further confirms the diagnosis of insanity necessary for continued imprisonment'.[13] One is reminded here of a later case, in the 1960s, when an investigator faked insanity to gain access to an asylum. When he took notes in the ward, to keep a diary, the attendant recorded this as: 'Patient engages in writing behaviour.'[14]

But the problem goes deeper. Hersilie's self-defence, writes Matlock, 'threatens to reinstate her in a network that makes her readable only in the terms of the system that marked her as mad'; her text invites us, as readers, 'to entangle ourselves in the regions between madness and sanity, fiction and nonfiction, experience and representation, discourse and silence, the interpretable, and that which resists interpretation'. After all, the asylum does its work all too well; knowing that she has passed through it, we are bound to wonder about her mental state. And even wondering whether Hersilie is sane works subtly to compromise her sanity; for when we consider the narrative of a person's life, is there *anything* that cannot pass as 'insane', viewed in a certain light? Or, conversely, is there *any* way to conclusively *prove* sanity?

A mad-doctor of the time, Trélat, writes that 'There are lucid madpeople who only reveal themselves when they write.' *La folie lucide*: in the world of madness, you can be mad not just when you appear to be mad, but when you appear to be sane, too. Thus we are warned that Hersilie may dupe us, that 'her writing may seduce us with its lucidity, lure us with its plausibility, but that at any moment it may betray her for what she really is – a lunatic – and catch us in her Unreason'.[15] Here we encounter the fateful link between madness and unreason that is central to the modern construction of madness: madness is never *only* itself; it is also unreason, the reason that cannot speak its name, the reason that is unaware of itself. Madness thus reveals 'a blindness *blind to itself*, to the point of necessarily entailing an illusion of reason', as Shoshana Felman puts it.[16] This will be explored later; but it is already apparent that this perspective gives an important role to the mad-doctor, the later psychiatrist. If madness is difficult to recognize, experts are clearly necessary. If, as Trélat wrote in 1861, 'a great number of lunatics live in our midst', then they must be identified and incarcerated. By mid-century, such mad-doctors are frequently referred to as 'alienists', experts in 'mental alienation', the mind that is alienated from itself, lost to reason, even though it may put on the appearance of rationality.

And Hersilie? Does she 'put on the appearance' of rationality? Is she one of the 'lucid mad'? Matlock suggests that, in her case, it is not quite as clear-cut as it has hitherto appeared to be, a case of arbitrary imprisonment: 'In paradoxical ways, Hersilie sets her own terms for analysis, leaving us unable to know whether she was sane or insane.' This is because 'her self-representation emerges as anything but stable'; instead, 'her passage through the mad-system seems to have left her unable or unwilling to resolve her identity into a narrative that would make her whole again'.[17]

To see what this means, we must return to her name. Hersilie was incarcerated under the name of Chevalier, and protested long and loud about this; in due course, the asylum authorities changed this to Chevalier-Rouy. And the duplicity of the system, in giving her a false name, could be said to invite duplicity as a response; if she is not allowed her own identity, why should she not play at identity, mock duplicity by taking it on, using it? John Perceval, too, suggests that no patient can escape confinement without recourse to 'deception and duplicity'.[18] In one set of letters, Hersilie asserts that she is incarcerated because of a scandal involving the Duc de Berry, close to the King – she is his daughter. She confides that she likes this identity 'because it *attracts attention*' (original emphasis). But she also writes that she has encountered strangers who tell her that she has been incarcerated because she was believed to have dangerous knowledge about a worldwide secret society. And there is the 'dark lady' who visited her both before, and during, her confinement, and who claimed to be the 'real' Hersilie. Indeed, Hersilie most frequently asserts that she is indeed not the 'real' Hersilie, but her double, a sacrificial substitute; because she is *not* Hersilie, she can tell Hersilie's story, and defend her against the plots of her family. . . .

It is all very confusing. Is this 'doubling' a conscious strategy, an attempt to 'double her way out of the crazy house'? Does she resort to multiple identities in order to make someone care about her plight? (If this is deliberate, it does after all succeed, in the end.) Is it strategy – or symptom? Clearly there is grist for the alienist's mill here. When Hersilie cries out that 'It is my very self they are out to get; it's me they want to annihilate, whatever name I call myself',[19] the mad-doctors will take this as evidence of paranoia. And if Hersilie's doubling hovers uncertainly between strategy and symptom, this same doubling can be taken, elsewhere, as clear evidence of a mental pathology. Here is Victor Tausk, writing of a patient of his, Natalia, half a century later:

> The patient is Miss Natalija A., thirty-one years old, formerly a student of philosophy. She declares that for six and a half years she has been under the influence of an electrical machine made in Berlin. . . . It has the form of a human body, indeed, the patient's own form, though not in all details. . . . The outstanding fact about the machine is that it is being manipulated by someone in a certain manner, and everything that occurs to it happens also to her. When someone strikes the machine, she feels the blow in the corresponding part of her own body.[20]

Here, the doubling has become a process wherein the self truly becomes other to itself, unknowable and alien through distancing in another body, which thereby becomes both symbol and explanation of one's sense of estrangement. As will be seen, this becomes apparent in the symptoms of what today is classified as 'schizophrenia'. The central problem, of agency and responsibility, is raised in this context by Brown, who writes that the question at issue is 'whether the patient's behaviour merely expresses his state of mind or whether the patient does what he does *in order to* express his state of mind'.[21] In the first case, the 'acting-out' can be presented as a *symptom*, not a deliberate *choice*. It is clear that Hersilie's behaviour, and her claims about herself, are undecidable in these terms; and the suggestion is that the issue is *in principle* undecidable, it can *never* be conclusively resolved, even if, in practice, some cases seem clearly on one side of the divide, and some, on the other.

So in the end we do not know whether, or to what extent, Hersilie is in charge of this doubling, this smokescreen, this dissolution of self. Is it conscious, strategic duplicity? Or is it that there is no self-identical 'she' there, that 'she' is broken among the fragments, dissolved in the separate, fractured identities? We can never know; and we can never know not just because she is long dead, taking her secret with her, but because it is not clear what the 'secret' is anyway, or how one could identify it. If madness is the other that cannot speak its name, it is not clear that anyone else can speak it either, or even recognize it; it is a mocking presence in the very heart of reason, ever-reproduced in its threatening, fearful immediacy even as it is exiled, expelled, rendered unthinkable. If Hersilie is not fully in charge of her self-identity, she commits the unthinkable crime of the modern self, but also reminds us that this self-identity is never something that we can be confident of knowing, of mastering, since it is always recalcitrant to our reflexive grasp, always other to itself, and who is to say that 'we' are so far from Hersilie?

> If Hersilie's text undoes the boundaries between madness and sanity, her continued doubling ensures that those lines will not be redrawn. . . . She has dissolved her identity, doubling her way out of it as she has doubled her way out of their system. She has scattered herself among the fragments of paper, and promised to be possibly everywhere herself Hersilie – or someone like her who knows the same pain.[22]

'Should I Return in My Absence, Kindly Detain Me Till I Come Back': The Psychotic Experience

Inevitably modernity enters into our experiences, influencing them, structuring them, even partially constituting them. It is perfectly possible that the modern world produces stresses that can be manifested in what we term 'mental illness', just as it is perfectly possible that some forms of 'mental illness' have genetic or other organic causes – nor are these hypotheses necessarily incompatible. But what matters here is that whatever we take to be the 'signs' or 'symptoms' are inherently cultural and social, since they inevitably render the very nature and possibility of thought, communication and relationship problematical; and that these 'symptoms', and the experiences they rest on, may be particularly challenging in the problems they pose to the modern world, even if that world is implicated in their production. If, as Bastide suggests, 'The madman . . . represents the chaotic part of ourselves', and consequently, 'normal man is the seed-bed in which madness takes root',[23] then we can add that a culture obsessed with controlling or denying its 'chaotic part' will necessarily regard its 'representation' through madness as particularly problematical, and its 'community' with the mad as a scandal.

We can explore this further through examining schizophrenia, the best-known of the so-called 'psychoses'. It has always been controversial; psychiatrists have disagreed widely over its nature, identification and causes, so that Sass can write that 'The schizophrenic, it seems, is psychiatry's quintessential Other – the patient whose very essence is "incomprehensibility" itself.'[24] And Showalter's remark that the term 'schizophrenia' has been 'extended to cover a vast assortment of odd behaviours, cultural maladjustments, and political deviations, from shabbily dressed bag ladies to Soviet dissident writers'[25] is certainly a fair comment on the way it has been embedded in the politics of social control, though it does not, of course, follow that this is *all* there is to say about it.

Let us take the case of John Perceval. After his recovery, he wrote an account of his incarceration, and the events leading up to it; and while he denounced his treatment, he had no doubt that he had experienced an episode of 'lunacy'. In present-day terms, it is likely that it would be categorized as an attack of acute schizophrenia. Perceval tells us that he heard voices – 'I heard the sounds of the cattle lowing and of other beasts in the fields, convey articulate sentences to me' – confused members of his family and the asylum attendants with the figures of the Holy Trinity, and held delusory beliefs.

Retrospectively, Perceval interpreted his madness as a trial, sent by God, which he had managed to survive through giving up his belief in the *literal* reality of his 'voices' and 'visions', which he now dismissed as illusory. He came to feel, *after* the event, that he had in effect taken the 'voice of conscience' as *literally* a voice, rather than metaphorically, and had therefore 'heard' it, as physically real; whereas actually the 'voice' was of his own making, a projection of his inner torment. Insightfully, he writes that delusion consists in 'mistaking a figurative or a poetic form of speech for a literal one', and that 'lunacy is ... the mistaking of a command that is spiritual for that which is literal – a command that is mental for one that is physical'. While these formulations vary, they amount to a claim that the conventional distinctions between the literal and the real, on the one hand, and the figurative and the unreal, on the other, cannot be made in 'lunacy'. Again, he comments that in these literal-minded interpretations, the capacity for humour and irony was lost to him. He gives an illustration:

> the lunatic takes the literal sense, and his imagination not being under his own control, he in a manner feels it. In like manner, when I was desired to suffocate myself on a pillow ... I conceive, now, that the spirit referred to the suffocation of my feelings – that I was to suffocate my grief, my indignation, or what not, on the pillow of my conscience; that I was not to abandon myself to my feelings, but to control them, as others did theirs around me.[26]

Here speaks modern man, trying to regain control of an imagination that has become undisciplined to the point where it even overflows into 'the real'. Porter suggests that, for Perceval, 'insanity was, first and foremost, loss of reason, or reason overwhelmed by imagination',[27] and this is very like Kant's Enlightenment vision: 'lawless fantasy comes close to madness. Here fantasy makes the man its mere plaything and the poor fellow has no control over the course of his ideas.'[28] In the modern world, it is taken as particularly important that these boundaries be maintained, that the literal be assimilated to the real, that representation and reality be strictly distinguished, and that symbolism be reduced to the 'unreality' of metaphor and fantasy, now seen as 'mere' products of the imagination; acceptable, even beneficial, in their way, but very much in need of control.

That a failure to 'live' these distinctions can have wide-ranging effects on both subjective experience and on social interaction is clear not just from Perceval's case but from others, too. The psychoanalyst Hanna Segal describes two patients: a neurotic whose dream of violin playing could be interpreted as masturbatory fantasy, and a psychotic who, asked why he had given up violin playing, replied 'Do you expect me to masturbate in public?' Commenting on these two successive examples, Jacqueline Rose suggests that 'The symbol first *represents* the object and then *becomes* it.'[29] And then we have Joseph, conversing in an asylum with others diagnosed as schizophrenic, and developing the theory that there are huge domes, miles high, above our towns and hospitals, domes that keep us secure but also frustrate us; the roads between the domes cannot be used, on pain of death; aeroplanes only *appear* to fly, due to the hypnotic gas in the domes, but actually they are stuck to them. . . . It is clear from Barham's account[30] that while we can try to understand Joseph – up to a point – by interpreting what he says metaphorically, he does not himself see it like this, since the conventional distinction between the literal and the metaphorical seems not to be available to him; he is simply describing the world as he experiences it, in all its distressing complexity.

Joseph seems to have no capacity to 'stand back', to *doubt*, to question the nature of his experience. He cannot police the boundaries, maintain the distinctions between what we take to be separate dimensions. Perceval, too, says as much: 'I perished from . . . fearing to doubt, and of taking the guilt of doubt upon my conscience.'[31] He himself suggests that it was when he began to doubt the reality of the 'voices', accept the 'guilt' of doubt, that recovery began. To doubt is always to doubt authority; and to be modern is to be able both to doubt, and to carry the burden of guilt that accompanies it. To fail to pay the price, in neurosis, is to risk paying the higher price, in psychosis, that results from the disavowal of guilt in the inability to doubt.[32]

Remembering the discussion, in a previous chapter, of the 'embodied self' – somehow 'inside', yet distinct from the body, and able to control it, and thereby able to act as an *agent* in the world – we can approach another main feature of these experiences. Consider this excerpt from a person's account of a previous schizophrenic episode:

> When I am melting I have no hands, I go into a doorway in order not to be trampled on. Everything is flying away from me. In the doorway I can gather together the pieces of my body. . . . Why do I divide myself in different pieces? I feel that I am without poise, that my personality is melting and that my ego disappears and that I do not exist anymore. Everything pulls me apart.[33]

We can see here quite clearly that the sense of self and its relation to body that was outlined above has more or less totally broken down here. Not only is the body experienced as fragmented, breaking up, melting, but the self, too, is disappearing. The precarious distance and unity of self and body are no more. Laing suggests that in these situations we find 'a disembodied self and a body that is a thing that the self looks at, regarding it at times as though it were just another thing in the world'.[34] One patient said that his saliva tasted strange to him. When this happens, one's body has become alien, other; and since one no longer experiences it as a taken for granted unity, it comes to seem fragmentary. Antonin Artaud, who had such experiences, wrote of 'images of limbs that are far away and not where they should be', and of 'this ill-assembled heap of organs which I was and which I had the impression of witnessing like a vast landscape on the point of breaking up'.[35]

Hence the self loses its moorings, any definite identity: withdrawal from the body, a body that carries the history of past interactions with other embodied selves, means that not only is there nowhere to withdraw to, but that the self has withdrawn from parts of itself, and itself disintegrates, becoming objects among objects. The conventional, taken-for-granted boundaries have collapsed, and as Laing remarks, 'Our culture . . . comes down very sharply on people who do not draw the inner/outer, real/unreal, me/not-me, private/public lines where it is thought to be healthy, right and normal to do so.'[36] Julie, the 'ghost of the weed garden', laments: 'I could be that wall. It's a terrible thing for a girl to be a wall.'[37] Hence Smith can suggest that the central features of this experience are 'expressive of a disorder of the perception of the boundary between the self and the outside world'.[38] And the result, as Barham points out in the case of Joseph, is that the person is in 'the painfully untenable position of an actor who is unable to leave the stage but can no longer render intelligible the dramatic action of which he is part'; we find that 'the story of his life ceased to be available to him as a potentially intelligible narrative'.[39]

The elements of strategy preserved in psychotic withdrawal can nevertheless have a bizarre effect; it is as though deliberate manipulation, irony and ridicule are present even though they cannot be 'deliberate'. Laing suggests that a good deal of schizophrenia is 'red-herring speech, prolonged filibustering', hence 'the schizophrenic is often playing at being psychotic, or pretending to be so'.[40] But if it is 'a special strategy that a person invents in order to live in an unlivable situation',[41] it is a 'strategy' that constantly re-creates its own unlivability, a strategy that ultimately parodies and subverts the very idea of 'strategy', since it guarantees that the subject of the strategy is constantly at its mercy, under its control. This was the point at which Perceval afterwards thought he had gone mad, the point at which he lost his 'restraining power' over his thoughts and beliefs: 'My will to choose to think orderly, was entirely gone.'[42] It is as though the person can now only react, not act, a reaction that enacts the impossibility of moving on, the collapse of agency; and this idea of uncontrolled lack of control is deeply troublesome in a self-consciously rationalist culture.

Ultimately, it is as though the self is no longer 'there'. Shoshana Felman claims that the issue of madness arises 'at that point of silence where it is no longer we who speak, but where, in our absence, we are *spoken*'.[43] A vivid utterance by a schizophrenic patient seems to encapsulate this: 'Should I return in my absence, kindly detain me till I come back.'[44] In its upside-down and back-to-front way, this seems to sum up what the schizophrenic's situation involves: being there and not there, so that one returns in one's absence, is present only when not there, and has indeed to be 'detained' by someone else. . . . Laing points graphically to the effect of this on other people; he describes the sense of 'being in the presence of another human being and yet feeling that there was no one there'.[45]

In probing further into the connections between these experiential facets of schizophrenia, it may also be possible to clarify its relations with modernity. For a start, Porter suggests that, historically, a key development was 'the heightened perception of mysterious, treacherous inner faculties capable of disturbing – and even disorientating – the individual, independently of rational will',[46] and a related clue is offered by Gutman in referring to paranoia, which is frequently associated with schizophrenia: 'Paranoia, the delusion of self-reference . . . would seem to be a historically-defined disorder, for it is dependent upon the sense of self that came into being with Rousseau and the Romantics.'[47]

We have seen that the schizophrenic experience seems to entail an inability to carry out the rituals and strategies of selfhood, as these involve the maintenance of reality/fantasy, literal/metaphorical and reason/imagination boundaries. Bateson comments on the importance of our normal ability to 'communicate about communication, to comment upon the meaningful actions of oneself and others', and suggests that 'This metacommunicative level the schizophrenic seems unable to use successfully.'[48] Schizophrenia indeed emerges as a self-destructive, extreme form of reflexivity, very much shaped by the modern development of the self-conscious, embodied self, indicative of defining attributes of modernity itself.

Developing these ideas, Sass points to what he calls the 'paradox of the reflexive', whereby the 'desperate attempt to constitute the self is precisely what tears the self apart', so that the self destroys itself in the very act of searching for itself. In this penetrating argument, he suggests that 'acute self-consciousness has the effect of *effacing* the self, while simultaneously obscuring its own role in this effacement', and hence that self-reflexive awareness can contribute to a *loss* of sense of self: 'Far from necessarily *sustaining* a sense of self, a strong observing ego may actually undermine it.' It is as though the harder we look at the subjective stream of experience, the more the feeling of selfhood dissolves; what is normally experienced as 'inner' and integral thereby becomes objectified and fragmented. Then, with the boundaries breaking up, the normally 'outer' becomes incorporated in the process; any ordered, subjective experience of an 'outer' world disintegrates. The observing eye constantly distances itself from what it observes; inner experiences and outer realities coalesce even as they break up; in trying to construct a secure sense of self, the self cripples itself:

> As the patient's own strange sensations and thoughts attract his attention, this attention itself, which takes the sensations as its object, can make the sensations seem all the more distant, external, and concrete. . . . Eventually, the patient who thus steps back from his involvement may begin to feel as if his sensations and thoughts originated outside his own body or mind.[49]

Hence the 'voices', or the feeling of 'being watched', the paranoia; the self, attempting to observe and control itself, becomes alienated as all-powerful other to itself, victim of its own surveillance, destroyed by its own all-seeing gaze.

Elsewhere, analysing the celebrated case of Schreber, examined previously by Freud, Sass comments that Schreber's paranoia seems to result from the way he ends up 'watching himself watching himself watching himself watch',[50] an endless regress of 'hyperreflexivity'. As usual, Nietzsche puts it all more simply: 'One *must not* eye oneself while having an experience; else the eye becomes "an evil eye".'[51] The modern self entails and presupposes a reflexive consciousness; but to *focus* on this, attempt to *know* it, catch it in the act, destroys it.

In the light of this, it is hardly surprising that schizophrenia seems to have considerable symbolic resonance in the arts and culture of modernity. In the modernist novel, after all, we frequently encounter an interest in the 'stream of consciousness', a sense that consistency of character and narrative unity become less important than an exploration of the fragmentation and incoherence of experience. The unity of self-consciousness dissolves, the sense of time as a linear flow collapses, clear boundaries and identities are elided, and we are left with unconnected images and memories, floating simultaneously, with no sense of rational project to connect them. The modernist celebration of the incoherence and diversity of experience, subverting the purposive, integrated self of the project of modernity, could thus be seen as homologous to the schizophrenic experience itself, summarized by Jameson as 'an experience of pure material signifiers, or, in other words, a series of pure and unrelated presents in time'.[52] And Showalter's claim that the 'schizophrenic woman' has become a central cultural figure in the twentieth century, appropriated by modernist literary movements as 'the symbol of linguistic, religious, and sexual breakdown and rebellion', suggests a gender dimension; she speculates that typical schizophrenic symptoms can be seen as having parallels in the social situation of women, notably the split between body as sexual object and mind as subject, and the vulnerability to conflicting messages about femininity and maturity.[53]

That these schizophrenic experiences, in their milder forms, could even have benefits for cultural creativity, has long been suspected. Perceval points out that 'lunacy' can mean the emancipation of the mental faculties from 'confused judgement', so that 'the talents become free which have before been cramped'.[54] The delusory flash of inspiration is not, after all, different in kind from the sudden creative insights of great scientists or artists. When James Joyce took his daughter Lucia to Carl Jung for treatment, Jung had no doubt that the daughter was indeed psychotic; but of Joyce himself, he wrote that 'His "psychological" style is definitely schizophrenic, with the difference, however, that the ordinary patient cannot help talking and thinking in such a way, while Joyce willed it and moreover developed it with all his creative forces.'[55]

In the end, then, the links between modern selfhood and the schizophrenic experience are strongly marked; yet this in turn means that the common view that such forms of 'mental illness' represent a regression, either to a childlike or pre-human state, is really just a misleading projection of the complacency of the modern self-image. The schizophrenic represents no more a 'regression' than Kurtz did – there can be no real return – rather, it is a parody of the very reflexivity of the modern consciousness itself, a reminder of its paradoxes and limitations, whereby modernity can fail to recognize its own involvement in the shaping and production of what it rejects and expels. If schizophrenia holds up a mirror to the modern self, it reminds us that what we see in the mirror is only a face, or mask, that the 'real' self is hidden, and anyway may only be a construct perched precariously on the boundaries between inner and outer, real and unreal, observer and observed.

Lunatics, Mad-doctors and the Crazy House

The mental hospital itself both rests on, and helps reproduce, a basic pattern of ideas about madness that runs deep in the modern period. First, we find a pervasive dichotomy between 'reason' and 'passion' in the characterization of madness itself. In the seventeenth century, Locke argued that 'having joined together some ideas very wrongly', the mad 'mistake them for truths', so that madness becomes a defect of reasoning, involving delusion. Hobbes, however, put the emphasis on 'passions unguided', so that madness becomes an upsurge of drives and emotions uncontrolled by intellect and rational will. Madness as loss of reason was frequently seen as a regression to childhood, and madness as passion involved comparison with 'brutes', since being unable to control one's drives rendered one animal-like; but these twin regressions were not mutually exclusive, and either way the effect is that the victim is 'lost to reason'.[56]

By the nineteenth century, with the further emergence of the modern sense of 'mind' and 'the mental', this state was seen as 'mental alienation', and the 'estranged of mind' had to be cared for by 'alienists'. Here we encounter a second important dichotomy, that of mind and body. It was widely held by alienists that although the mind, as such, could not but function perfectly, it could nevertheless be affected by its physical substratum, the brain, which could indeed be 'diseased', and, potentially, 'cured'.[57] This idea is still common today: a patient diagnosed as schizophrenic and trying to make sense of the condition is quoted as saying that he could make no sense of the idea of a 'split mind', whereas a 'malfunctioning brain' presented no such problem of intelligibility; hence the hallucinations, in coming from part of the brain, could be seen as 'not-me'.[58] If this perspective can be described as 'Cartesian' in any sense, it is in the implicit assimilation of 'mind' and 'reason', with the latter seen as central to self-regulation. Given this, the state of being 'estranged of mind' must entail either a brain dysfunction, or the overwhelming of reason by the passions, thus reinforcing the first dichotomy.

This also gives a clue to the third dichotomy, of organic and 'moral' causes, with the latter category, in the broad nineteenth-century sense, incorporating much that would today be seen as 'social'. In practice, the two potential causes were – and are – usually seen as operating together, so that Boyne can claim that 'The essence of modern madness is to be undecidable between these two poles.'[59] Typically, madness became both illness and deviance; 'unreason' operates both through physical causes and as 'the psychological effect of a moral fault', as

Foucault puts it, adding that psychiatry itself only developed when madness was 'alienated in guilt'.[60] Hysteria, for example, was a condition to which women were biologically predisposed, but hysterical attacks themselves could well be encouraged by behaviour that flouted the conventions of respectable womanhood.

However, this example also shows the instability of the 'moral' category itself: for could it not be that it was these very conventions – the restrictions of 'respectable' marriage and the 'private sphere' – that contributed to the tensions that produced hysteria in the first place? Here we encounter the 'discourse of stress', the idea that the civilizing process is inevitably accompanied by pressures and strains. In the eighteenth century, 'stress' had developed as a category for making sense of the way civilization was alleged to engender anxieties, lead to 'excesses', enervate the system, and encourage the 'morbid' growth of the imagination.[61] Gordon points to a 'reflexive consciousness at work in such eighteenth-century notions as hysteria, hypochondria, nerves and vapours, where certain classes of mental ailment are seen specifically as ills of modernity and its vices'.[62] Hirst and Woolley summarize these themes in writing that 'The "nervous" constitution is a disease of civilisation; and overdeveloped "sensibility" leads to a magnification of the physical and mental effects of sensation and passion.'[63] And just as such problems were a product of civilization, so were the resources to cope with them, notably self-discipline and will-power.

But a move the other way was equally possible, towards arguing that the major cause of 'mental illness' was congenital; hence what Ray calls 'psychiatric Darwinism', dominant in the late nineteenth century. Ultimately, the mentally and physically 'degenerate' were viewed as evolutionary regressions, posing a danger to the purity and intelligence of 'the race'. This spectre of 'chronic insanity' haunted the late Victorian imagination, in an era when the asylum population was rising twice as fast as that of the population as a whole.

The above pattern of mental illness constructions both permits, and reflects, the existence of experts and institutions that are in some sense 'medical' yet also distinct from the medical profession and the ordinary hospital. Essentially, then, psychiatry and the asylum presuppose first, that as a medical problem, mental illness is in principle curable (or at least, the symptoms can be controlled), and second, that the techniques involved will differ in some ways from those of general medicine, while overlapping in others (psychotherapy, occupational therapy, and so on, as well as drugs or electroconvulsive therapy). But there has always been tension over whether totally separate institutions are called for. Thus Ray points out that asylum superintendents were in 'the awkward position of having to stress both the unity of mental and physical disorders (to legitimate medical dominance), and their different forms (to legitimate separate institutions)'.[64] And since the mentally ill cannot, by definition, cope for themselves, and may not even recognize they have a problem, curing must involve elements of custody. Separation and surveillance are necessary. In short, the asylum develops as an institution poised uneasily between hospital and prison, with elements of the workhouse thrown in, and this midway point turned out to be inherently unstable.

Suppose, to take the first case, we drop the assumption that mental illness was curable, as was often done in the early eighteenth century, and the late nineteenth to early twentieth centuries. The asylum then becomes a purely custodial institution, swinging dangerously close to the model of the prison. And this affects the status of psychiatry, threatening to marginalize it; psychiatrists are liable to become little more than humane prison wardens. But if the second assumption is dropped, and cure involves merely drugs and surgery, then we are swinging close to the hospital model, and the case for a separate psychiatric profession and separate asylums becomes dubious. There are clearly signs of this in the present situation, with the closure of mental hospitals.[65]

Episodes in the history of the asylum illustrate these tensions. 'Moral management', pioneered by the Tukes at the York Retreat from the 1790s, rejected the mechanical restraints and other abuses of the eighteenth-century asylum regime; the key to therapy was to restructure the environment, relationships and work habits of the patient, so that the virtues of hard work, conscientiousness and decency could be instilled. The imposition of moral discipline by the therapist would result in self-discipline in the patient. The fact that, as Ann Digby puts it, 'The mad were in some sense authors of their own misfortunes since their control over their passions was inadequate'[66] both justified their custody and held out the promise of cure. But in swinging away from a narrowly medical notion of cure, it becomes difficult to justify both the asylum and psychiatry: how can the custodial aspects be justified in the absence of any clear biomedical rationale? And what price psychiatry, if enlightened moral guidance is really all that is needed? In effect, the prison looms again: an enlightened prison, no doubt, dedicated – in utilitarian spirit – to reforming its inmates and returning them to society, but a prison nonetheless. We can see that humanitarianism is perfectly compatible with domination.

Gradually the reformed mad-doctors revived medical theory in this area, incorporating certain 'moral management' ideas, and moved in to establish control over the new wave of asylums in the mid-nineteenth century; thus do professionalization and institutionalization reinforce each other. By the 1870s the psychiatric profession was in full control. There was little hope of therapy in the huge asylums, nor did the doctrine of congenital disease make this a plausible aspiration, and it is clear from Warner's research that a systematic denigration of the claimed success rates of the earlier moral managers occurred.[67]

In many ways, though, it is the 1950s – when asylum populations first showed serious signs of a major downturn – that still provide us with the most potent imagery of the asylum, with novels like Kesey's *One Flew Over the Cuckoo's Nest*, and pathbreaking texts like Goffman's *Asylums*, suggesting as they do that much behaviour that is taken to indicate 'mental illness' can actually be seen as the effects of the institutionalization itself, or of the drugs used.[68] However, we can perhaps most appropriately give the last word to John Perceval, even though his experiences date from much earlier: 'My delusions, though they often made me ridiculous, did not derange my understanding unaided by the poisonous medicines and unnatural treatments of my physicians.' And looking at the other inmates, he even concludes that 'this mad state may be the necessary effects of the situation in which we are placed'.[69]

Madness and Unreason

Crucial to the emergence of the modern way with madness is the link between madness and unreason that was originally forged in the seventeenth century. Foucault argues that in the late medieval and Renaissance periods

> madness was allowed free reign; it circulated throughout society, it formed part of the background and language of everyday life, it was for everyone an everyday experience that one sought neither to exalt nor to control. . . . Up to about 1650, Western culture was strangely hospitable to these forms of experience.[70]

The mad had a role on the margins – simultaneously dangerous yet necessary – as in the symbolism of paintings of the 'ship of fools', depicting the mad sailing from town to town, or in the incarceration of the so-called 'raving mad' in the city walls; but their major significance was that they brought the margins into the centre. Mostly, they remained in the community, a reminder that madness was part of the human condition, an inescapable part of our lives since the Fall.

This should not, however, be misconstrued; madness was not romanticized. Madness was like death – it enforced an awareness of the nearness, the possibility, of damnation. In Foucault's words, 'the head that will become a skull is already empty. Madness is the *déjà-là* of death.'[71] MacDonald asserts that 'The idle speech of raving lunatics was mystical in a sense, for like the delirious utterances of dying men and women it was spoken by people nearer the unseen world than we, but it held no peculiar authority.'[72] It was not what the mad had to say, but the fact of madness itself, that was significant. Madness revealed the menace beneath the surface, but also reminded us of the 'madness' of heavenly bliss; true wisdom means understanding the limits of reason. To reach God, humans must fathom the depths of the non-rational; Luther himself described reason as a whore. Only thus can humanity comprehend what Foucault calls 'the madness of the cross . . . the great unreason of sacrifice'.[73] Painters such as Bruegel and Bosch depict madness entering the very heart of the world. Porter concludes that 'If mankind was radically sinful, the gulf between *homo rationalis* and the fool was neither clear-cut nor crucial under God, for all are sinful, all mad.'[74]

It could be said that 'folly', as a broad category, encompassed both madness and sanity, thereby maintaining a precarious dialogue between them. In his influential Renaissance text *In Praise of Folly*, Erasmus suggested that just as all life is foolish, so the fool is wise, since he *knows* that life is foolish and behaves accordingly; his very existence testifies to the madness in our lives. MacDonald points out that the Jacobean stage 'teemed with idiots and lunatics', and popular writers filled their works with 'natural fools, counterfeit madmen, Mad Toms, melancholy gentlemen and distempered lovers'.[75] We are reminded of King Lear going into exile, a mad king pretending to be sane, accompanied by a retainer, who is sane and pretending to be mad, and a wise Fool. . . . Thus does the fool ridicule the pretensions of earthly authority, and the frailties of reason; he stands at centre stage as the guardian of truth. Indeed, this view lingers on, later, in secular form, becoming a trope for the denunciation of the world; thus Thomas Tryon insists that 'the world is just a great Bedlam, where those that are more mad, lock up those that are less'.[76]

Then, in the seventeenth century, this whole universe of experience gave way; with the folly of Carnival increasingly driven out, folly itself ceased to mediate madness and reason. Instead, we encounter the master contrast that contains, latent within it, the later history of madness in its relation to society: that of reason and unreason. For Montaigne, still sympathetic to the earlier attitude, to ignore or disparage unreason is to close oneself off from otherness and difference; it is unreasonable to make reason the measure of all things. But Descartes will have none of this. With Descartes, we have the birth of the self-confident 'rational subject', confident that rationality can be stretched over the surface of the world and leave no mysterious residue; what cannot be grasped by reason does not exist, and reason can become a regulating practice of selfhood.[77]

For Descartes, rational thought is totally incompatible with madness; madness becomes unreason, mere exclusion or negativity. There can no longer be a *relationship* between sanity and madness, at least not a relationship of communication. By the eighteenth century, writes Porter, it was widely thought that madness had 'nothing authentic to say'.[78] Thus is the sense of community and continuity broken. With madness excluded from life and devalued as a possible source of insight, with its demotion to the empty category of unreason, the possibility of *confinement* is opened up: madness becomes subject to power. The asylum looms. To begin with, the mad were often incarcerated indiscriminately with vagrants, the poor, and criminals, all seen as manifestations of this central – and scandalous – 'want of reason'. The specialist mental hospital itself only develops extensively in the early nineteenth century, hand in hand with the development of psychiatry itself, now the dominant mode of constituting and assimilating what had become 'mental illness'.

Psychiatry itself is, as Boyne remarks, a part of the Enlightenment project, which affirms that 'no part of the social condition is beyond analysis', and thus that 'the orderly workings of social power can be guaranteed through the development and application of knowledge'; a project which thereby 'enshrines a denial of otherness, of difference'.[79] Thus Foucault claims that psychiatry constantly continues to reproduce the very barrier between 'reason' and 'unreason', that defined its possibility in the first place; it is a 'monologue of reason *about* madness', established on the basis of a silence, a 'broken dialogue' that testifies to the way 'sovereign reason' is also 'sovereign power'.[80]

It is important to focus further attention on the reason/unreason dichotomy. Foucault argues that madness in the classical period ceased to be the sign of another world. . . . Confinement merely manifested what madness, in its essence, was: a manifestation of non-being; and by providing this manifestation, confinement thereby suppressed it, since it restored it to its truth as nothingness. Confinement is the practice which corresponds most exactly to madness experienced as unreason, that is, the empty negativity of reason; by confinement, madness is acknowledged to be *nothing*.

Madness as unreason is madness as non-being; it cannot have a meaning, for there is nothing there that could 'mean'. It is a degree zero of deviance, an absolute void; it cannot speak, and it cannot have a role. It cannot confirm the absolute plenitude and self-sufficiency of reason, for its very existence contradicts that – unless its existence is rendered knowable through capture and confinement, in which case it escapes in itself even as it is trapped in its 'manifestation', in the mad. Hence 'unreason defined the locus of madness's possibility',[81] since madness was unreason's empirical form, its disclosure: 'the paradox of this *nothing* is to *manifest* itself, to explode in signs, in words, in gestures'. This paradox is elaborated as follows:

> For madness, if it is nothing, can manifest itself only by departing from itself, by assuming an appearance in the order of reason and thus becoming the contrary of itself . . . madness is always absent, in a perpetual retreat where it is inaccessible, without phenomenal or positive character; and yet it is present and perfectly visible in the singular evidence of the madman. . . . All that madness can say of itself is merely reason, though it is itself the negation of reason. In short, *a rational hold over madness is always possible and necessary, to the very degree that madness is non-reason.*

Hence unreason is everything that 'presents itself to reason in familiar structures', thus 'authorizing a knowledge, and then a science', but is also 'all that is constantly in retreat from reason, in the inaccessible domain of nothingness'.[82]

What this seems to suggest is that while it would be possible to see madness as traversed by modernity, bearing its mark, it is not obvious that this would justify claims to *understand* it. If schizophrenia can be presented as a paradoxical, extreme form of modernist reflexivity, does this give us warrant to assert that we comprehend the madness it embodies? Would this not be to subsume it under the categories of rationalizing analysis, dissect it in a language not its own, and one that betrayed it? Would it not be to confirm the subordination of the mad – and the escape of madness – yet again? Writing of the 'silence' of the mad since the breaking of the dialogue, Derrida suggests that

> The misfortune of the mad, the interminable misfortune of their silence, is that their best spokesmen are those who betray them best; which is to say that when one attempts to convey their silence *itself*, one has already passed over to the side of the enemy, the side of order, even if one fights against order from within it, putting its origin into question.

Thus the attempt to 'listen' to their silence, 'restore' it to speech, would be a 'subtle restoration . . . of the act perpetrated against madness – and be so at the very moment when this act is denounced'.[83] This implies that if the classic exemplars of madness – from John Perceval to Julie and Joseph – can be said to produce a language that is indeed intelligible, up to a point, that would only be because it could be interpreted as 'metaphor', thus giving it a derivative, second-order truth, or because we can see it in functional terms, as a 'response' (to family traumas, and so on). Either way, we simply stretch the nets of rationalism over it. And besides, we can never do this without residue, or the 'madness' itself threatens to disappear: what is left, an irrationality of behaviour or intention in context, remains construed as a crucial 'want of reason'.

Furthermore, if this ability to 'understand' madness – as meaningful and/or as product of underlying organic pathology – seems to be a testimony to reason's power, really it only confirms reason in its empty self-sufficiency, its self-validating circularity: a 'reason' that can only grasp what it has itself produced can only attain chimerical victories. If we could understand the mad, either we're mad or they're not; and either way, it is both madness, as unreason, and reason itself, that come into question. It is not that madness is a message 'from elsewhere', conveying a 'deeper' meaning, or that, conversely, it is problematical because it falls foul of some universal reason, but that madness and reason, in their modern senses, come into being *together*; we here encounter a sociocultural reality, not just a philosophical polarity. If madness can speak, it is only in the language of reason; and if reason can speak, madness exists as its impossible backdrop. And if reason exists, it does so by positing a boundary, to safeguard itself. But the boundary is impossible; not only can one not cross it, one cannot even conceive of crossing it. What lies 'beyond' is unthinkable, absolute lack or undifferentiation, the poles between which madness swings: absolute void and absolute excess, nothingness and chaos.

Madness must therefore be known – for there is nothing that cannot be known – yet it also defies knowledge in the very act of its appropriation. What *counts* as madness, how it can be *recognized*: there is not, there never has been, there never could be, any decisive, agreed solution to this, and the answers shift constantly through the modern period. Madness always carries the element of *undecidability*; Hersilie's plight is ineliminable, for the uncertainty over Hersilie's status as mad or sane is precipitated by anyone about whom the question is posed. And if, in our time, madness has acquired the unconscious as one of its zones of operation, this same unconscious notoriously throws up parallel problems of interpretation. A culture can only know madness if it surrenders any firm sense of its boundary as the limit of the sane, the rational, if the reason/unreason dichotomy is itself subverted. Perhaps this is what Felman means when she writes that 'madness stands in our contemporary world for the radical ambiguity of the inside and the outside', and that 'a discourse that speaks of madness can henceforth no longer know whether it is inside or outside, internal or external, to the madness of which it speaks'.[84]

Madness Represented, Madness Reproduced

The problem remains: if madness has been characterized as a negation of reason, an absence, it must nevertheless be represented in some form, if it is to be identified and controlled. What, then, are the 'images of madness' that have developed in modernity? And do they merely 'reflect' madness, or *shape* it?

This problem can be traced through the history of modern madness. In theory, madness in the seventeenth and eighteenth centuries was easily recognized; Porter suggests that 'it was of the essence of lunacy to be visible, and known by its appearance', and he quotes Tryon's claim that because men of reason were such hypocrites, it was really *only* the mad whose nature could be read in their faces. Madness meant behaving, talking and looking crazy; it always gave itself away. But we also find the idea that madness could be a trickster: 'It impersonated civility, yet laughed behind its back', hence 'What was so maddening about madness was that it was simultaneously real, terrifying and catastrophic, yet also chimerical, duping both its victims and society at large.'

By the nineteenth century, psychiatry was firmly committed to a view of madness as something difficult to recognize and decode, 'fearsomely latent', yet open to the 'expert diagnostic gaze'.[85] Increasingly, attempts were made to develop a typology of madness, using *visible* features of the mad as signifiers of their 'inner state' of distress. If objective features of physical appearance could be pointed to, then the patient could become a specimen, one of a 'type', exemplifying the possibility of a scientific classification of the forms of madness. The rationale is stated clearly enough by a Dr Morison in 1825: 'The appearance of the face, it is well known, is intimately connected with, and dependent upon, the state of the mind.'[86] In the hands of the phrenologists, this became the doctrine that brain and skull shape would reveal mental health or its opposite; criminality and insanity, as deviations from normality, would both thus be manifested in physical deformities. Showalter suggests that 'the set of an ear, the shape of a brow, even the quiver of an eyebrow, were "stigmata of degeneration"', and she quotes Henry Maudsley: 'few persons go mad . . . who do not show more or less plainly by their gait, manner, gestures, habits of thought, feeling, or action, that they have a sort of predestination to madness', and his conclusion that 'outward defects and deformities are the visible signs of inward and invisible faults which will have their influence in breeding'.[87]

What result, however, are pictures that testify to a deep instability in the strategy of madness representation. On the one hand, the pictures can be like parodies; they so exaggerate the alleged diagnostic features that they are useless as guides to the diversity of individuals. Charles Bell's book on madness (1806) illustrates this, as does Esquirol's 'atlas' (1838) – the first of many such – which contains a collection of pictures to exemplify the types of madness. One of Bell's grimacing caricatures is used by him to draw revealing conclusions about the recognition and nature of madness and madmen:

There is a vacancy in their laugh, and a want of meaning in their ferocious-
ness. . . . To learn the character of the human countenance when devoid of expression, and reduced to the state of brutality, we must have recourse to the lower
animals. . . . If we should happily transfer their expression to the human countenance, we should, as I conceive it, irresistibly convey the idea of madness, vacancy
of mind, and mere animal passion.[88]

Madness as unreason is madness as absence, represented in the presence of the
brutish. . . .

On the other hand, accurate portrayals of specific individuals fail to capture
what is supposedly 'mad' about them altogether. Portraits of the mad by great
artists like Géricault and Van Gogh are in this sense self-defeating. When we look
at Géricault's superb depiction of an old woman (see plate 4), would we have
known that she was suffering from 'monomania of envy', had we not been told in
the caption? When sent photos of the 'mentally ill', Darwin confessed his
bewilderment: 'He completely failed to see the categories, the complex tax-
onomies that . . . underpinned nineteenth century theories of madness', writes
Janet Browne, concluding that 'For Darwin, there was no face of madness.'[89]
Again, works of art painted by the allegedly mad posed – and pose – much the
same problem. It has proved impossible to find any clear-cut way to distinguish
these by criteria of form or content, particularly in an era of modernist questioning and parody of orthodox canons of representation.[90]

Increasingly, then, it was not appearance but behaviour that came to be
relied on as the outward manifestation and 'proof' of the madness within.
Madness is no longer 'read' on the surface of the body; the mad are known
through their *acts*. This shift of emphasis can be seen in the work of Charcot,
whose lectures at the Salpêtrière asylum in Paris in the 1880s gave him an
international reputation.

His aim was to demonstrate the features of hysteria as a form of mental illness,
using his patients, invariably women; and the climax of the demonstration would
come when he hypnotized a patient and made her perform the *grande hystérie*, the
hysterical seizure, culminating in the classic, swanlike *arc en cercle* movement.
Heath writes:

> The pictures and engravings of the period capture the scene: the audience rapt in
> attention, the assistants, the master, and then the young woman, in the pose of a
> convulsion, head thrown back, body arched forward, she fixed for the gaze, the
> offered object of the lesson.

It was, in short, intensely theatrical; and one might suspect that the 'actresses', as
it were, came to know their lines. Heath suggests as much:

> It was too perfect. The same patients were used time after time, like so many
> actresses. Expectation of what should happen was high and what was wanted was
> more or less well known to these women. . . . Patients, who were entirely dependent
> on Charcot and the Salpêtrière, knew hysteria and went with the pattern. Some,

indeed, were rehearsed beforehand by the zealous assistants eager to please the master.[91]

One patient, Blanche Wittmann, could 'do' the *grande hystérie* so well that she became known as the 'Queen of Hysterics'; she later confessed that even under hypnosis she had known perfectly well what she was doing. Even the supposedly unique *arc en cercle* symptom turns out to have had a long history in conventional representations of madness.[92] Hence when the Victorian actress Ellen Terry visited an asylum to see what madness was 'really like', in order to improve her performance in madwoman roles, she came out complaining that the inmates were 'too theatrical' to teach her anything. It is as though the spectacle of madness had been irredeemably corrupted by its own representations.

And Charcot's own photographs confirm this general impression; what purport to be photos of the unadorned mad state actually tell us about gender-related conventions of decorum and civility. What we see is not madness, but its management. Not surprisingly, then, Showalter claims that Charcot's hospital became an environment in which female hysteria was 'perpetually presented, represented, and reproduced'.[93] In effect, we find here the shaping and production of madness, rather than simply the exhibition of something 'already there'. The mental hospital becomes the means whereby the modern world can simultaneously *expel* madness, withdraw it from the everyday world, while forming it according to its own *image* of madness. Whether you are mad when you enter the mental hospital, you certainly have madness thrust upon you. If madness is exiled in modernity, it is nonetheless shaped, structured and represented by that very reason that proclaims itself other to it.

Madness, as heir to the folly of carnival, must be captured in representation, yet defies this fate. And this is because of what it represents in itself: the threat of the ineffable, the impossible communication, the very possibility of experience that cannot be communicated and therefore cannot be *known*, even to those who experience it. Madness intervenes *in* representation, parodies it; what is mad is unrepresentable, what is unrepresentable is mad. Madness is the alienated revenge of the otherness at the very heart of reason.

Notes

1 J. Matlock, 'Doubling Out of the Crazy House: Gender, Autobiography, and the Insane Asylum System in Nineteenth-century France', *Representations* (1991), 34.
2 P. S. Penfold and G. Walker, *Women and the Psychiatric Paradox* (Open University Press, 1984), ch. 6. See also B. S. Turner, *Medical Power and Social Knowledge* (Sage, 1987), ch. 5, and J. Ussher, *Women's Madness* (Harvester Wheatsheaf, 1991).
3 G. Bateson (ed.) *Perceval's Narrative* (Stanford University Press, 1961).
4 G. Bateson, introduction to *Perceval's Narrative*, p. xvii.
5 E. Showalter, *The Female Malady* (Virago, 1987), p. 52. See also D. Russell, *Women, Madness and Medicine* (Polity, 1995).
6 Matlock, 'Doubling', p. 70.

7   Cited in Penfold and Walker, *Psychiatric Paradox*, p. 73.
8   Showalter, *Female Malady*, p. 124.
9   Ibid., ch. 1.
10 R. Porter, *Mind Forg'd Manacles: A History of Madness in England from the Restoration to the Regency* (Penguin, 1990), p. 203.
11 Showalter, *Female Malady*, pp. 61, 81.
12 V. Skultans, *English Madness* (Routledge, 1979), p. 95.
13 Matlock, 'Doubling', p. 68.
14 D. Rosenhan, 'On Being Sane in Insane Places', in O. Grusky and M. Pollner (eds.) *The Sociology of Mental Illness* (Holt, Rinehart and Winston, 1981), p. 312.
15 Matlock, 'Doubling', pp. 68, 68, 69, 72.
16 S. Felman, *Writing and Madness* (Cornell University Press, 1986), p. 36.
17 Matlock, 'Doubling', pp. 89, 68, 79.
18 Perceval, in Bateson, *Perceval's Narrative*, p. 125.
19 Matlock, 'Doubling', pp. 80, 79, 81, 84.
20 V. Tausk, 'On the Origin of the Influencing Machine in Schizophrenia', *Psychoanalytic Quarterly* (1933), 2, pp. 529–30.
21 R. Brown, 'Psychosis and Irrationality', in S. I. Benn and G. H. Mortimore (eds.) *Rationality and the Social Sciences* (Routledge, 1976), p. 336.
22 Matlock, 'Doubling', pp. 85, 82.
23 Cited in A. C. Smith, *Schizophrenia and Madness* (Allen and Unwin, 1982), p. 139.
24 L. Sass, 'Introspection, Schizophrenia and Fragmentation of Self', *Representations* (1987), 19, p. 4.
25 Showalter, *Female Malady*, p. 204.
26 Perceval, in Bateson, *Perceval's Narrative*, pp. 265, 270, 279, 271.
27 R. Porter, *A Social History of Madness* (Weidenfeld and Nicolson, 1989), p. 175.
28 J. Schulte-Sasse, 'Imagination and Modernity: On the Taming of the Human Mind', *Cultural Critique* (1986–7), 5, p. 33.
29 J. Rose, 'The Man Who Mistook His Wife for a Hat or A Wife is Like an Umbrella – Fantasies of the Modern and the Postmodern', in A. Ross (ed.) *Universal Abandon: The Politics of Postmodernism* (Minnesota University Press, 1988), p. 239.
30 P. Barham, *Schizophrenia and Human Value* (Blackwell, 1984).
31 Perceval, in Bateson, *Perceval's Narrative*, p. 37.
32 G. Bateson, 'Towards a Theory of Schizophrenia', in his *Steps to an Ecology of Mind* (Paladin, 1973), p. 182.
33 Sass, 'Introspection', p. 1.
34 R. D. Laing, *The Divided Self* (Penguin, 1965), pp. 161–2.
35 Cited in Sass, 'Introspection', p. 25.
36 R. D. Laing, *Self and Others* (Tavistock, 1969), p. 19.
37 Laing, *Divided Self*, p. 198.
38 Smith, *Schizophrenia*, p. 37.
39 Barham, *Schizophrenia*, pp. 149, 150.
40 Laing, *Divided Self*, pp. 163, 164.
41 R. D. Laing, *The Politics of Experience* (Penguin, 1967), p. 95.
42 Perceval, in Bateson, *Perceval's Narrative*, p. 44.
43 Felman, *Writing and Madness*, p. 55.
44 Smith, *Schizophrenia*, p. 28.
45 Laing, *Divided Self*, p. 195.
46 Porter, *Manacles*, p. 196.

47 H. Gutman, 'Rousseau's *Confessions*: A Technology of the Self', in L. H. Martin (ed.) *Technologies of the Self: A Seminar with Michel Foucault* (Tavistock, 1988), pp. 119–20.

48 Bateson, 'Towards a Theory', p. 187.

49 Sass, 'Introspection', pp. 8, 23, 8, 18, 16. See also the more developed version, *Madness and Modernism* (Basic Books, 1992).

50 L. Sass, 'Schreber's Panopticism', *Social Research* (1987), 54: 1, p. 144.

51 W. Kaufmann (ed.) *The Portable Nietzsche* (Viking Press, 1964), p. 157 (original emphasis).

52 F. Jameson, *Postmodernism* (Verso, 1991), p. 27. It will be apparent that I have reservations about Jameson's attempt to link schizophrenia with the *post*modern.

53 Showalter, *Female Malady*, pp. 204, 213; and see Sylvia Plath's account in *The Bell Jar* (Faber and Faber, 1988). See also broader linkages with modernism in Sass, *Madness and Modernism*.

54 Perceval, in Bateson, *Perceval's Narrative*, p. 282.

55 Cited in Smith, *Schizophrenia*, p. 143.

56 Porter, *Manacles*, p. 192.

57 A. Scull, *Museums of Madness* (Penguin, 1982), pp. 159–60.

58 J. Wing (ed.) *Schizophrenia from Within* (National Schizophrenia Fellowship, 1975), p. 31.

59 R. Boyne, *Foucault and Derrida* (Unwin Hyman, 1990), p. 47.

60 M. Foucault, *Madness and Civilization* (Tavistock, 1967), pp. 158, 183.

61 Porter, *Manacles*, p. 84.

62 C. Gordon, '*Histoire de la folie*: An Unknown Book by Michel Foucault', in A. Still and I. Velody (eds.) *Rewriting the History of Madness* (Routledge, 1992), p. 26.

63 P. Hirst and P. Woolley, *Social Relations and Human Attributes* (Tavistock, 1982), p. 176.

64 L. J. Ray, 'Models of Madness in Victorian Asylum Practice', *European Journal of Sociology* (1981), 22, p. 252.

65 See Scull, *Museums of Madness*, and K. Doerner, *Madmen and the Bourgeoisie* (Blackwell, 1981), for discussions of aspects of this.

66 A. Digby, *Madness, Morality and Medicine: A Study of the York Retreat* (Cambridge University Press, 1985), p. 3.

67 R. Warner, *Recovery from Schizophrenia* (Routledge, 1985), pp. 119–25.

68 See, for example, P. Brown and S. Gunk, 'Tardive Dyskinesia', *Journal of Health and Social Behaviour* (1986), 27:2.

69 Perceval, in Bateson, *Perceval's Narrative*, p. 277.

70 M. Foucault, *Mental Illness and Psychology* (California University Press, 1987), p. 67.

71 Foucault, *Madness*.

72 M. MacDonald, *Mystical Bedlam* (Cambridge University Press, 1983), p. 147.

73 Foucault, *Madness*, p. 79.

74 Porter, *Manacles*, p. 20.

75 MacDonald, *Mystical Bedlam*, p. 121.

76 Porter, *Manacles*, p. 28.

77 Boyne, *Foucault*, ch. 2.

78 Porter, *Manacles*, p. 281.

79 Boyne, *Foucault*, p. 33.

80 Foucault, *Madness*, pp. xii–xiii, xii.

81 Ibid., pp. 115, 115–16, 83.

82   Foucault, *Madness*, p. 107 (original emphasis).
83   J. Derrida, 'Cogito and *Histoire de la Folie*', in his *Writing and Difference* (Routledge, 1978), pp. 36, 35.
84   Felman, *Writing and Madness*, pp. 12–13.
85   Porter, *Manacles*, pp. 35, 17, 35.
86   S. Gilman, *Seeing the Insane* (Wiley, 1985), p. 92.
87   Showalter, *Female Malady*, pp. 106–7.
88   Cited in Gilman, *Seeing the Insane*, p. 90.
89   J. Browne, 'Darwin and the Face of Madness', in W. Bynum et al., *Anatomy of Madness*, Vol. I (Tavistock, 1985), pp. 161, 162.
90   See D. Maclagan, 'Outsiders or Insiders?', in S. Hiller (ed.) *The Myth of Primitivism* (Routledge, 1991) and S. Gilman, 'The Mad as Artists', in his *Difference and Pathology* (Cornell University Press, 1985).
91   S. Heath, *The Sexual Fix* (Macmillan, 1982), pp. 35, 35–6. On hysteria, see also J. Beizer, *Ventriloquized Bodies: Narratives of Hysteria in 19th Century France* (Cornell University Press, 1994).
92   Gilman, *Seeing the Insane*, p. 22.
93   Showalter, *Female Malady*, pp. 92, 150.

5 Modernity's Sphinx:

Woman as Nature and Culture

In the picture in plate 5, a man sits, rigid, implacable, face towards us as we look in. On the right, women display ostentatious grief and horror. Our eyes travel to the object of their distress, a procession bearing corpses, entering their household. The contrast between the masculine left of the picture, and the feminine right, is all the more marked in that the man sits in the darkness, while the anguish of the women is bathed in light; the emotional dissonance ruptures space itself.[1] Clearly there is a fundamental sense in which this is a painting 'about' gender, even though that is not alluded to in its title, nor has it been central to art-historical discussions of the painting. For this is *Brutus Receiving the Bodies of His Sons*, painted in the 'Year of Revolution', 1789, by the Revolution's greatest painter, Jacques-Louis David; and it depicts an event in the early history of the Roman Republic when a founder of the Republic, Brutus, himself a regicide, orders the execution of his sons on learning that they had engaged in a plot to restore the monarchy. Indeed, we are informed in the original sources, Plutarch and Livy, that he watched as the execution was carried out.

The next picture (see plate 6) again displays masculine violence, this time in battle, but the woman's role is in complete contrast; now, she is a commanding public figure, waving the *tricolore* as she leads armed men over the corpses of the already fallen. We are not surprised that this is *Liberty Guiding the People*, also known as *Liberty on the Barricades*, and it dates from another revolutionary context: Delacroix painted it in the aftermath of the 'July Revolution' of 1830, when the 'bourgeois monarchy' of Louis-Philippe was installed. The title tells us to 'read' the woman as allegory, and certainly reading her is difficult: intensely political, she yet has her breasts exposed, as though she also crosses other barricades, between the private and the public, the respectable and the transgressive, nature and culture. . . . Taken together, then, these two pictures present a consistent portrayal of men as active on the public stage, whereas there are paradoxes and challenges in the portrayal of women. How can this be accounted for?

Returning to the painting by David, one can note that it was painted at a time when not only was political revolution imminent, but a revolution that had been going on in the relation between the sexes was reaching its culmination, inaugurating the modern regime of gender relations. For the emotionalism of women, while portrayed as 'natural', is very clearly the work of culture. In the case of France, Outram suggests that the Revolution was crucial in destroying what had hitherto been experienced as a shared continuum, with men, too, involved in the expression of *sensibilité*. Earlier in the century, men and women had 'sighed and wept together' over the novels of Richardson, Rousseau and Goethe; but now that kind of reaction was confined to one sex only.[2] Tears, no longer gender-neutral, were now clearly marked as feminine, and by the next century it was firmly established that 'the man who sobbed found himself relegated to femininity and childhood'.[3] The 'closed man' of Elias is not accompanied – to the same extent – by 'closed woman'.

While it was still accepted, by the time of the 1789 Revolution, that the woman *could* be capable of public heroism, it was held to be different in kind, reactive rather than a manifestation of autonomous 'Stoic virtue': 'They react with warm and generous outrage, and through maternal or married love . . . perform acts of courage and sacrifice.'[4] Men act, through remorseless self-control; women *re*act, through emotional involvement. Men thereby gain a *public* dignity and status denied to women, whereas women have access to a 'private' virtue, based on emotional generosity and insight within the domestic context. Here we encounter the clear emergence of the public and private as gendered worlds: the public world of politics and business, the private world of family and domesticity; and the latter, while idealized, through association with the idea of love as the glue that binds the family together, also amounts to a 'new model of female confinement'.[5] And in David's picture, after all, we note that while the women are bathed in light – their 'private' sphere is open to the gaze – they are semi-blinded. They are, as Bryson puts it, 'to be seen, not to see'.[6]

Lynn Hunt observes that there was also a class dimension here, in that the exclusion of the feminine from the public went along with 'the violent rejection of aristocratic degeneracy'.[7] Throughout the eighteenth century, conduct and courtesy books directed at the middle-class woman, extolling wifely and motherly virtues, flooded the market, both in France and England, and this coincides with the rise of the novel of manners. Neither aristocratic idleness nor manual labour were acceptable for a woman; indeed, education for domesticity became crucial. The aristocratic woman became less desirable as a model: 'She represented surface rather than depth, embodied material as opposed to moral value, and displayed idle sensuality instead of unflagging concern for the well-being of others', as Nancy Armstrong puts it.[8]

It can, of course, be pointed out that although women under the Old Regime were excluded, in the main, from formal political channels – as were most men – nevertheless, in practice they participated in public and political life. Indeed, the first half of the eighteenth century seems to have been a period when women suffered fewer gender restrictions than would be the case for at least a century and a half afterwards. Defoe's heroines are level-headed, intelligent, and capable of participating in business ventures; but Dijkstra suggests that already by 1740, with Samuel Richardson's *Pamela*, this was changing. The wife should be at home, helping her husband by 'the very intensity of her purity and devotion'.[9] Thus it can be seen that the emerging social relations of modernity present a pattern of gender role-specialization that excludes women from what is seen as the central dynamic of the modernizing process itself. As Tester suggests, 'since the private realm was the natural place of women, they were defined through the defining act of men as by themselves incapable of modernity'.[10] Men, on the other hand, come to be seen as having what Poole calls a 'doubly representative' role: in the public sphere, they represent the private, and within the sphere of domesticity they represent 'the public realm of reason, order and duty'.[11]

This does not necessarily imply any straightforwardly positive evaluation of the public realm however; often, indeed, it is the reverse. Herbert is surely right in his comment, on the Brutus painting, that 'The heart of the picture is a family torn asunder in the private misery brought on by the public act',[12] and Bryson elaborates as follows:

> The male world of heroism and political action is not shown as superior to the world of the females and their emotionalism: it is true that while the men do great deeds, the women are at home sewing, that on seeing the body they react but do not and cannot act, that they are cordoned off or coralled inside the house and seem without access to the outside world; all this is obvious, and equally obvious is the sinister quality of Brutus.[13]

It is no accident that Brutus sits in the dark; after all, Plutarch himself, considering the horror of the deed, asked whether Brutus was indeed more brutish than human. . . .

This all seems to make the paradox of Liberty all the more acute. Yet if the women in David's painting represent woman as simultaneously enclosed yet excluded – the 'other inside' – and certainly as occupying a fixed position, the woman in the Delacroix seems to set this position in motion, making it problematical; she seems to represent woman as the transgressive force that both straddles and threatens the boundary in powerful yet ambiguous ways. And this painting draws on a history; for the French Revolution, a landmark in the masculine appropriation of the public sphere, was nonetheless symbolized by a *woman*, Marianne, a woman attacked by her enemies as 'dirty', probably from humble origins, probably a whore – which is how the 'public woman' will be construed in the nineteenth century – and these qualities are still present in her iconic portrayal in Delacroix.[14]

Liberty's nudity crystallizes these issues, and two recent commentators, Marcia Pointon and Marina Warner, elaborate its significance. Warner writes:

> By exposing vulnerable flesh as if it were not so, and especially by uncovering the breast, softest and most womanly part of a woman, as if it were invulnerable,

the semi–clad figure expresses a strength and freedom. . . . It presents itself as a zone of power, through a primary connotation of vitality as the original sustenance of infant life, and . . . through the erotic invitation it extends, only to deny.[15]

And as Pointon adds, 'The central paradox of Liberty as a concept (freedom is good but licence is bad) is represented through the visual paradox of the exposed body in which nakedness symbolises Truth but nudity suggests sexuality'; hence, while nakedness as Truth can inspire, sexuality is inherently dangerous, and it is this that leads to the naming of Liberty as a whore. Also, sexuality involves power; Liberty strides over male corpses, 'sexually dominant in a world of male carnage'.[16] The breasts carry this tension most vividly, increasingly coded in the nineteenth century as a highly charged, erotic, tabooed zone, while also embodying the powerful idea of nation or republic as 'mother', the reproductive, generative force that men can attempt to direct but can never really control, just like nature itself. . . . Thus 'power' is ambiguous here: Liberty as the power to transform positively, a force for progress and liberation, but also as elemental, uncontrollable, dangerous; a force of nature, yet also a force *for* culture, when directed by it. Warner expands on this as follows:

> Cast as a wild thing, who breaks the bonds of normal conventions, Liberty prolongs the ancient associations of women with Otherness, outsiderdom, with carnality, instinct and passion, as against men, endowed with reason, control and spirituality, who govern and order society. But she also subverts the value normally ascribed to these categories and, in so doing, she places women in a different relation to civilization, to its content and happiness as well as its discontents. . . . [She] belongs to that unruly land beyond society's borders, where the wearers of Phrygian caps also dwell; this is also the conventional ascribed site of women, close to the natural processes, those mysteries of death and birth, which refuse to yield up to reason and social control. Yet the figure of Liberty lives up to her name by affirming nature within culture itself, as a necessary and intrinsic part of it.

Thus is otherness feared yet necessary, excluded yet incorporated; and a woman, who might be censured or ridiculed for wearing the cap of Liberty in everyday life, can nevertheless occupy a position of symbolic pre-eminence. So if 'Otherness is a source of potential and power, but it cannot occupy the centre', it is also true that, in this case, it cannot *simply* be excluded, exploited; the question of 'power' in gender relations is not straightforward. Being the sphinx, the carrier of contradictions, is not without its possible strategic benefits.

Warner concludes that 'It is because women continue to occupy the space of the Other that they lend themselves to allegorical use so well.'[17] And indeed, Marianne is still with us, and not necessarily only in France: Pointon reminds us of the reports of a naked woman posing on a taxi with a National Union of Mineworkers banner in the 1984 miners' strike. . . .[18]

Subject, Object and Agency

Throughout the modern period, then, we find 'woman' posing these problems of consistency. Women are pure and impure, capable of self-sacrificial and redemptive love yet also selfishly carnal and sensual; women are virgins and exemplifications of the ideal of motherhood – preferably both at once, an act that is difficult to carry off unless you happen to be the Virgin Mary – but are also witches and whores; provocative sexual agents and 'natural' sexual victims. Simone de Beauvoir puts this well:

> woman is at once Eve and the Virgin Mary. She is an idol, a servant, the source of life, a power of darkness; she is the elemental silence of truth, she is artifice, gossip and falsehood; she is healing presence and sorceress; she is man's prey, his downfall, she is everything that he is not and that he longs for, his negation and his *raison d'être* . . . woman incarnates no stable concept.[19]

In principle, these ambiguities of identity may serve as sources of creativity as well as of danger; boundaries are not necessarily a problem. But what happens with modernity is that a clear boundary *is* constituted, and 'woman' is simultaneously constructed as a boundary being, both a full participant in human society, yet also 'other', not fully 'acculturated'. We thus find the distinction between the 'bad' aspects of femininity, requiring control, and the 'good' aspects, defined as complementary to the attributes of masculinity; and this distinction can be drawn within each woman, or between groups of women. Hence the crisis over the feminine in the gender politics of modernity: on the one hand, woman is closer to nature, potentially dangerous, in need of restraint; on the other hand, woman is a subject, an agent, and this dimension becomes increasingly important as the question of 'rights' and 'responsibilities' gradually forces its way on to the political and legal agenda of modernity. Outram refers to 'a decisive sectioning of the public realm' between 'men who are subjects alone, and women who are both subject and object'.[20] This conjunction of woman-as-object (of control, and desire) and woman-as-subject has implications for the structure of feminine selfhood and for the psychology of men and women themselves; as Janet Sayers points out, 'women's psychology is conditioned by their being treated at one and the same time as both the same as, and different from, men'.[21]

In practice, this can mean that women-as-agents can find that their status as autonomous individuals is compromised, in ways blatant or subtle. The forms this can take are historically quite varied. Thus Belsey points out that for much of the early modern and modern periods, married women were conceived, legally and morally, as simultaneously independent and dependent. They had power over their children, but their husbands had authority over them, so in effect they *controlled* children and yet also *were* children:

> Neither quite recognized as adults, nor quite equated with children, women posed a problem of identity. . . . In other words, the wife is aligned with the children, the

mother with the father. These subject-positions, offered to the same woman, cannot be held simultaneously without contradiction. . . .

Permitted to break their silence in order to acquiesce in the utterances of others, women were denied any single space from which to speak for themselves. . . . To speak from a place of independence, from an autonomous position, to be, in other words, a subject, is to personate masculine virtue.[22]

Again, women as adults would be free to enter into the marriage contract, yet as children, they could not do so, falling 'naturally' under the domination of father or husband, denied rights to control either the choice of partner or their subsequent fate, resulting not only in tensions in gender relations, but in liberal political theory as well.[23] Thus women were at the margins, allotted the place of 'the body outside discourse';[24] yet were also 'uneasily, silently at the heart of the private realm'.[25] Access to public language is access to public power; hence the very core of the gender politics of modernity has revolved around this access to speech, and the grounds on which it can be asserted and denied. From seventeenth-century witches to nineteenth-century hysterics and beyond, this remains a constant theme. Of witches, Christina Larner claims that their 'essential individual personality trait does seem to have been that of a ready, sharp and angry tongue';[26] and Showalter adds that if the hysterical woman is at one end of the spectrum of resistance, feminism is at the other, as 'the alternative to hysterical silence, and the determination to speak and act for women in the public world'.[27]

Ideologically and politically, then, we find that this nexus of assumptions, these tensions in the characterization of 'woman', can facilitate both incorporation and exclusion. If women are culture, they can be attributed responsibility, and blamed if things go wrong, since responsibility is fundamental to the modern notion of the person as subject, as free agent; if they are nature, they can be denied access to important areas, and blamed if they transgress the limits. The point at which this structure of assumptions becomes clearly apparent is the time of the witch-hunts and trials, even though witchcraft beliefs in themselves would conventionally be seen as a last gasp of the pre-modern, rather than an early formative stage of the modern. Modern notions of legal responsibility are emerging clearly in this period, and in ways that link them with attributions of independent agency to women in some areas, though not others. Now, they are seen as increasingly able to enter, freely, into pacts with the devil, hence can be *blamed* for doing so. This is spelt out clearly by Larner, who writes that 'Witchcraft as a choice was only possible for women who had free will and personal responsibility attributed to them', and that 'Without the concept of personal religion and personal responsibility there could be little meaning in the Demonic Pact.' The devil's temptations are all around; but those who succumb are therefore responsible for their fate, and deserve their punishment. Larner points out that this is also the period when another 'woman's crime', infanticide, reaches the statute books; in France, as many women were executed for infanticide as for witchcraft. In short, the extension of legal status to women can be an ambiguous benefit.[28]

However, women's 'closeness to nature' was also part of the witchcraft debate. An opponent of the witch-hunts, Weyer, argued that although women did fall for the devil, this was because of their 'natural weakness', and when they confessed to crimes they had not really committed, this was because their brains were 'addled by melancholy'.[29] Here we see the beginnings of the modern medical discourse on women, the argument that they are 'naturally' prone to illness, an argument that can be used both as an extenuating circumstance, and as an implicit denial of full citizenship, for example in job discrimination. We are not, in short, so far from the PMT debate of recent decades, with the medicalized 'premenstrual syndrome' making an appearance in the law courts. When a medical text from 1970 informs us that 'from 25% to 100% of women' are affected by it, and that 'the few women who do not admit to premenstrual tension are basically unaware of it but one only has to talk to their husbands or co-workers to confirm its existence', the breathtaking vagueness and circularity of the claim is entirely reminiscent of those earlier debates.[30]

But it is the arena of sexuality that furnishes the best examples of the twisted logic of these debates on agency and blame. All too often, it is the actual *victim* of sex crimes who is implicitly or explicitly blamed; what is done *to* her thereby becomes her own fault. She 'led him on', the judge will say, she 'asked for it', she should not have accepted the lift, she was wearing provocative clothes. . . . One of the most recent in a long history of judicial statements in this vein comes from Judge Dean at Cambridge in 1990: 'When women say no they don't always mean no. Men can't turn their emotions on and off like a tap as some women can.' Lucy Bland elaborates the point:

> Informing judicial precedent (case law) and court procedure is a conception not of female sexual passivity or asexuality but female *precipitation* – of inciting the man to commit sexual assault or in some way contributing to its commission. Thus, in effect, women are not only held responsible for their own sexual behaviour . . . they are frequently also held responsible for *male* sexual behaviour, in the sense of encouraging the man to act. . . . In effect, the woman is put on trial and to establish *his* guilt she has to prove *her* innocence.[31]

What seems to happen here is a subtle combination of two strands: it is precisely *because* the woman can be presented as a free, autonomous agent, that she can be blamed for what happens to her, as she precipitated it through her own wilfulness or recklessness; and the man's responsibility for sexual violation is thereby projected on to her. Women *represent* sexual desire; they provoke it, wittingly or unwittingly. And again, this is because they represent *nature*, that threat to masculine rationality and self-control. Seidler writes:

> It has been a male identification with reason that has supposedly allowed an escape from a state of servitude in which reason is enslaved to the passions. . . . It is women . . . who have subsequently been seen as constantly tempting men away from the path of reason and morality. It is as if women are to be blamed for reminding men of their sexuality. But this also becomes part of a history of men forsaking

responsibility for male sexuality since, once aroused, sexuality is supposedly beyond the control of reason. It threatens the very sense of self-control that defines men's rationality.[32]

Adding that 'A woman's body evokes the self-knowledge a man tries to forget', hence producing fear, Susan Griffin traces the wider cultural ramifications of this, in pornography, for example: 'in the pornographic fantasy, whenever the virgin is raped, she is told that she has always wanted to be raped'. By her very beauty, a woman can make a man into a rapist, and 'lead him into the world of flesh and the devil'.[33] And the rape victim becomes a substitute witch; if she does not 'bewitch' the man literally, she certainly does metaphorically. . . .

The 'Dual Vision' and Separate Spheres

By the second half of the nineteenth century, the tensions and possibilities inherent in the modern construction of womanhood had increasingly become concentrated around two poles, a 'dual vision' that laid bare the underlying pattern all the more clearly. This 'dual vision', in its relation to notions of civilization and the idea of separate male and female spheres, the public and the private, is summarized by Sally Shuttleworth in these terms:

> Victorian medical textbooks demonstrated not only woman's biological fitness and adaptation to the sacred role of homemaker, but also her terrifying subjection to the forces of the body. At once angel and demon, woman came to represent both the civilizing power that would cleanse the male from contamination in the brutal world of the economic market and also the rampant, uncontrolled excesses of the material economy.[34]

The crucial notion of the links with nature is further elaborated by Elisabeth Bronfen:

> Using the feminine form as allegory of nature, European culture could express nature as the mother and bride, whose primary life-giving functions were to comfort, nurture and provide. Yet nature also embodied unruly disorder, uncivilised wilderness, famines and tempests. . . . In the equation with nature, earth, body, Woman was construed as Other to culture, as object of intense curiosity to be explored, dissected, conquered, domesticated and, if necessary, eliminated.[35]

Woman represents both an original, paradisical wholeness, and the corruption of the flesh after the Fall, together with the artifice and decoration with which this corruption is masked.

One of the poles of this duality, then, posits woman as disorder, as danger. A woman who escapes the control of (masculine) culture is inherently destructive. And in this period, the danger becomes strongly sexualized; in the course of the century, 'the erotic woman becomes the devouring demon',[36] and Gay adds that 'no century depicted woman as vampire, as castrator, as killer so consistently, so programmatically, and so nakedly as the nineteenth'.[37] Dijkstra argues that by 1900 the prevailing view among scientists, doctors and painters seems to have been that a woman who rejected the domesticity stereotype had inevitably regressed to the bestial, and was represented in the art of the time as a true 'idol of perversity', a 'snake-encircled, medusa-headed flower of evil'.

Not surprisingly, it was the sphinx that became the classic image of this state. After all, the sphinx in the Greek myth had been half-woman, and half-animal (usually a lion); all men who failed to answer her riddle had been killed. The sphinx is depicted in these representations as the devouring mother, outwardly nurturing but with deadly claws. Describing Khnopff's picture *The Supreme Vice*, Dijkstra writes that

> behind every man's vulnerable, statuesque, nude virgin-sister standing haloed on her pedestal there loomed formidably the evil sphinx of holy motherhood turned barren aggressor, her enticing breasts – the enlarged echo of the breasts of the virgin standing before her – guarded by the claws of polyandry and the death's-head of bestial passion.[38]

One variant of this is discussed by Jacqueline Rose in her book on Sylvia Plath. She points to a deep strand in modern cultural theories of feminine creativity, the positing of a vengeful, repressed 'nature goddess', an all-devouring female force, outside law and (male) control, and cites the poets Ted Hughes – 'If you refuse the energy, you are living a kind of death. If you accept the energy, it destroys you' – and Robert Graves, whose 'White Goddess' or 'Muse' is 'the Mother of All Living, the ancient power of fright and lust – the female spider or the queen bee whose embrace is death'.[39] If, through the association with 'culture' and 'progress', more conventional theories of creativity have presented it as a masculine attribute, we see here its repressed other, its association with destructiveness and death. And this influences women writers also: Sandra Gilbert and Susan Gubar argue that the figure of the madwoman in Victorian women's novels is 'usually in some sense the *author's* double, an image of her own anxiety and rage', a representation of her own distorted creativity, her debilitating 'anxiety of authorship'.[40] In our own time, something of this tradition persists in Hollywood films, in the portrayal of the *femme fatale*.[41]

Death itself runs like a *leitmotif* through these cultural constructions; the feminine can be lethal to itself, as well as to the masculine, after all, and this is just as true when the opposite pole of the duality is brought into view. The woman who can control her passions – which really means that she has to allow her husband to control her, as she does not have the strength – attains a state of purity, becomes capable of great love and redemption. Her nature has become angelic, as it were; in that favourite Victorian phrase, she is 'the guardian of the hearth'. But what does this 'purity' *mean* here? Essentially, it is about self-denial. A 'pure' woman cannot attain autonomy, the masculine status of independent selfhood. She is essentially a *giver*; in Balzac's words, 'Woman is man's equal only when she makes her life a perpetual offering.'[42] The only self she can come to have is the self of self-denial, self-sacrifice; and the ultimate self-sacrifice is, after all, that of one's own life. Here we encounter that well-known strand in late nineteenth-century representations that presents women as weak, frail, prone to early death, *because* of this very purity. Physical weakness becomes a signifier of mental or inner purity; there is a sort of spiritual transference from the wife to her husband and children that gradually but remorselessly kills her. In a sense, claims Dijkstra,

> As every properly trained, self-denying woman knew, true sacrifice found its logical apotheosis in death. . . . Death became a woman's ultimate sacrifice of her being to the males she had been born to serve. To withhold from them this last gesture of her exalted servility was, in a sense, an act of insubordination, of 'self-will'.[43]

In this sense, the 'pure' woman always dies a virgin, virginity being an attitude of asexual self-denial, a refusal of pleasure in the act, with sex itself being a form of sacrifice – almost religious – in which the victim 'gives' herself. And such religious terminology could also colour descriptions of the role of motherhood: thus Ida Sée, in 1911, wrote that 'Mothers had to consecrate themselves to this holy office', and that it seemed perfectly 'natural' to Michelet that a mother would give up her life to save her child.[44] Lynda Nead suggests that motherhood was regarded as 'woman's main reason for being and her chief source of pleasure'.[45] We are not so far from the 1950s spectre of Winnicott's 'ordinary devoted mother', able to be preoccupied by her child to the exclusion of any other interest. Elisabeth Badinter points out that this is in marked contrast to the attitude prevailing in most of the eighteenth century, an age of 'maternal indifference', when most infants were farmed out to poor foster parents, and over half died before their second birthday; only gradually do we find medicine constructing the 'maternal instinct' that will later come to have a taken-for-granted status, even in our own time.[46]

If all this giving is a kind of delayed suicide, the most direct form of self-sacrifice would of course be suicide as such; but this act itself is censured, and anyway, to *act* to end one's life is rather too masculine. The way to resolve this is to present the self-sacrifice as occurring through illness, and it is above all TB that is cast as the active agent here; to die of tuberculosis was presented as a suitably passive, painless, gradual way for a virtuous woman to 'slip away'. But the 'fallen' woman would not generally have this chance to redeem herself; for her, the way out was via the suicide that could be presented as least suicidal and least active, death by drowning, a drifting away on the tide, an effortless floating towards eternity. Hence the portrayals of Ophelia in her watery grave, bedecked with flowers, positioned as if on the deathbed of the virtuous woman, and thus attaining a kind of redemption.[47]

The respectable middle-class woman, then, would inevitably be fragile: 'In these delicate vessels is borne through the ages the treasure of human affections', in George Eliot's rapturous tones.[48] One can see how the result could indeed be her 'canonization as a priestess of virtuous inanity'.[49] Nevertheless, given the critique of the aristocratic woman for her life of pointless display, there is a problem here: the middle-class woman has to 'do nothing', in a sense, while nevertheless doing her 'domestic duty'; and she has to do the latter without it being assimilated to 'mere labour', domestic *work*. And of course this *does* involve labour: both real labour, and a labour of concealment. Recent research has made it clear that the number of servants has been exaggerated; inevitably the 'respectable woman' had to do domestic work. 'Her life took shape around the contradictory imperative of laboring while rendering her labor invisible', as Anne McClintock puts it, and 'Her success as a wife depended on her skill in the art of both working and appearing not to work.' And where there were servants, their 'invisibility' helped to confirm the 'invisibility' of domestic labour generally.[50] The tensions are resolved ideologically by presenting the woman of virtue as above all an *exemplary* figure, a guide and model, thereby passive yet meritorious, presiding effortlessly over her household as a paragon of virtue, invisible yet vigilant, indeed active, in the background, visible yet inactive when on public display.

Here it can be seen that the 'pure' woman could actually slide into having an active role, as the carrier of morality, while the man, having to survive in the competitive world outside, may have to act in ways that are far from morally ideal. The private world of love is, in a moral sense, superior, and women could act as 'civilizers' of men. Hence Leonore Davidoff suggests that while the man represents the Head of the household, 'Middle-class women represented the emotions, the Heart, or sometimes the Soul, seat of morality and tenderness.'[51] Sylvana Tomaselli points to a strong Enlightenment tradition in which women are seen both as beneficiaries of the civilizing process – Montesquieu linked political servitude with the domestic servitude of women, for example – and as agents of civilization themselves.[52] As 'motherhood' was increasingly coded as a 'natural' attribute of womanhood, so it was given a fundamentally educational dynamic. For the educational philosopher Froebel, writing in the 1840s, the ideal teacher of the young was essentially 'a mother made conscious', and this conjunction has continued to influence both childcare and teaching.[53]

Hence we see a paradox, a fundamental tension in the gender politics of 'civilization'. While the growth of a rational, civilized society could be seen as involving the imposition of masculine control in the interests of 'progress', with 'woman' constructed as one of the 'others' to whom Enlightenment must be brought, it was also true that men were in need of 'civilizing' themselves; whereas women, through their very *lack* of full autonomy and selfhood, their purity and self-denial, could be exemplars of 'true' civilization, bearers of moral superiority. Jordanova suggests that

> The notion that women are closer to nature than men contained numerous elements, including the claims that women are more emotional, credulous, superstitious and less analytical than men. It could equally effectively express the idea that they were the carriers of a new morality through which the artificiality of civilization could

be transcended. Similarly, taking men as cultural could imply either the progressive light of masculine reason or the corruption and exploitation of civil society.

The favoured way of resolving the tension, or keeping it latent rather than overt, was to invoke the 'separate spheres' argument, so that 'the feminine form of the civilizing process stressed emotional and moral rather than scientific, economic, technological or political progress'.[54] On the different roles of man and woman, the contemporary critic John Ruskin concluded that 'Each has what the other has not: each completes the other, and is completed by the other.'[55]

Ruskin's comment has far-reaching ramifications; in developing this, it can be useful to distinguish two dimensions of the doctrine and practice of 'separate spheres'. First, the 'private' can refer to the construction of 'the personal', coded as the arena of emotional life and intimacy, whereas the 'public' refers to the 'impersonal' façade of social life, the structuring of relationships through 'civility'. And second, the private can refer to a range of activities, those associated with 'the domestic' as it comes to exist in the last couple of centuries or so, while the public refers to 'civil society', the activities of political and economic life. And both sets of distinctions in effect become superimposed, as gender becomes the key signifier of identity and difference in modernity.

The first of these sets of distinctions implies that women are encouraged to specialize in expressiveness and subjectivity, men in instrumentality and abstraction. Thus Giddens is led to claim that 'Women have prepared the way for an expansion in the domain of intimacy in their role as the emotional revolutionaries of modernity.'[56] This notion of intimacy can help to clarify the sense in which women can be said to 'exemplify' morality. Poole develops the point as follows:

> Femininity is constructed, at least in part, through exclusion from the ideals of reason. It is constructed, not through abstraction and separation, but through relationships. To be a woman is to exist within specific relationships to specific others and it involves specific activities with respect to those others. It is to be wife, mother, nurturer, and so on. . . . Morality does not here take the form of an impartial and impersonal consistency but of working through one's specific responsibilities to specific others. . . .
>
>   Here, morality is a form of character. To be moral is to be a certain kind of person, to know how one should act in order to express that identity.

And above all, as has been seen, there is a sense in which it is not action but state, 'being', which is crucial to the purity of women; and when action *is* called for, it should be interpreted as self-denial, expressive of self even in its absence. For a man, on the other hand, action is vital, for it is through action that separation and selfhood are brought about; through action comes the objectification of otherness and the subordination of self to the abstractions of formal and instrumental reason, the impersonal sphere of law and civility. Poole therefore suggests that this abstract masculine subjectivity 'exists only by constituting everything with which it comes into contact as other', and thereby a threat.[57] And it is this abstract subjectivity that is celebrated in the Kantian tradition of moral philosophy wherein moral action becomes universalizable, subject to a law that is willed for all. Seidler suggests that this tradition

> has only served to confirm the greater freedom and autonomy of men. They are thought to be able to act out of a sense of duty, since they are supposedly more able to control the influence of feelings and desires. In this sense men have been taken to be free men, and women only able to achieve their freedom through accepting their subordination to men.[58]

This is a tradition of thought that runs quite deeply in modern Western culture: the idea of masculinity as 'emancipation', transcendence of nature, implying a rigidly bounded sense of identity, and a propensity for dualism. This perspective is summarized by Carol McMillan in these terms:

> Man reaches beyond himself, relates himself to a beyond that results in the splitting of the unity of life into the forms of subject-object, judge/judged, means/end, with which he aims to establish the unity he has lost; woman, on the other hand, is in a pre-dualistic stage.[59]

And again this serves to reinforce the ideological identification of masculinity with progress, change and culture, 'transcending and transforming things through the superimposition of abstract categories and transpersonal values', as Sherry Ortner puts it, whereas women represent immanence and embeddedness in nature and tradition.[60]

For Nancy Chodorow, the result is that masculine identity is precariously based on a denial of relation and connection, and 'it becomes important for masculine identity that certain identities are defined as masculine and superior, and that women are believed unable to do many of the things defined as socially important'; a man's contempt for female activities serves to free him not only from mother but also from 'the femininity within himself'.[61] It can be added that the masculine 'drive to self-sufficiency' and the resulting loss of the otherness within can have serious emotional consequences.[62] Thus the very psychology of masculinity and femininity can be seen to reflect and reproduce the gender relations of modernity.

To return to the second set of distinctions, Weeks brings out one way to show the contrast between the spheres:

> The decency and morality of the home confronted the danger and pollution of the public sphere; the joys and the 'naturalness' of the home countered the 'corruption', the artificiality of the streets. . . . The double standard of morality relied upon this separation between the public and the private. The private was the nest of domestic virtues: the public was the arena of prostitution, of vice on the streets.[63]

The 'double standard' is essentially an institutionalized version of the 'dual vision', in which the 'bad' aspect of womanhood was projected on to the prostitutes, and, to a lesser extent, working-class women generally; while such women were censured for their illicit activities, a veil was drawn over the men who were their clients, so long as they maintained the public façade. And while there has, subsequently, been a greater acceptance of women in the public sphere, together with a decline in the status of the private – which is also, after all, the arena of wife-battering and child abuse – at least as important, in relation to the 'separate spheres', was the rise of the 'housewife'. With the decline of the servant system in the middle- and upper-class households, already apparent before the First World War, and accelerating towards total collapse by the 1920s, the housewife emerges as the symbolic core of the private sphere, reaching her apotheosis in the glorification of the housewife-as-mother-and-consumer in the 1950s.

In her stimulating discussion of housework, Bernice Martin emphasizes the issue of power, suggesting a sense in which the 'purifying rituals' of housework necessarily give women a controlling function, since

> housework as the ritual creation of order also confers a form of domestic power on women which is so 'natural' and habitual that we have largely ceased to recognise its existence. . . .
>
> Women not only create the basic framework of order, but *we police it*. The job of keeping it in repair necessarily involves the exercise of control, particularly over the other members of the family. . . . Housework as magic *is* power. . . . Mother wields power.[64]

Again, we see a suggestion that the 'separate spheres' doctrine cannot *simply* be dismissed as necessarily unequal, exploitative; the question of power in gender relations is always difficult. Certainly, nineteenth-century male ideologists were very concerned that, as Nussbaum suggests, 'the domestic woman gains power to shape the public realm, particularly the nation, through pro-creation and education'.[65] And in recent years, feminist scholars have been concerned to revalue the significance of these gender distinctions and social practices, while not denying their restrictive aspects. Nancy Armstrong goes so far as to claim that we encounter here the emergence of a new form of power:

> This power emerged with the rise of the domestic woman and established its hold over British culture through her dominance over all those objects and practices we associate with private life. To her went authority over the household, leisure time, courtship procedures, and kinship relations, and under her jurisdiction the most basic qualities of human identity were supposed to develop.[66]

Jordanova's conclusion is that women 'may be subordinate in some areas of life, such as legal rights, and superordinate in others, such as control of the household', and '*both* of these could be based on their putatively natural qualities'.[67] It is now necessary to examine these 'natural qualities' in greater depth.

Plate 1. Pieter Bruegel: *The Battle of Carnival and Lent*, 1559. Kunsthistorisches Museum, Vienna.

Plate 2. Francisco de Goya: *The Burial of the Sardine*, 1815. Museo del Prado, Madrid.

Plate 3. Georges Rochegrosse: *Death of Babylon*, 1891. From Antonin Proust, *Le Salon de 1891* (Paris, 1891).

Plate 4. Théodore Géricault: *The Madwoman (Monomania of Envy)*, 1822–3. Musée des Beaux Arts, Lyon.

Plate 5. Jacques-Louis David: *Brutus Receiving the Bodies of his Sons*, 1789. Musée du Louvre, Paris.

Plate 6. Eugène Delacroix: *Liberty Leading the People*, 1830. Musée du Louvre, Paris.

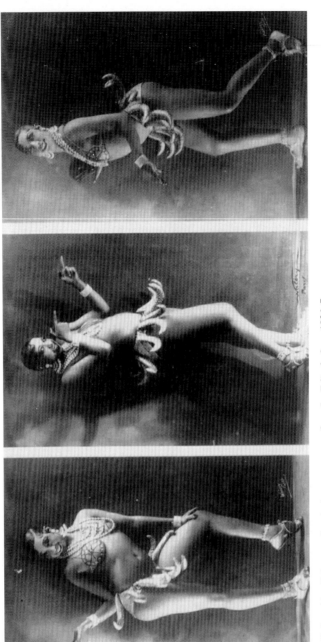

Plate 7. Josephine Baker wearing the banana costume from *La Folie du Jour*, 1926–7.

Culture, Biology, and Two Sexes

The idea that the two sexes, and sex itself, might be said to be in some sense historical products is implicit, and frequently explicit, in recent scholarship, suggesting as it does that the rigid sexual identities we cultivate, and which are popularly assumed to be 'natural' and given at birth, are really fictions elaborated in the last few centuries.[68] The recent work of Laqueur is useful for exploring this. He suggests that it is only relatively recently that sex as a taken-for-granted, biological attribute, the foundation for gender identity, has existed:

> The dominant, though by no means universal, view since the eighteenth century has been that there are two stable, incommensurable, opposite sexes and that the political, economic, and cultural lives of men and women, their gender roles, are somehow based on these 'facts'. Biology – the stable, ahistorical, sexed body – is understood to be the epistemic foundation for prescriptive claims about the social order.

Before that, to be a man or woman was essentially a gender identity based on social rank; it was not a matter of two totally distinct and biologically separate sexes. In a sense, the sexed body was secondary, while this gender/rank fusion was what really counted.[69] This seems to fit with Lynne Friedli's suggestion that '"woman" is invented as a social category from around the end of the seventeenth century',[70] out of this gradually emerging sense of a biology/gender relation.

And the body? In this older view, 'there was but one sex whose more perfect exemplars were easily deemed males at birth and whose decidedly less perfect ones were labelled female'. On this essentially Galenic 'one-sex' model, sexuality was a continuum, with no sharp line between male and female. Men who associated too closely with women could lose their 'hardness' and become effeminate; and rapid physical movement could produce a sudden sex change. Paré and Montaigne both give an account of a girl who jumped across a ditch while chasing pigs and who developed a penis. This would not have been so difficult; on the Galenic model, it is only 'heat' that causes the vagina to 'pop out' into the penis anyway; one is simply the reversal of the other. A woman was simply a man inside out, so to speak. The vagina, as an inverted penis, did not even have a distinctive medical name until the early eighteenth century, and 'ovaries', similarly, were referred to by the term also used for 'testicles', again as though simply a version of the latter. Uterus and scrotum were also equivalent. Even when Renaldus Columbus discovered the clitoris in 1559, this was not seen as shattering the symmetry of the penis/vagina equation – no New World was opened up here – indeed Columbus claimed that semen flowed from it, thereby assimilating it to the tip of the penis. This model remained influential throughout the early modern period, and when it came under increased attack, it was as much because it was seen as an aspect of the 'grotesque body' as for intellectual reasons; it was socially subversive as much as scientifically questionable.[71]

And sexuality, as sexual behaviour? Laqueur claims that 'The commonplace of much contemporary psychology – that men want sex while women want relationships – is the precise inversion of pre-Enlightenment notions' that equated 'friendship with men and fleshliness with women'.[72] On this earlier view, orgasm was thought necessary for women to conceive – again the symmetry with men – and the 'lustfulness' of women was cited frequently by sixteenth- and seventeenth-century authors. The Restoration dramatist Aphra Behn noted that a young wife often exhausted her husband sexually, as was evident in the 'paleness of his face, the lankness of his cheeks, the thinness of his calves'.[73] By the early nineteenth century, all this has changed, and women are being comprehensively desexualized; 'woman's sexual pleasure is newly imagined as unnecessary to reproduction, orgasm unnecessary to conception, and sexuality separated from motherhood', as Nussbaum puts it, and hence 'Women become the object of impregnation rather than participants in reproduction.'[74] Here the stereotype of female 'passionlessness' emerges;[75] and increasingly the clitoris becomes a problematical site, cause of nymphomania, hysteria and marital distress. Biological difference is constructed as foundation for social difference, and its influence is seen everywhere; and this new model develops *before* the occurrence of the scientific discoveries that will in due course be used to legitimize it. (For example, not until 1928 was the relation between hormones, ovulation and the menstrual cycle incorporated into scientific discourse.[76])

By the middle years of the last century, then, it was taken for granted that the otherness of woman was 'natural', biological, and that there was a sense in which woman was *closer* to nature; woman's embeddedness in 'natural cycles' reveals her 'essence'. And this can pose a threat; as Cathérine Clément suggests, women can be seen as

> allied with what is regular, according to the rules, since they are wives and mothers, and allied as well with those natural disturbances, their regular periods, which are the epitome of paradox, order and disorder. It is precisely in this natural periodicity that fear, terror, that which is offside in the symbolic system, will lodge itself.[77]

A woman's reproductive function defined her character, position and value, and her biological periodicity was linked with her propensity for 'nervous disorders'; hence, in Mary Poovey's words, woman was constructed as 'a creature who needed constant and expert superintendence by medical men'.[78] Indeed, this medical control has already been firmly established in the arena of childbirth; since the seventeenth century, the traditionally female midwife had been increasingly driven out. Carolyn Merchant argues that for these medical men, 'The midwife symbolized female incompetence in her own natural sphere, reproduction, correctable through a technology invented and controlled by men – the forceps.'[79] In a sense, childbirth could be presented as not 'natural' at all; since so much could go wrong, it always bordered on the pathological, hence had to be fully appropriated by culture, under male control. The word 'natural', with its inherent fluidity, could thus be a potent resource for ideological shifts and medical manipulation. In effect, it was male biology that was implicitly defined as the standard: 'while appointing the male reproductive system as normal, this viewpoint calls abnormal any aspect of the female reproductive life cycle that deviates from the male's'. The influential physician Rudolf Virchow captured all this in a vivid, crude formulation: 'Woman is a pair of ovaries with a human being attached, whereas man is a human being furnished with a pair of testes.'[80] And the result in practice was widespread medical and surgical intervention, including ovariotomies and clitoridectomies, advocated for a range of conditions (from 'troublesomeness' to 'erotic tendencies'),[81] together with a strong rationale for the restriction of women to the domestic sphere. Even higher education could be dangerous, putting a strain on the reproductive system.[82]

Notions of control and self-control are basic here. A man needs only his own resources for self-control, though this is not to say that it is necessarily easy. In this light, masturbation appears as the symbolically appropriate male pathology, an illicit male 'spending', simultaneously sexual and economic, an offence against 'the autonomous accumulation of male energies'.[83] And menstruation, defined in a 1910 medical text as 'belonging to the borderland of pathology',[84] appears as the crucial symptom of female biology, inherently dangerous to men and women alike, unhygienic, polluting. . . . However, Sally Shuttleworth, in her interesting account, stresses that while a woman, 'rendered helpless by the tyranny of her body', must resort to medical help and supervision, it was 'not the menstrual flow *per se* that caused alarm, rather its suppression and retention'. The contrast with men is clear: 'While male health was believed to be based on self-control, woman's health depended on her very *inability* to control her body.' Hence

> female identity was defined by the condition of *excess*, an excess that had to be sluiced away through her 'dark drains' if it was not to flow back and pollute the entire system. . . .
>
> menstruation became an obsessive focus for the male imagination, symbolizing, with its bloody, uncontrollable flow, the dark otherness of womanhood, the suppressed terms behind the ideological projections of female purity and spirituality. . . .
>
> Womanhood itself is thus figured as a form of pathology: only when polluted and out of control (and thus not 'feminine') could females be socially accredited with the title of true woman.[85]

Woman thus epitomizes both the transcendence of physicality, through purity, and the continuing, latent presence of the 'grotesque body' under the civilized veneer. Indeed, women had a general problem with boundaries, of body and behaviour; they were 'given to constitutionally structured fits of weeping, fainting and uncontrollable laughter',[86] due to 'the mobility of their fibres, especially those in their uterus'. Hysteria was never far away. Woman as 'naturally' docile, under (male) cultural control, can represent benevolent nature, nature in harmony with culture; woman as unruly becomes wild, untamed, dangerous nature. And just as nature is predictable and controllable when the laws governing it are understood, so also with woman.[87]

Darwin's own work represents the culmination of these developments. In *The Descent of Man*, he argued that natural selection had led men to possess a 'higher eminence' in any activity requiring 'deep thought, reason, or imagination', and 'Thus man has ultimately become superior to woman', although apparently woman manifests 'greater tenderness and less selfishness', again illustrating the moral ambiguities of 'superiority'.[88]

In the end, then, we can see the clear emergence and consolidation of the modern structure of gender relations. The production of modern biological notions of 'nature' was simultaneously the production of two sexes, and of gender identities as based on these. It is clear that this emerged precariously and laboriously. Indeed, while female sexuality was taken for granted in the early modern period, it has had to be 'rediscovered' – in ways that amount to a reinvention – during this century, with the collapse of the 'asexuality' model and the development of psychoanalysis. Eve Kosofsky Sedgwick therefore writes that

> What *was* new from the turn of the century was the world-mapping by which every given person, just as he or she was necessarily assignable to a male or a female gender, was now considered necessarily assignable as well to a homo- or a hetero-sexuality, a binarized identity that was full of implications, however confusing, for even the ostensibly least sexual aspects of personal existence.[89]

What can be seen is that the project of modernity has involved an attempt to construct and enforce a *consistency* between the three spheres of sex, gender and sexuality, with 'sex' seen as biological difference, 'gender' as social role, and 'sexuality' as sexual desire. Thus men are biologically male, play a masculine role, and are heterosexual in orientation, and these dimensions are not only consistent and mutually reinforcing, but are based on the underlying cultural construction of the 'two sexes' as biologically distinct. But whereas men are 'naturally' equipped to transcend the limitations of nature – that, in modernity is what culture *means* – the identity of woman has been fixed through the language of nature itself, a language that does not permit the autonomous, independent selfhood of the masculine subject. Hence woman's 'closeness' to nature is rationalized through science, and women are precluded from full participation in modernity as project, and there is a resulting tension between woman as subject, responsible agent, and woman as object, of masculine control.

Anyway, the underlying nexus has always proved controversial and unstable. Once it becomes possible, in the modern period, to make distinctions between sex, gender and sexuality, it becomes clear that they have a fluidity that resists assimilation to the biological 'two-sexes' model. It is as though they *have* to be assimilated at the very point when their *non-identity* becomes manifest. The self attempts to preside over and enforce this identity, in the public world of bodies and roles, to perpetuate this illusion of continuity or identity between sex, gender and desire, the desperate attempt to maintain a 'phantasized biology of the "real"'.[90] Yet the very interiority of the self, this zone of fantasy, also guarantees the impossibility of success. The attempt to exclude certain identities, summarized by Judith Butler as 'those in which gender does not follow from sex and those in which the practices of desire do not "follow" from either sex or gender', has served, in the end, only to encourage them.[91]

Overall, then, it is as though modernity has offered women a deal: you can have an identity that purports to respect your biological difference through 'protecting' you in the domestic sphere and thereby giving you high status, as complementary and, in that sense, equal, although the restrictions may cause you stress, even illness; or you can insist on full autonomy and independence, in which case you are liable to be repressed as deviant, again driven into illness, or denounced as 'unnatural'. It is hardly surprising that so many have rejected the deal, preferring to take up the 'equal rights' agenda that is present as the other strand in modern gender politics and culture, as suggested earlier, and which must, in turn, result ultimately in a questioning of these gender distinctions themselves: if it is essentially our qualities as individuals that are to determine our activities and opportunities, what place can there be for 'gender' anyway?

Secret, Enigma and Paradox

The idea that 'woman' somehow embodies a powerful secret – that woman both *is* mystery, and yet is also the *key* to mystery – runs as an insistent theme through the modern period, as does the idea that to attempt to 'penetrate' the secret is just as likely to produce enigmas and paradoxes as to resolve them. In the context of conventional Hollywood cinema, Neale argues that 'women are a problem, a source of anxiety, of obsessive enquiry; men are not'. While masculinity is implicit, taken for granted, 'Femininity is, by contrast, a mystery.'[92] An important aspect of this is suggested by Evelyn Fox Keller:

> Secrets function to articulate a boundary: an interior not visible to outsiders, the demarcation of a separate domain, a sphere of autonomous power. And if we ask whose secret life has historically been, and from whom it has been secret, the answer is clear: Life has traditionally been seen as the secret *of* women, a secret *from* men. By virtue of their ability to bear children, it is women who have been perceived as holding the secret of life.[93]

Thus the 'male gaze' is drawn to watch, analyse, examine; but there is always the hint of danger beneath the self-awarded power to control and probe the objectified femininity. The bravado is certainly apparent. With the invention of the speculum in the mid-nineteenth century, doctors could begin to examine the interior of the female reproductive system, and Shuttleworth captures the exultant tone: 'Technology here offers the fulfilment of the male erotic dream: the male gaze could follow the fingers and penetrate into the most hidden recesses of the female anatomy.'[94] Experimenting with a speculum in 1845, the gynaecologist Sims experienced himself as 'a colonizing and conquering hero', and 'an explorer in medicine who first views a new and important territory'. But the apprehensiveness and doubt is also revealed, the sense in which knowledge of the other is inseparable from knowledge of self, and may well engage with forbidden and disturbing aspects of the latter; doctors opening up a female corpse are thus 'maintaining the illusion of their own invulnerability and destroying the terrifying female reminder of their impotence and uncertainty'.[95] Giddens adds that:

> The enquiries which men carried on into the nature of women were not just an expression of traditional sexual otherness; they were investigations into un-acknowledged arenas of self-identity and intimacy, as reordered areas of social life to which men had little entry.[96]

The 'secret of woman' – that is, both the solution to the mystery of woman and to the mystery of the otherness that woman serves to symbolize – is thus a source of both desire and fear: 'Unveiling women is not just a prelude to possession but an encounter with risk and danger and also with excitement and pleasure.'[97]

What, then, is the truth *of* woman and the truth that is sought *in* woman? It is already clear that in practice the 'meaning of otherness' is a sterile, imposed truth, reflecting the categories of the investigator, the assumptions of the gaze. Success here is also failure, and such success as is achieved is never enough; one is reminded of Freud's increasingly hysterical attempts to solve the puzzle of Dora's hysteria, and of the greater failure that already threatened: that neither hysteria nor anything else would in the end solve the enigma of the 'dark continent' of the feminine. The hysteric always has the last laugh; in this sense, whatever her plight, she also embodies a power of resistance: in Heath's words, 'she's having problems with the identity, with the knowledge and its system held out to her, choking on that, entering a protest, but unheard'.[98] Is it that, Alice Jardine suggests, 'the true' is 'that which can never be seen, which never presents itself as such but rather captures, points, withdraws, hides itself in its veils: and that *true* is seen as being "woman"'? But she adds that, for others, '"woman" is precisely that element which disturbs even that presupposition'.[99]

Two possibilities are implied here: that woman is an allegory of a truth that men cannot attain, or that woman mocks truth, represents the indefinable, promises a truth that is not there, constantly shifts, represents a difference that denies identity. On one model, woman hides the truth; on the other, she hides the truth that there is no truth there, that there is nothing to hide. She is both 'the enigma and its impossibility'.[100] Either way, she captivates: the secret of the other that awaits unlocking.

Truth as unsolvable temptation, woman as riddle: what is the deeper source of these paradoxes, these oscillations, this 'problem of woman'? One perspective on this is offered by Christina Crosby's claim that, in the nineteenth century,

> history is produced as man's truth, the truth of a necessarily historical Humanity, which in turn requires that 'women' be outside history, above, below, or beyond properly historical and political life. Constructing history as the necessary con-

dition of human life . . . ensures that 'man' can emerge as an abstraction, can know himself in history, find his origin there and project his end – but only if there is something other than history, something intrinsically unhistorical. 'Women' are the unhistorical other of history.

'Women' are here identified as the intimate core of social life, representing unchanging repetition, cyclical nature; that which man must transcend in order to progress, but which he must therefore understand, interrogate. Hence we see the 'ceaseless asking of the woman question', which is 'the price of discovering the truth of man in the far reaches of history'.[101] Woman becomes the necessary presupposition, the grounding, 'the exteriorised factor which grounds the system'.[102]

If masculinity has been the defining principle of identity – the master signifier of identity – the corollary is its taken for granted status, its indefinability. It is the 'I is I', the tautology at the heart of modernity. If masculinity is indefinable but defining, then femininity becomes the endlessly defined, the play on definition, that which constantly escapes definition even as it is defined. Woman as other represents the inevitable slide of otherness into difference, the way otherness can never be pinned down save in positive terms that thereby escape the negation implicit in 'otherness' itself, leading to a frantic plethora of alternatives around the two poles of excess and lack, oscillating between them, the hysteria at the heart of the system. This dialectic, in its Freudian version, is articulated clearly by Heath:

> What works is identity, genital organization, the phallus, *that* difference . . . with the woman as other to the man, *his* difference, less and more, falling short and beyond; she lacks the phallus, is less, but since she is therefore different, she is also more, excessive, beyond him, an enigma.[103]

This is revealed not only in the dichotomies already discussed, and their empirical manifestations, but in some of the most commonplace clichés of sexist language: that woman is inconstant, fickle, you 'never know where you are with her', she 'doesn't know her own mind', she talks a lot but it makes little sense. . . . Luce Irigaray pinpoints this in her suggestion that

> 'She' is indefinitely other in herself. That is undoubtedly the reason she is called temperamental, incomprehensible, perturbed, capricious – not to mention her language in which 'she' goes off in all directions and in which 'he' is unable to discern the coherence of any meaning.[104]

Bringing these points together, Bronfen suggests that since 'self' is itself coded as masculine, this has sweeping implications for characterizing the feminine:

> As Other, Woman serves to define the self, and the lack or excess that is located in the Other functions as an exteriorisation of the self, in respect to both gender and death. Woman comes to represent the margins or extremes of the norm. . . .

> Woman . . . is constructed as the place of mystery, of not knowing. . . . She is desirable because distant, absent or not quite there, a dream, a phantom, a mediatrix, a muse . . . a limit and excess.[105]

A link is suggested here between femininity and the other great enigma of modern discourse, death, the inexplicable and meaningless incursion that offers the key to life, a key that must be found, but, in a post-religious age, never can be. Showalter also makes the link: 'The veiled woman who is dangerous to look upon also signifies the quest for the mystery of origins, the truths of birth and death.'[106] If woman possesses the secret to life, she can only do so through having the key to death; and in reverse, death becomes a key to woman, her most intimate destiny, the fate of purity in self-sacrifice. Death and femininity are yoked together, representing the inscrutable and inexpressible; enigmas to be solved, yet enigmas that cannot, *must* not, be solved, 'must be left open, undecided, indeterminate, marking the limit a system sets itself'.[107]

Femininity as representation: if masculinity is the power to define, femininity becomes the representation of the defining power that can never know or possess itself as such, can never be self-identical. Thus Teresa de Lauretis can write that 'Woman, the other-than-man' is the term that simultaneously designates 'the vanishing point of our culture's fictions of itself and the condition of the discourses in which the fictions are represented'. Woman is hence the foundation of representation yet is 'nowhere': Western representations tell 'the story of male desire by performing the absence of woman and by producing woman as text, as pure representation'.[108]

Masculinity is thus the key term, the baseline against which 'femininity' is measured. Masculine identity is above all about masculine *identity*: it is a matter of boundaries, separation, the coherence of identity.[109] Feminine identity, on the other hand, is primarily 'difference', the exploration of relation, the dissolution of boundaries, the non–identity of identity, the gradations of 'otherness'. Identity becomes one possible mode of existence of difference; from being master signifier of identity, masculinity in the end risks becoming exposed either as merely one variant in a set of possibilities, or as the destructive and authoritarian myth of bounded self-sufficiency and self-identity: either hysteria or paranoia. And femininity emerges as the reflexive, questioning, unstable mode of identity, always other in itself.

Seeing woman as 'difference' has shown how 'woman' has come to designate what has eluded and challenged orthodox (masculine) discourses, yet such a placing designates elements not *inherently* linked – 'woman as nature', for example – but only linked relative to the discourse that puts 'masculinity' in the place of 'self'. Examining this, in the case of Western 'grand narratives', Alice Jardine suggests that we find that what has both eluded and engulfed them, this 'other-than-themselves', is 'almost always a "space" of some kind (over which the narrative has lost control), and this space has been coded as *feminine*, as woman'.[110] The feminine has come to stand in for 'otherness' itself, and otherness in its multiplicity has invaded the content of the feminine, leaving it crucially unstable, a resource for cultural paradox and manipulation. If 'man' is a master signifier for identity, then 'woman' is a master (!) signifier for otherness, and can in turn be represented *by* 'otherness' in many forms; it can as easily be these 'other' forms that represent the unrepresentable, mysterious 'woman' as vice versa.

In modernity, woman can represent lack not because *she* lacks something – she doesn't – or because she lacks *something* – the penis? – but because she signifies difference, non-identity with the marked term. She can therefore represent the man's lack, his desire, the other that is constitutive, through exclusion, of masculine identity. Femininity, suggests Shoshana Felman, should be conceived as 'masculinity's uncanny difference from itself. It inhabits masculinity as Otherness, as its own disruption.'[111] And again we encounter the mystery of power. Judith Butler suggests, following Lacan, that 'power is wielded by this feminine position of not-having', since masculinity can necessarily only exist when confirmed as such: a man's

> seemingly self-grounded autonomy attempts to conceal the repression which is both its ground and the perpetual possibility of its own ungrounding. But that process of meaning-constitution requires that women reflect that masculine power and everywhere reassure that power of the reality of its illusory autonomy.[112]

Men have power because their autonomy enables them to control women; yet this autonomy rests on recognition and 'reassurance' from women, and disappears without it, as though power depends on the other it is exercised over. Women have power, but only the power to reassure or withhold reassurance, a power that limits, even denies itself in its very manifestation. It is this very ambivalence of power that generates the potential for women's oppression, which is rendered possible by the paranoia inherent in the very assertion of this 'illusory autonomy'.

In the Greek myth, many men fail to solve the riddle of the sphinx, and pay with their lives. Oedipus solves the riddle; the sphinx kills herself; and Oedipus goes to meet his destiny: the knowledge of his own criminality, the gouging out of his own eyes, the living death of wandering exile. The riddle has to be attempted; but success and failure seem to amount to the same thing. If woman is constructed as modernity's sphinx, posing the riddles of life and death, immanence and transcendence, nature and culture, self and other, it is not clear that the outcome could be any different.

Notes

1 A. Brookner, *Jacques-Louis David* (Chatto and Windus, 1990), p. 92.
2 D. Outram, *The Body and the French Revolution* (Yale University Press, 1989), p. 87. See also J. Landes, *Women and the Public Sphere in the Age of the French Revolution* (Cornell University Press, 1988).
3 A. Vincent-Buffault, *The History of Tears* (Macmillan, 1991), p. 246.
4 Outram, *Body*, p. 84.

5   E. Fox-Genovese, Introduction to S. Spencer (ed.) *French Women and the Age of Enlightenment* (Indiana University Press, 1984).

6   N. Bryson, *Tradition and Desire: From David to Delacroix* (Cambridge University Press, 1984), p. 74.

7   L. Hunt, 'The Many Bodies of Marie Antoinette', in her *Eroticism and the Body Politic* (Johns Hopkins University Press, 1991).

8   N. Armstrong, 'Some Call It Fiction: On the Politics of Domesticity', in J. F. MacCannell (ed.) *The Other Perspective in Gender and Culture* (Columbia University Press, 1990), p. 73. See also her *Desire and Domestic Fiction* (Oxford University Press, 1987), ch. 2.

9   B. Dijkstra, *Idols of Perversity: Fantasies of Feminine Evil in Fin-de-Siècle Culture* (Oxford University Press, 1987), p. 8.

10 K. Tester, *Civil Society* (Routledge, 1992), p. 135.

11 R. Poole, 'Modernity, Rationality and "the Masculine"', in T. Threadgold and A. Cranny-Francis (eds.) *Feminine, Masculine and Representation* (Allen and Unwin, 1990), p. 55.

12 R. L. Herbert, *David, Voltaire, Brutus and the French Revolution* (Allen Lane, 1972), p. 43.

13 N. Bryson, *Word and Image: French Painting of the Ancien Regime* (Cambridge University Press, 1981), p. 234.

14 See M. Agulhon, *Marianne into Battle* (Cambridge University Press); and M. Iversen, 'Imagining the Republic', in P. Hulme and L. Jordanova (eds.) *The Enlightenment and Its Shadows* (Routledge, 1990).

15 M. Warner, *Monuments and Maidens* (Weidenfeld and Nicolson, 1985), pp. 277–8.

16 M. Pointon, *Naked Authority: The Body in Western Painting 1830–1908* (Cambridge University Press, 1990), pp. 72, 74, 81 (original emphasis).

17 Warner, *Monuments*, pp. 292–3, 293, 292.

18 *Guardian* (16 April 1984).

19 S. de Beauvoir, *The Second Sex* (Cape, 1972), p. 163.

20 Outram, *Body*, p. 85.

21 J. Sayers, *Sexual Contradictions* (Tavistock, 1986), p. x.

22 C. Belsey, *The Subject of Tragedy: Identity and Difference in Renaissance Drama* (Methuen, 1985), pp. 153, 155, 149, 181. See also E. Goffman, *Gender Advertisements* (Macmillan, 1979), arguing that this assimilation of male/female to parent/child runs on into the present.

23 C. Pateman, *The Sexual Contract* (Polity, 1988), especially pp. 51–5.

24 F. Barker, *The Tremulous Private Body: Essays on Subjection* (Methuen, 1984), p. 100.

25 Belsey, *Subject*, p. 150.

26 C. Larner, *Enemies of God* (Blackwell, 1983), p. 97.

27 E. Showalter, *The Female Malady* (Virago, 1987), p. 161.

28 Larner, *Enemies*, pp. 101, 193, and ch. 8. See also C. Merchant, *The Death of Nature* (Wildwood House, 1982), ch. 5.

29 Merchant, *Death of Nature*, p. 141.

30 Cited in S. Laws, 'The Sexual Politics of Pre-menstrual Tension', *Women's Studies International Forum* (1983), 6:1, p. 19.

31 L. Bland, 'The Domain of the Sexual: A Response', *Screen Education* (1981), 39, pp. 64–5.

32 V. Seidler, 'Reason, Desire and Male Sexuality', in P. Caplan (ed.) *The Cultural Construction of Sexuality* (Tavistock, 1987), p. 87.

33 S. Griffin, *Pornography and Silence* (Women's Press, 1981), pp. 19, 23, 30.
34 S. Shuttleworth, 'Female Circulation: Medical Discourse and Popular Advertising in the Mid-Victorian Era', in M. Jacobus (ed.) *Body/Politics* (Routledge, 1990), p. 55.
35 E. Bronfen, *Over Her Dead Body: Death, Femininity and the Aesthetic* (Manchester University Press, 1992), p. 66.
36 K. Theweleit, *Male Fantasies*, Vol. I, *Women, Floods, Bodies, History* (Minnesota University Press, 1987), p. 360.
37 P. Gay, *The Bourgeois Experience*, Vol. I, *Education of the Senses* (Oxford University Press, 1984), p. 207. And, in the context of contemporary film, see B. Creed, *The Monstrous-Feminine* (Routledge, 1993).
38 Dijkstra, *Idols*, pp. 325, 331.
39 J. Rose, *The Haunting of Sylvia Plath* (Virago, 1991), p. 151.
40 S. Gilbert and S. Gubar, *The Madwoman in the Attic* (Yale University Press, 1979), pp. 78, 59.
41 See L. Hart, *Fatal Women* (Routledge, 1994), and Creed, *Monstrous-Feminine*.
42 Cited in de Beauvoir, *Second Sex*, p. 632.
43 Dijkstra, *Idols*, pp. 28, 29 (original emphasis).
44 E. Badinter, *The Myth of Motherhood* (Souvenir Press, 1981), p. 235.
45 L. Nead, *Myths of Sexuality: Representations of Women in Victorian Britain* (Blackwell, 1988), p. 26.
46 Badinter, *Myth*, pp. 273, xix.
47 See Dijkstra, *Idols*, ch. 2; Showalter, *Female Malady*, pp. 10–11.
48 G. Eliot, *Daniel Deronda* (Penguin, 1967), p. 160.
49 Dijkstra, *Idols*, p. 4.
50 A. McClintock, *Imperial Leather: Race, Gender and Sexuality in the Colonial Contest* (Routledge, 1995), p. 162, also pp. 160–5 and ch. 3. See also L. Davidoff and C. Hall, *Family Fortunes: Men and Women of the English Middle Class, 1780–1850* (Hutchinson, 1987) and N. Armstrong, 'The Rise of the Domestic Woman', in N. Armstrong and L. Tennenhouse (eds.) *The Ideology of Conduct* (Methuen, 1987).
51 L. Davidoff, 'Class and Gender in Victorian England', in J. Newton et al., *Sex and Class in Women's History* (Routledge, 1983), p. 19.
52 S. Tomaselli, 'The Enlightenment Debate on Women', *History Workshop Journal* (1985), 20, p. 113.
53 Cited in C. Steedman, '"The Mother Made Conscious": The Historical Development of a Primary School Pedagogy', *History Workshop Journal* (1985), 20, p. 149.
54 L. Jordanova, *Sexual Visions: Images of Gender in Science and Medicine* (Harvester Wheatsheaf, 1989), pp. 21, 37.
55 In 1865; cited in Nead, *Myths*, p. 34.
56 A. Giddens, *The Transformation of Intimacy* (Polity, 1992), p. 130.
57 Poole, 'Modernity', pp. 54, 55, 55. See also G. Lloyd, *The Man of Reason* (Minnesota University Press, 1984), on the philosophical background; and my *Exploring the Modern: Patterns of Western Culture and Civilization* (Blackwell, 1998), ch. 6, on the novel and the relational model of morality.
58 Seidler, 'Reason', p. 86.
59 C. McMillan, *Woman, Reason and Nature* (Blackwell, 1982), p. 3.
60 S. Ortner, 'Is Female to Male as Nature is to Culture?', in M. Evans (ed.) *The Woman Question* (Fontana, 1982), p. 501.
61 N. Chodorow, *The Reproduction of Mothering* (California University Press, 1978),

p. 181.

62   Giddens, *Transformation*, p. 116.

63   J. Weeks, *Sex, Politics and Society* (Longman, 1981), p. 81.

64   B. Martin, '"Mother Wouldn't Like It!": Housework as Magic', *Theory, Culture and Society* (1984), 2:2, pp. 20–1, 24.

65   F. Nussbaum, '"Savage" Mothers: Narratives of Maternity in the Mid-eighteenth Century', *Cultural Critique* (1991–2), 20, p. 126.

66   Armstrong, *Desire*, p. 3.

67   Jordanova, *Sexual Visions*, p. 41.

68   See, for example, J. Weeks, *Sexuality and Its Discontents* (Routledge, 1985).

69   T. Laqueur, *Making Sex* (Harvard University Press, 1990), pp. 6, 8. See also L. Schiebinger, *The Mind Has No Sex?* (Harvard University Press, 1989), chs. 6–8.

70   L. Friedli, '"Passing Women": A Study of Gender Boundaries in the Eighteenth Century', in G. S. Rousseau and R. Porter (eds.) *Sexual Underworlds of the Enlightenment* (Manchester University Press, 1987), p. 250.

71   Laqueur, *Making Sex*, pp. 124, 127, and passim.

72   Ibid., pp. 3–4.

73   B. Easlea, *Science and Sexual Oppression* (Weidenfeld and Nicolson, 1981), p. 78.

74   Nussbaum, '"Savage" Mothers', pp. 127, 128.

75   N. Cott, 'Passionlessness', *Signs* (1978), 4:2.

76   Weeks, *Sex, Politics*, p. 43.

77   C. Clément, 'The Guilty One', in H. Cixous and C. Clément, *The Newly Born Woman* (Manchester University Press, 1987), p. 8.

78   M. Poovey, *Uneven Developments: The Ideological Work of Gender in Mid-Victorian England* (Chicago University Press, 1988), p. 37.

79   Merchant, *Death of Nature*, pp. 155, and ch. 6.

80   A. Fausto-Sterling, *Myths of Gender* (Basic Books, 1985), pp. 121, 90.

81   G. Barker-Benfield, 'The Spermatic Economy: A Nineteenth-Century View of Sexuality', in M. Gordon (ed.) *The American Family in Social-Historical Perspective* (St Martin's Press, 1978), p. 388.

82   J. Sayers, *Biological Politics* (Tavistock, 1982), ch. 2.

83   Barker-Benfield, 'Spermatic Economy', p. 377.

84   Weeks, *Sex, Politics*, p. 43.

85   Shuttleworth, 'Female Circulation', pp. 51, 56, 57, 57, 59, 62.

86   B. Turner, *Medical Power and Social Knowledge* (Sage, 1987), p. 89.

87   Jordanova, *Sexual Visions*, pp. 28, 42.

88   C. Darwin, *The Descent of Man* (Murray, 1874), pp. 564, 565, 563.

89   E. K. Sedgwick, *The Epistemology of the Closet* (California University Press, 1990), p. 2.

90   A. R. Jones and P. Stallybrass, 'Fetishizing Gender: Constructing the Hermaphrodite in Renaissance Europe', in J. Epstein and K. Straub (eds.) *Body Guards* (Routledge, 1991), p. 106.

91   J. Butler, *Gender Trouble: Feminism and the Subversion of Identity* (Routledge, 1990), p. 17. See also ch. 7 of this volume, and my *Exploring the Modern*, ch. 5.

92   S. Neale, 'Masculinity as Spectacle', in S. Cohen and I. R. Hark (eds.) *Screening the Male* (Routledge, 1993), p. 19.

93   E. F. Keller, 'From Secrets of Life to Secrets of Death', in M. Jacobus (ed.) *Body/Politics* (Routledge, 1990), p. 178.

94   Shuttleworth, 'Female Circulation', p. 63.

95 E. Showalter, *Sexual Anarchy* (Virago, 1992), pp. 129, 134.

96 Giddens, *Transformation*, p. 178.

97 Jordanova, *Sexual Visions*, pp. 96–7.

98 S. Heath, *The Sexual Fix* (Macmillan, 1982), p. 49.

99 A. Jardine, *Gynesis: Configurations of Woman and Modernity* (Cornell University Press, 1985), p. 154.

100 Bronfen, *Dead Body*, p. 264.

101 C. Crosby, *The Ends of History: Victorians and 'The Woman Question'* (Routledge, 1991), pp. 1, 3.

102 Bronfen, *Dead Body*, p. 223.

103 Heath, *Sexual Fix*, p. 47.

104 L. Irigaray, 'This Sex Which Is Not One', in E. Marks and I. de Courtivron (eds.) *New French Feminisms* (Harvester Wheatsheaf, 1980), p. 103.

105 Bronfen, *Dead Body*, pp. 181, 205.

106 Showalter, *Sexual Anarchy*, p. 145.

107 Bronfen, *Dead Body*, p. 255. See also the discussion of death in my *Exploring the Modern*, ch. 7.

108 T. de Lauretis, *Alice Doesn't: Feminism, Semiotics, Cinema* (Indiana University Press, 1984), pp. 5, 13.

109 On tensions and paradoxes of masculinity, see M. Simpson, *Male Impersonators* (Cassell, 1994) and V. Seidler, *Unreasonable Men* (Routledge, 1993).

110 Jardine, *Gynesis*, p. 25.

111 Bronfen's summary, in *Dead Body*, p. 189.

112 Butler, *Gender Trouble*, pp. 44, 45.

6 The Rape and Romance of 'Nature'

Having lived among the native hunter-gatherers of northern Canada, Nelson tells us that

> Traditional Koyukon people live in a world that watches, a forest of eyes. A person moving through nature – however wild, remote, even desolate the place may be – is never truly alone. The surroundings are aware, sensate, personified. They feel. They can be offended. And they must, at every moment, be treated with proper respect. All things in nature have a special kind of life, something unknown to contemporary Euro-Americans, something powerful.[1]

'The uncounted voices of nature,' adds a Tuscarora Indian, 'that for the Whites are dumb, are full of life and power for us.'[2] What we seem to find here is a notion of nature as community, of humanity as just one member of a community of beings that are bound by reciprocal ties and obligations; or, more fundamentally, an *experience* of nature in these terms, for it is not necessarily the case that there will be any explicit conception of 'nature' as such. This experience of nature entails a sense of *limits*; that human existence is bounded by constraints set by the existence of other creatures. And along with this, the suggestion that such a conception, and experience, of nature has become impossible in the modern world; that nature has become 'silent'; and that nature only becomes silent when silenced. . . . Thus ecologists call on us to relearn the 'language of nature', and hear 'the passions, pains and cryptic intents of the other biological communities that surround us and silently interpenetrate our existence'.[3]

It is, indeed, within the ecological tradition that this submerged conception of nature has most forcefully been articulated. When John Muir, in the 1870s, writes that 'The whole wilderness . . . is alive and familiar' and 'the very stones are talkative, sympathetic, brotherly',[4] he is not so far from the Koyukon. And today, one of the leading philosophers of deep ecology, Arne Naess, can write an article entitled 'Self-Realization in Mixed Communities of Humans, Bears,

Sheep, and Wolves',[5] and much the same idea is present in Aldo Leopold's vision of the 'land-community'.[6] Todorov denounces 'the illusion that all communication is interhuman communication', and claims that the triumph of Western civilization has been bought at the cost of communication with the natural world.[7]

If we look back at the medieval period in the West, we again encounter a sense of nature as community or continuum. Animals shared moral attributes, like wickedness, with humans. Old Germanic law extended the right to peace, guaranteed by royal authority, to animals, and the beast was 'thus invested with human rights and inferentially endowed with human responsibilities'. Animals were recognized as witnesses when burglary was committed at night; the owner could lodge a formal complaint, bringing his animals with him to court. These ideas and practices lie behind the apparently extraordinary cases of animal trials recorded in Evans's book *The Criminal Prosecution and Capital Punishment of Animals*. The cover shows a contemporary picture of a pig that had been formally tried for murder in a French court in 1386; it was found guilty and hanged. And the book gives numerous other examples; as late as 1587, weevils were brought to trial for damaging the vineyards. Alas, in this case we do not know the outcome, because, as Evans tells us,

> the last page of the records has been destroyed by rats or bugs of some sort. Perhaps the prosecuted weevils, not being satisfied with the results of the trial, sent a sharp-toothed delegation into the archives to obliterate and annul the judgment of the court.[8]

This is the universe in which the English friar Bartholomew, writing a work of natural history in the thirteenth century, could provide us with the following description of the cat:

> He is a full lecherous beast in youth, swift pliant and merry . . . and is led by a straw and playeth therewith: and is a right heavy beast in age and full sleepy, and lyeth slyly in wait for mice . . . in time of love is hard fighting for wives, and one rendeth the other grievously with biting and with claws.

Berger is surely correct in observing 'the writer's pleasure in identifying himself with the animal while he is describing it';[9] there is a lack of distance here. In short, there is no clear-cut distinction between the legal, moral, social and behavioural attributes of animals on the one hand, and humans on the other; and even after the line became more firmly drawn, it remained true that, in many ways, 'domestic beasts were subsidiary members of the human community', and might well live under the same roof.

By the seventeenth century, this had all been changing rapidly. Thomas points out that for Descartes, 'A transcendent God, outside his creation, symbolized the separation between spirit and nature. Man stood to animal as did heaven to earth, soul to body, culture to nature.'[10] A sharp dichotomy now ruptures the continuity of the medieval 'great chain of being'; and when the chain is reconstituted, in the late nineteenth century, under the influence of Darwinism, it is a celebration of human – or specifically masculine – triumph, with Man at the apex of the chain. Harriet Ritvo suggests that

> The circumscription of the legal role of animals reflected a fundamental shift in the relationship between humans and their fellow creatures, as a result of which people systematically appropriated power they had previously attributed to animals, and animals became significant primarily as the objects of human manipulation.[11]

Human power over animals could symbolize power over nature, but could also symbolize status distinctions between groups, often simultaneously (fox hunting, dog shows); but whereas the civilizing process initially permitted human distancing from 'the animal' to be appropriately celebrated through the killing and eating of animals, this has, for a long time, been changing. Tester suggests that kindness to animals now reflects embarrassment about the 'animality' of life and a kind of 'social repudiation of beastliness'.[12] It is through non-killing rather than through killing that we can now manifest human superiority.

But, of course, the symbolic and ritual significance of animals in modern culture ranges more widely than this. Leach, for example, has argued that the 'otherness' of animals can be mapped as circles of distance from the human centre: 'pets' are closest, may share the human home, and are coded as inedible; then come farm animals, 'livestock', edible if young, female or castrated; 'field' animals, or 'game', are protected but not tame, and may be killed when sexually intact, but only at specific times and in ritual ways; and finally, 'wild' animals, totally 'other', and again inedible.[13] Ultimately, animals intrigue because they can be seen both *as* nature, a flesh and blood embodiment of something that can otherwise become too abstract, vast and complex to grasp, and as mediators *between* humans and nature. They can exemplify the modern sense of nature in which, as Willis suggests, 'the animal' is 'both within us, as part of our underlying biological heritage as human beings, and also . . . outside and beyond human society';[14] we can project outwards, on to animals, our uneasy relations with the 'nature within'.

The modern view of nature replaces continuity with dichotomy, community with distance, participation with manipulation. We see the emergence of the twin notions of 'humanity' as somehow separate from 'nature', and nature as an abstract other that must be mastered, or a mysterious force that must be propitiated. The world thus becomes the world-as-nature, free of any divine plan or principle, a resource to be utilized, whether for technological development or moral or artistic enrichment. Connolly summarizes this by writing that, in modernity, 'Nature becomes a set of laws susceptible to human knowledge, a deposit of resources for potential use or a set of vistas for aesthetic appreciation.'[15] The implications of this will be explored in the remaining sections.

The Body of Nature

'Nature as community' is not necessarily so far from 'nature as body', particularly when the idea of community as organic, a living entity, is emphasized. And it is nature as a *gendered* body. A central strand in the pre-modern popular conception of nature in the West is of nature as a kind of living womb, a female body, a powerful procreative and regenerative force. This can in turn be related to carnivalesque notions of the 'grotesque body', which characteristically had female imagery associated with it; and this body, both destructive and regenerative, was above all *active*, a dynamic embodiment of cosmic creativity. Not only was nature seen in a generalized sense as female, then, but the earth specifically was seen as a nurturing mother, sensitive and responsive to human action; humans and other animals were her offspring, at times troublesome, but always dependent on her.[16] This perspective could be said both to reflect, and to contribute to maintaining, a world in which the actual capacity to transform and manipulate nature was rather restricted; such a view of nature does indeed seem to incorporate a sense of the necessary limits of human powers. As Carolyn Merchant puts it,

> The image of the earth as a living organism and nurturing mother had served as a cultural constraint restricting the actions of human beings. One does not readily slay a mother, dig into her entrails for gold, or mutilate her body, although commercial mining would soon require that. As long as the earth was considered to be alive and sensitive, it could be considered a breach of human ethical behavior to carry out destructive acts against it.[17]

Indeed, mining is a useful illustration. The modern attitude is that mining stands in no particular need of justification; but in most cultures, and certainly in pre-modern Europe, mining is seen as inherently controversial and quite probably sacrilegious, involving a kind of rape of the earth. Clearly such an overall conception of nature would have seriously inhibited the transformation of the world wrought by modernity, but it was in decay well before the seventeenth century. However, it has retained a certain hold, and has even had a revival in our own time; for an influential theory found in contemporary green cultural and political movements, embedded in their critique of the modern construction of nature as an expendable resource, is the so-called 'Gaia hypothesis'. Put forward by the scientist James Lovelock, and named after the Greek goddess of the earth, this is the idea that the earth can be regarded as an organism, involving a network of interdependent life-processes whereby the different species and natural cycles can interact to maintain the balance of the whole, a balance that one species, humanity, is threatening to upset: the nurturing mother and her recalcitrant offspring, again.[18]

With the Renaissance, we encounter two associated images of nature that hold considerable significance for the future. First, the prevalence of Arcadian or pastoral imagery. In the poetry of Spencer, or the paintings of Cranach and

Botticelli, nature is tamed, idealized: it has become a garden for nymphs to recline in. Merchant comments that in pastoral imagery, 'both nature and women are subordinate and essentially passive'; thus 'They nurture but do not control or exhibit disruptive passion.' Passivity is here being constructed as a property both of nature and of the feminine. But at the same time, we find a second perspective, apparently pulling in the opposite direction: one that portrays nature as disorderly, disruptive, bringer of tempests and disease. This, too, is associated with the feminine, and fits easily with the attitude that makes the witch-hunts possible. In effect, this is the 'dual vision' of woman, previously discussed. And the implication of *both* images of nature as female – pastoral idyll and destructive disorder – is to propel *man* to centre stage, as the necessary spectator, controller and regulator of nature.[19]

Baconian science, as it emerged in the seventeenth century, was from the start a self-consciously masculine project. Nevertheless, it took a long time to establish complete hegemony. For much of the seventeenth and eighteenth centuries, 'science' and 'reason' were portrayed iconographically as *female*. In Renaissance iconography, 'Scientia' had been pictured as a woman with stately robes, and 'Physica' was a goddess with a globe at her feet. Galileo invoked the feminine icon for the title page of *Il Saggiatore*. Londa Schiebinger therefore argues that

> When it came to science, there were at least two distinct allegories vying for power of representation. Baconians championed a masculine symbol – virile, ready to act and command. Others championed a feminine symbol, discreetly mediating between the demands of male scientists and the secrets of 'female' nature.

With this latter model, it is as though 'science' was female, but 'scientists' male. Neoplatonists held creativity to be a fusion of opposites: 'In order to unite in a creative union with the female, the male scientist images his science as opposite, or feminine', and thus he will be led to the secrets of nature. As late as the 1760s, that great product of the Enlightenment, the *Encyclopédie*, sported a frontispiece that presented an elaborate allegory of feminine hegemony in science, with Truth and Reason – both female – presiding over the search for knowledge.

But by the early nineteenth century, any remaining equivocations had been swept away: not just scientists, but science itself, had become decisively masculine, and 'With the passing of the feminine icon also passed the classical appreciation of women's contribution to the sciences.'[20] Nature, as the object of scientific investigation, had become the passive, feminized body, for male scientists to penetrate and dissect. As Jordanova suggests, science and medicine were 'drawn both to personifications of nature as woman and to the image of unveiling in order to represent their privileged relationship to Truth and to Nature'.[21] And the rise of modern anatomy and medicine since the seventeenth century was quite centrally linked to, and dependent on, the practice of dissection, in which the corpses of criminals were handed over to scientists for what was, in effect, 'part of the legal system of revenge'.[22] If you want to find out about life, cut up a few corpses, as the anatomist Bichat remarked.[23] The road to understanding life runs through death; and given the increasing prevalence of the portrayals of *women's* bodies in medical texts and artistic representations of anatomical practice, the body of nature has become not just lifeless, but feminine, too. Even recently, the biologist René Dubos observed that biologists feel most at ease when the object they are studying is no longer living.[24] The live body of nature has become a corpse; the principle of regeneration, a practice of dissection.

The set of assumptions implicit in this emergence of anatomy as a privileged route to the investigation of life can be explored further through examining the emergence of modern biology itself. The 'natural history' of the seventeenth and eighteenth centuries had been based on the assumption that, as the biologist Jacob puts it, 'What was read or related no longer carried the weight of what was seen'; in other words, 'The visible structure of living organisms became the object of analysis and classification.' Nor was there any clear distinction between the animate and the inanimate: 'that particular quality of organization called "life" by the nineteenth century was unrecognized. There were not yet functions necessary to life; there were simply organs which function.' It was the revolutionary transformation of these assumptions that made modern biology possible:

> A living being is no longer a simple association of organs, each working autonomously. It becomes a whole whose parts are interdependent, each performing a particular function for the common good. . . . Thus at the end of the eighteenth century there was a change in the relations between the exterior and the interior, between the surface and the depth, and between organs and functions of a living being. What becomes accessible to comparative investigation was a system of relationships in the depth of a living organism, designed to make it function. Behind the visible forms could be glimpsed the profile of a secret architecture imposed by the necessity of living.[25]

Nature becomes life, the dynamic capacity for self-organization; in Foucault's words, 'the enigma of a force inaccessible in its essence, apprehendable only in the efforts it makes here and there to manifest and maintain itself'.[26] And if the living being captures the power of life in some way, Jacob reminds us that it can only do so momentarily; it is doomed to die, since 'it is destroyed precisely by what has made life itself spring forth'.[27] The idea of 'organism' as entailing organization, change, dynamism and decline – 'historicity' itself – here enters the agenda of modernity. And again, we find that the biologist kills the organism to find its principle of life, only finding thereby a greater knowledge of the hidden structure left behind when life departs: the paradox of dissection chasing holism that constitutes the grounding of biology itself, constantly questioning its achievements even as it makes them possible, reflected even today in disputes between reductionists who seek to understand an organism by 'dissecting' it into its constituents (genes), and those who seek its principles of organization at higher levels of complexity and interdependence.

The implication of these perspectives for the human body can in turn best be examined through considering medicine. The medieval body, linked to other bodies and organisms by criss-crossing 'signs', was in effect part of a cosmic 'text' that could, with the appropriate skills, be 'read'; and the 'meanings' of the body were always as much social, cultural and cosmological as physical. The afflictions of the body had to be 'read' in this way; 'plague', for example, was experienced in moral and religious terms, and was not a 'disease' in the modern sense, engendering little interest in what we would see as its biological distinctiveness and epidemiological characteristics.[28] The modern body, on the other hand, is not only individualized, it is 'naturalized', seen in physical terms; it occupies space, it has *depth*. This depth makes possible the use of metaphors like 'unveiling', the idea that it is necessary to probe 'beneath' the surface, that the surface carries 'symptoms' that are causally, but problematically, related to underlying, hidden processes. Here we encounter the modern notion of 'disease' as the biological dysfunction that causes the symptoms of the 'illness' experienced by the individual. The implications are spelt out by Osherson and Amarasingham:

> The localization of illness changed the status of the patient's body; no longer was it primarily the seat of subjective impressions interpreted by the patient to the doctor, but rather it became the site of specific disease entities to be detected and evaluated by the doctor independently of the patient.

Thus we see a shift from the idea of a person with an affliction to that of a patient with a disease, a shift that simultaneously involves a decisive role for medical intervention; the patient 'alienates' his or her body to the doctor, and receives it back, 'repaired'. The patient is subject to the 'clinical gaze'. The same authors add that 'The notion of the body as the possession of a consumer of services who is able to buy "repairs" for it became current at the same time that the buying and selling of services for other possessions became a major economic force.'[29] So while biomedicine in its contemporary form is inseparable from the work of Pasteur and other researchers of the late nineteenth century who established the framework of germ theory, this did not alter the basic structure of what was by then a highly distinctive set of cultural practices of body management and intervention. And Engel, in the course of a critique of the limitations of modern medicine, complains that biomedicine is still based on 'the notion of the body as a machine, of disease as the consequence of breakdown of the machine, and of the doctor's task as repair of the machine', calling for a revival of the other perspective in modern biology, referred to above.[30]

Finally, this has implications for the status of the modern self, housed in a body construed as 'other', part of the 'nature' that has to be controlled. As Barker-Benfield writes, 'Man's command of the unrefined, passionate part of himself formed the model for his conquest of nature',[31] and Merchant adds that

> A new concept of the self as a rational master of the passions housed in a machine-like body began to replace the concept of the self as an integral part of a close-knit harmony of organic parts united to the cosmos and society. Mechanism rendered nature effectively dead, inert, and manipulable from without.[32]

The self becomes a kind of transcendental observer of the world, able to intervene *in* it, through *using* the body, yet not really *of* it. In its capacity as observer and thinker, 'self' in effect means 'mind', and we see here the mind/body dualism that has been central not only to modern medicine but the whole modern orientation to the world. And this dualism embodies paradox, for there is a sense in which mind is embedded in body just as culture is embedded in nature. Modern culture, surveying and controlling nature, cannot escape it, yet constantly alters it in the very attempt to escape. Culture becomes the reflexive mode of nature; nature becomes self-conscious, thereby always other to itself.

The Universe of Nature

The early modern world in which the Scientific Revolution took place was a world in which the devil was still very active; and for a long time, his magical practices, far from being incompatible with those of science, seem to have coexisted with them, even been part of the emergent universe of scientific discourse. What is significant is that his activities are now clearly seen as part of the *natural* world. Francis Bacon, philosopher of the Scientific Revolution, himself urged that 'superstitious narratives' should be investigated, as 'it is not yet known in what cases, and how far, effects attributed to superstition participate of natural causes'; magic might produce remarkable results, but only by manipulation of 'natural' causes. Satan himself could not transcend natural laws; and as Clark remarks, 'where his power to produce real effects gave out, his ingenuity in camouflaging weakness by illusory phenomena took over'. The devil was a gifted natural magician, and could influence people and events in subtle ways – hence the dangers of witchcraft – but he remained part of what was increasingly distinguished as the world of 'natural', law-governed processes. Thus Clark concludes that 'Demonology was one of the "prerogative instances" of early modern science', and was a genuine vehicle for what could be called a scientific debate, premised on assumptions about the 'natural order', and the ability to intervene in it and manipulate it, that were shared with other sciences.[33]

The universe of nature was, however, increasingly a world that God himself was withdrawing from. In the earlier view, God frequently intervened in his creation; miracles, after all, were evidence of this. But now the view developed that once God had created the universe, he did not subsequently interfere in its workings. If he did, he would frustrate his own purposes; the regularity and rationality of his design would be subverted. Once created, the universe would run like clockwork. The increasing distance of God reinforced this sense of the universe as 'natural', bereft of spiritual intervention; this was the universe of silent, infinite spaces that so terrified Pascal. Nevertheless, in one respect God's status was crucial; he acted as a guarantor of the *order* of the world. Nature's laws could run remorselessly, unaffected by caprice; they were really *there*, and there was no reason why they could not be discovered using human reason. This shift is momentous; it makes possible the emergence of 'nature' as a rational order, intelligible through scientific investigation. And it makes possible the epistemo-logical correlate: 'the notion of knowledge as a matter of rightly ordered inner representations – an unclouded and undistorted Mirror of Nature', in Rorty's words.[34]

Clocks and machines became 'root metaphors' for this conception of nature. Merchant suggests that the rise of mechanism 'laid the foundation for a new synthesis of the cosmos, society, and the human being, construed as ordered systems of mechanical parts subject to governance by law and to predictability through deductive reasoning'.[35] The laws governing the universe could be ascertained by a combination of mathematical abstraction and detailed empiri-cal experimentation, the regularities of the whole coexisting with the relative separability of the parts for purposes of scientific investigation. Materialism frequently accompanied mechanism; the world is ultimately made up of particles in motion, intelligible through the laws of Galileo and Newton. As the philoso-pher Descartes put it: 'Know that by nature I do not understand some goddess or some sort of imaginary power. I employ this word to signify matter itself.'[36] Merchant suggests that this 'removal of animistic, organic assumptions about the cosmos constituted the death of nature – the most far-reaching effect of the Scientific Revolution',[37] and in a sense this is true, though there is also a sense in which this is the *birth* of nature, the modern sense of 'nature' as a separate, intelligible, law-governed and controllable world. Perhaps the birth of the one is inseparable from the death of the other.

If 'nature as mechanism' is a metaphor, it is nevertheless both based on, and productive of, a very specific kind of human artefact: a machine. A machine has parts, each part being functionally specific, empirically separable, and in principle replaceable; and the machine is designed to achieve specific goals in the transformation of the world. World and machine become mutually reinforcing products of one another; the world of technology is oriented towards the production of a world that is intelligible and transformable through technology. There is, in effect, both a conceptual and a practical link between science and technology here; both Bacon, in the early seventeenth century, and the group of scientists who gathered in the Royal Society later in the century, had no doubt that the aims of science were to serve human needs through the manipulation of nature's laws. Bacon proclaimed that 'Human knowledge and human power meet as one.'[38] We can 'command nature by obeying her', and the point of learning about the world is to intervene in it. Nature simply *is* the world as transform-able in the light of human interest; it is a law-governed mechanism with parts that can be combined, recombined or replaced, depending on our needs. Under-standing and intervention go together. Summarizing the implications of the Galilean–Newtonian universe, Starobinski points out that

> homogeneous space lends itself to the measurement of speeds, masses, rela-tionships: it therefore reveals laws of matter which can then be exploited. The cal-culations of mechanics were to allow man to increase and direct his forces. The 'point of view' of the individual was not only the center for his abstract contem-

plation, but the support for his practical transforming activities . . . in proportion to the growth of his knowledge he saw his powers increasing. . . . Industry and commerce established a systematic basis for the exploitation of nature. The profit anticipated would be obtained with even greater certainty if man dominated nature by wielding effectively the uniform laws governing natural phenomena.[39]

It can be seen that 'nature as mechanism' slides easily into 'nature as resource', a picture of the world in which those natural resources that are not infinite can always be replaced by technological ingenuity, through the creation of substitutes.

Another implication of this is that nature is evacuated of any moral or teleological dimension. Taylor argues that 'We demystify the cosmos as a setter of ends by grasping it mechanistically and functionally as a domain of possible means';[40] indeed, this is the death of the cosmos in its traditional sense, as an all-encompassing source of meaning and purpose. Eder adds that this in turn reconstitutes our notion of rationality:

> Modern culture has so far been dominated by a conception of rationality that takes nature as a means to other ends. This rationality in fact excludes any moral considerations from the realm of nature . . . the subjugation of nature to ends defined by culture becomes the model of rationality.[41]

And this conception of nature as threat, as antagonist, is a central strand in the modern orientation; it would be difficult to argue with the general justice of Schumacher's conclusion that 'Modern man does not experience himself as a part of nature but as an outside force destined to dominate and conquer it. He even talks of a battle with nature, forgetting that, if he won the battle, he would find himself on the losing side.'[42]

The Garden of Eden

Not surprisingly, the idea of nature as a resource, or as a challenge to human domination, has generally been accompanied by the view that the actual experience of nature is not something to be sought after. Sometimes, this rejection of any wider interest in nature was based on straightforward utilitarian grounds; the gardener Samuel Collins spoke for many contemporaries in 1717 when he said that the best of all flowers was a cauliflower. But very often, the unproductive was also seen as unaesthetic, unattractive. Mountainous country, for example, was particularly to be avoided. In the 1670s Chief Justice North shuddered at the 'hideous mountains' of the Lake District, full of horrid waterfalls and ghastly precipices.[43]

If nature *could* be a source of pleasure, it could only be nature as strictly subordinated to human design, nature as an excuse for the exercise of human rationality. Beauty could not be derived *from* nature; rather, it has to be imposed *on* it. The French formal garden of the seventeenth and eighteenth centuries embodied these principles, and was widely copied. The epitome of this was reached in Le Nôtre's gardens at Versailles and other royal palaces, influencing Hampton Court and Chatsworth, with the long, symmetrical vistas, the straight lines, the precise, rigid layout of paths and beds, designed to geometrical precision, and the carefully trimmed and manicured plants, grouped in rows with each plant of an identical shape and height, like a regiment lined up and standing to attention – the more ambitious and imaginative ancestor of many a boring municipal and suburban garden in our own time. This is hardly a celebration of nature; it is a celebration of the power of culture to shape the 'formlessness' of nature in accordance with human reason.[44] Mukerji suggests that such gardens were constituted as 'models of the exercise of power over nature, narratives for describing the virtues of discipline'; as such, if they embodied the power of reason, it was a reason that also manifested the territorial hegemony of the ruler or owner.[45] And this latter aspect of power was to remain significant even when the style of garden design changed fundamentally, in the eighteenth century; it was the enclosure movement, sometimes flattening whole villages, that made 30- or 50-acre landscape gardens like Capability Brown's possible.[46]

A relationship between pleasure and power can also be traced in the arena of 'natural history', a mode of relating to nature that at times, in the eighteenth and nineteenth centuries, reached levels of considerable popularity. Central to natural history is the power to name, the capture of nature in the nets of classification that nevertheless purport to reflect what is 'really there'; human reason can grasp nature through immersion in it, but it is an immersion that also implies detachment, the retention of control, 'objectivity', and this vicarious involvement can give pleasure. Sparrman, a pupil of the great taxonomist Linnaeus, accompanied Cook on one of his voyages, and described his pleasures in 'a-botanizing' in the same way as did Adam in his 'State of Nature'. And again, this blissful activity clearly involved a subtle dispossession of the local inhabitants, as Mary Louise Pratt points out:

> Where, one asks, is everybody? The landscape is written as uninhabited, unpossessed, unhistoricized, unoccupied even by the travelers themselves. . . . In the writing, people seem to disappear from the garden as Adam approaches – which, of course, is why he can walk around as he pleases and name things after himself and his friends back home . . . natural history asserted an urban, lettered male authority over the whole of the planet; it elaborated a rationalizing, dissociative understanding which overlaid functional, experiential relations among people, plants and animals. In these respects, it figures a certain kind of global hegemony.[47]

And Donna Haraway adds that Linnaeus

> referred to himself as a second Adam, the 'eye' of God, who could give true representations, true names, thus reforming or restoring a purity of names lost by the first Adam's sin. . . . The role of the one who renamed the animals was to ensure a true and faithful order of nature, to purify the eye and the word. . . . Indeed, this

is the identity of the modern authorial subject, for whom inscribing the body of nature gives assurance of his mastery.[48]

The 'mirror of nature' is also an act of appropriation, yet presented in innocent, hence pleasurable, terms: 'See, this belongs to you. You never thought you were so rich. This is what the scholars have obtained for you. Now learn to enjoy it all.'[49] The appropriation could become yet more direct, for the 'enjoyment' could easily include collecting; Adam might not only name the plants after his friends back home, he might take some back for them, too. Science slides easily into consumerism; most of the plants that are taken for granted in contemporary gardens have their origins in these overseas expeditions. Tulips, hyacinths, anemones and crocuses arrived in the sixteenth century, followed in the next two centuries by daisies, lupins, sweet peas and dahlias.[50] Seed catalogues were being produced by the late eighteenth century; Joseph Banks and the other naturalist-collectors introduced 7,000 new species during the reign of George III. By 1865 half a million people per year were visiting Kew Gardens.[51] Botany and gardening alike were becoming incorporated in the consumer spectacle.

Nevertheless, the continuities in this account conceal a major transformation. For the Enlightenment period, nature ceased to be an inert resource and became a living force, and a force for good; human social and cultural arrangements should harmonize with nature, not challenge it. 'One now did something in a certain way because it was more "natural",' writes Ann Bermingham; 'one said something in a certain way because it sounded more "natural"; something worked as it did because it was its "nature" to do so.'[52] Landscape gardening now sought to reconcile nature and culture; nature was to be shaped, rather than dominated. Starobinski suggests that such landscaping aimed to 'encourage perfection in nature, instead of wrongly conflicting with it'; returning to the 'original paradise' of nature, but without giving up the benefits of culture.[53] Passmore suggests, that, as with landscape painting, so also the landscape gardener was to 'take his materials from nature, to treat them reverently, but to arrange them in a better composition. To "perfect" was not to *impose* form, but to *improve* form.' The landscape garden becomes nature as a form of art. He brings out the wider significance of this in these terms:

> The two leading traditions in modern Western thought, then can be put thus: the first, Cartesian in inspiration, that matter is inert, passive, that man's relationship to it is that of an absolute despot, reshaping, reforming, what has in it no inherent powers of resistance, any sort of agency; the second, Hegelian, that nature exists only *in potentia*, as something which it is man's task to help to actualise through art, science, philosophy, technology, converting it into something human, something in which he can feel thoroughly 'at home', in no sense strange or alien to him, a mirror in which he can see his own face. Man, on this second view, *completes* the universe not just by living in it . . . but by actually helping to make it.[54]

Raymond Williams makes a similar point, though with more emphasis on the creativity of nature:

> Two principles of Nature can then be seen simultaneously. There is nature as a
> principle of order, of which the ordering mind is part, and which human activity,
> by regulating principles, may then rearrange and control. But there is also nature
> as a principle of creation, of which the creative mind is part, and from which we
> may learn the truths of our own sympathetic nature.[55]

Thus Lancelot 'Capability' Brown, arguably the most influential of the English
school of eighteenth-century landscape design, acquired his nickname through
his habit of describing sites as 'having capabilities' which it was his task to
'realize', thus enabling nature to be 'perfected'. The great eighteenth-century
gardens, such as Stowe, Stourhead, the Leasowes, and Rousham, were intended
to embody organic relations, rather than geometric precision; they 'improved' on
nature, while restoring the 'natural' look. Shrubberies and rolling parkland
took the place of straight avenues and clipped hedges; trees would be placed in
irregular clumps, footpaths would wind, hills would be used to diversify the views
from different points on the estate. The ideal is stated by Mukerji:

> The English garden was a place of study and contemplation of a nature that was
> other, and perfect in its otherness. It was something beyond human control, and yet
> under control because people had come to understand and work within its
> autonomous movements.[56]

Above all, such landscape gardens were to be sites where pleasure was to be had,
a certain kind of pleasure involving immersion and detachment, identification and
possession, otherness manifested yet restrained.

'Gardens are, first and foremost, about pleasure', writes Pugh, adding 'A
garden is, often, the only place I want to be'; yet he describes his own evolution
from 'a mindless, regressive immersion in the pleasures of the garden to an unease
about what the garden represents and why'. For Kant, the garden was a composition both pleasing and purposeless, and Pugh adds that the pleasure of the
garden is 'an elusive delight just because it seems to abjure more completely than
other pleasures any common point with the real world that it is in opposition to'.
Apparently so marginal and purposeless, the garden yet offers clues to key aspects
of the experience of modernity.

Purporting to restore the 'truth' of nature, the eighteenth-century garden
became, writes Pugh, 'a site of paradise lost and regained';[57] but can paradise lost
ever be regained? We encounter here what Bermingham describes as a pattern of
'actual loss and imaginative recovery', in that as a large part of the countryside
was being decisively marked by historical change, 'it was offered as the image of
the homely, the stable, the ahistorical'.[58] The garden becomes an idealized image
of a disappearing past. Nature is an original that has been lost; and what comes
after can only be nostalgia. It is through the garden gate that nostalgia enters the
experience and consciousness of modernity. 'The garden was a country of the
memory', suggests Starobinski; instead of being 'a throbbing center of presence
regained', the garden 'was a meeting place for nostalgic anxiety'.[59]

This can be explored further through considering the place of the ruin in the eighteenth-century imagination of landscape. William Shenstone, of the Leasowes, suggested that the 'melancholy or pensive' scene could mediate between the sublime and the beautiful in a landscape, and could most effectively be embodied in a ruin, with its simultaneous connotations of antiquity and transience.[60] Culture and nature can here attain a precarious balance, in a human work rendered 'natural' through the corrosion of time. Starobinski thus argues that 'the aesthetics of the ruin express a minor form of idyll: a new union of man and nature, through the intermediary of man's resignation to death'. Ruins represent a 'reverie before the encroachment of oblivion'.[61] Yet all is not what it seems, and this can take us further into the paradoxes posed by these pleasures taken in otherness: for the ruins are very often fakes.[62] Landscape designers and builders became expert in the production of 'Gothic' ruins, and these ruins contribute to a sense of unease in the presence of these gardens of Eden. Do we again find that the 'restoration' or 'recovery' of nature could rather be seen as its construction? That the cult of 'nature' means the exile of nature? Gardens have a multifaceted significance: if they introduce the modern sense of nostalgia, they also hint at our contemporary (postmodern?) concerns about authenticity and simulation.

This can be further examined by looking at the relationship between the landscape garden and the surrounding countryside. This is symbolised by the ha-ha, a deep ditch dug around the perimeter of the estate, often accompanied by an embankment or low wall. This boundary effectively prevented sheep getting in, but as it was invisible until one was relatively close to it, it was a boundary that seemed to deny itself, a sort of joke;[63] and its more significant effect was to obliterate any sense of contrast between the estate and the countryside beyond, enhancing the sense of 'nature' as a ubiquitous but carefully restrained power. But of course, this could only happen under certain conditions. Brown and Repton were careful to exclude 'unpleasing' views of the countryside, anything that hinted at the massive social and economic transformations taking place. What remained was a safe and pleasing vision of the countryside: 'as the real landscape began to look increasingly artificial, like a garden, the garden began to look increasingly natural, like the preenclosed landscape', as Bermingham puts it. She adds that

> Whereas the formal garden had stood between art and nature, the landscape garden tended to collapse the distinction altogether. In this sense, it became a *trompe l'oeil*. By conflating nature with the fashionable taste of a new social order, it redefined the natural in terms of this order, and vice versa.

Hence we can see how the landscape garden, and the genre of painting associated with it, represent the other side of the Enlightenment coin, the ease with which the critique of the old social order as 'unnatural' can slide into a conservative espousal of the emergent social order as 'natural'.[64] Pugh therefore suggests a distinction between 'countryside' and 'landscape'. If 'landscape as a piece of nature suggests what all of nature *ought* to be like, but in no sense *is* like', then we can say that 'a working countryside is never a landscape, and a landscape or a garden . . . represent separation from the working countryside'.[65]

The issue of 'work' is of further significance here, pointing to a tension in the idea of a 'natural' garden. If nature is 'capability', to be 'realized' by human labour, how can we be sure that our 'shaping' of nature indeed respects its potential, rather than just imposing our will on it? Human labour needs to be both present, to do the shaping, and absent, so as to ensure that it is truly 'nature' that results. The 'natural' garden is a human product that must above all conceal that fact. I sense this tension in my own gardening practice; that my wanting the garden to be 'natural' – albeit rather more on the model of the late nineteenth-century 'cottage' garden – is itself paradoxical, since in this case why don't I just leave it alone and let 'nature' take its course? A weed has just as much right to be there. . . . I can certainly understand Pugh's conclusion that 'The garden dissembles' since it is 'a repression of nature that masquerades as a mimesis of what it represses but which is really a total reconstruction';[66] and Hunt's claim that 'gardens are special sites of artifice pretending to be nature'.[67] This, indeed, reminds us of the paradoxes in our contemporary cult of 'the natural', carrying a powerful reference to a supposedly untouched, 'wholesome' nature while simultaneously being a product and tool of the advertising industry.[68]

Gardening has anyway, of course, become heavily implicated in the development of modern consumerism. Repton's designs in the early 1800s already marked a shift towards the smaller garden, with greater use of flower beds; and this is taken further in Loudon's work later in the century, with his advocacy of the 'gardenesque': 'the suburban gardenesque gardener had to impress not with land but with plants',[69] new varieties of which were constantly feeding the market. Repton was also able to abstract his designs into 'styles'; clients could choose between Classical, Gothic, Chinese, Turkish. . . . Taste was increasingly becoming something which 'each person constructed for him or herself', as Hunt puts it.[70] But by now, many no longer sought Eden in the garden; nature had escaped elsewhere.

Wilderness and the Sublime

'A gentleman's park is my aversion', asserts Constable. 'It is not beauty because it is not nature.'[71] Clearly there is a marked change in attitude here. Green suggests that by the 1830s we find the first examples of the modern notion of a guidebook, intended to encourage the exploration of scenery and 'natural beauty' as values in their own right; he claims that 'what was implicitly foregrounded was the use or enjoyment of the countryside *for and in itself*', rather than through its association with some famous author or building.[72]

If we take this further, we find the idea that the very 'wildness' of nature can be taken as desirable; it becomes an otherness that possesses a powerful presence and attraction. Hunt suggests that 'The wilderness became fashionable precisely because it occasioned highly personal experiences of sublime *frissons*, in contrast with the 'socially engineered and sanctioned attitudes available within the landscape parks and gardens'.[73] By the late eighteenth century, mountains had become goals for artists and travellers to explore precisely because they had come to represent this 'otherness'; they were seen as undomesticated, wild places, where true, uncontaminated nature could be found. Mountains still produced horror, but it was now 'agreeable horror', and this, together with 'pleasing melancholy', became an experience to seek out.[74] 'Previously, precipices had been hideous and largely uninteresting', writes Starobinski. 'Now, they were still hideous, but they attracted uneasy souls aspiring after the aesthetic emotion of terror.' What the artist meets on the summit is 'the dangerous face of that Nature from which genius draws its power'.[75] Hence Thomas can claim that

> By the late eighteenth century the appreciation of nature, and particularly wild nature, had been converted into a sort of religious act. Nature was not only beautiful; it was morally healing. . . .
>
> The feeling of awe, terror and exultation, once reserved for God, was gradually transposed to the expanded cosmos revealed by the astronomers and to the loftiest objects discovered by explorers on earth: mountains, oceans, deserts and tropical forests. . . . The mountains themselves . . . had become the highest form of natural beauty.[76]

This search by town dwellers for spiritual regeneration through the wild will become a constantly recurring theme in the modern period.

Nash points out that the original German *Wildnis* captures the twofold appeal: 'On the one hand it is inhospitable, alien, mysterious and threatening; on the other, beautiful, friendly, and capable of elevating and delighting the beholder.'[77] This duality could well serve as a definition of the category of the sublime, which forged an important link between art, nature and individual experience. For Edmund Burke, a leading theorist of the sublime, the Welsh mountains produced 'ideas elevating, awful and of a magnificent kind'.[78] The sublime – in contrast to the beautiful – pointed *beyond* the human dimension, communicated a sense of the majesty and power of the natural order; it promised access to transcendence in an era when God's own transcendence had become problematic. Nature was now sovereign power, an awesome, implacable force, pursuing its way independently of human will. Taylor suggests that this orientation was concerned with

> the sentiments which nature awakens in us. We return to nature, because it brings out strong and noble feelings in us: feelings of awe before the greatness of creation, of peace before a pastoral scene, of sublimity before storms and deserted fastnesses, of melancholy in some lonely woodland spot. Nature draws us because it is in some way attuned to our feelings, so that it can reflect and intensify those we already feel or else awaken those which are dormant. Nature is like a great keyboard on which our highest sentiments are played out. We turn to it, as we might turn to music, to evoke and strengthen the best in us.[79]

Genius itself was the working of an obscure power of nature. The artist should strive to image the 'invisible perfection' of nature, but this was not mimesis, rather an activity of the creative imagination. 'Art', writes Starobinski, 'was the human extension of the fecundity of the cosmos.'[80] Nature was totality, and this could only be grasped by the creative imagination, not by scientific analysis: 'To dissect is to murder', wrote Wordsworth, and that was no way to understand life.[81] These links are summarized by Hampshire in these terms:

> This romantic idea of the need to recapture naturalness, otherwise lost in the exercise of reason, comes near to explaining the metaphysical emotions which can take the place of those associated with transcendental religions; particularly Kant's theory of genius and of originality in the imagination as being the channel through which natural insights, otherwise lost, return to the human mind, as it were, un-observed and by unknown paths. We seem to ourselves to be brought into contact with a permanent natural order through works of imaginative art . . . [which] reveal an otherwise concealed or muffled reality, not accessible to science or to any conscious reflection.[82]

Taylor adds that 'this relation to nature is predicated on the modern identity',[83] and this needs to be explored further.

For Romanticism, our access to nature is through the 'inner voice' itself, even though this 'inner voice' may be more clearly articulated in the presence of natural wilderness. For the artist Caspar David Friedrich, 'A painter must not paint merely what he sees before him, but also what he sees within himself.'[84] In looking at nature, Coleridge claimed that he sought 'a symbolical language for something within me'; and Wordsworth admitted that 'I was often unable to think of external things as having external existence, and I communed with all that I saw as something not apart from, but inherent in, my own immaterial nature.'[85] For Rousseau, at the source of these ideas, social corruption separates us from the 'inner voice' of nature by subordinating us to artifice and opinion. Romanticism is an aspect of modern subjectivism; it both rests on, and deepens, the modern sense of the individual self as having depth, a depth that involves both a separation from nature, and from other selves, and a paradoxical potential for a sense of nature itself as depth, as the ground of all being.

This individualism is just as evident in the contemporary variants of these ideas. Probing the claim that 'it is virtuous to be natural', and the evidence of widespread ideological rejection of 'artificiality' and 'processing', Rosalind Coward argues that, on this model,

> Nature is vital forces and energies running through all things, vital forces which lie behind the process of renewal or recovery. The main source of knowledge of these forces is the individual body. These forces of nature are beneficial and healing. Indeed, nature is health . . . nature is something innate, to be found through a journey inwards, implying a relation of mind, body and outside. We can find this natural force by a process of readjustment to a proper balance and harmony with nature lost or alienated by our own modern culture.[86]

Romanticism, then, is a central strand in the modern construction of a self for which the experience of nature is aesthetic and individualizing. This self, in its relation to nature, is, suggests Green, both active and passive: 'active in its pictorial ordering of nature, passive in the immersion in sensation'. In this sense, nature can become an unthreatening source of pleasure in itself, something to 'escape into' while retaining the coherence of the observing self. 'If on the one hand the subject was subsumed in the organic wholeness of nature', writes Green, 'on the other it was distanced, the eye behind the viewing aperture, pictorially ordering the visual field into a sequence of tableaux'. And Green refers to the 'mix of consumption and immersion framing the nineteenth-century urban experience of the countryside'; we see here the transformation of nature into scenery, offered as a commodity for human consumption through aesthetic pleasure, 'a spectacle which slotted easily into the consuming rhetoric of the city'.[87]

Of course, day trips into the countryside hardly provided access to nature as wilderness; to find that, the British were increasingly driven abroad, where there was thought to be more of it. But in the case of North America, the whole idea of 'wilderness' came to have a central role in the culture, as a foundation myth. 'Wilderness was the basic ingredient of American civilization', claims Nash; and with the idea or symbol of wilderness, Americans 'sought to give that civilization identity and meaning'. This is worth further discussion, giving us clues to the significance of 'wilderness' in modern culture.

It is important to realize that the actual content of these attitudes to 'nature as wilderness' varied significantly and systematically. To begin with, wilderness was a challenge to be overcome. American pioneers, immersed in it, had no love of it, and were frequently seen by their more 'civilized', home-loving contemporaries, as being polluted by it. After all, the 'frontier', that key component in the American self-image, was precisely the frontier of civilization; beyond it lay barbarism. Nevertheless, as the frontier moved steadily westwards, so attitudes began to change, first towards giving a positive evaluation to the challenges posed by wilderness, and the heroism needed to overcome them, but then towards regarding wilderness itself in positive terms, particularly since it was clear that the increasing stream of European visitors regarded what lay beyond the frontier as having value.

Of course, some of these encounters with 'wilderness' were really just an opportunity to continue exploitative activities without having to be subject to the constraints of normal life. One traveller in the USA in the 1850s was accompanied by a huge retinue of 40 assistants, 112 horses and 3 cows, and proceeded to shoot 4,000 assorted game (buffalo, deer, elk and bears).[88] The British in India and Africa furnished many similar examples. Indeed, three million acres of Scotland were converted from pasture to moor and forest in the nineteenth century, for the convenience of the hunting and shooting elite, thus producing a 'planned wilderness' that was converted by travel writers and artists into 'natural' wilderness itself.[89]

But increasingly, the rationale for wilderness became the possibility it offered for the encounter with otherness, the experience of the *difference* of non-human nature, the grandeur and isolation of it. Wilderness 'had to do with emptiness and otherness' and was 'the antipode of civilization and all its myths, including those concerning wilderness'; it was a mirror held up to civilization itself, revealing *its* emptiness. Wilderness represented regeneration. The frontiersman was now looked at in a different light; his very *lack* of civilization gave him insight and power. Wilderness now became something to be cherished and preserved; and from this, the idea of 'stewardship' can develop, the idea that the role of 'preserving' nature inevitably slides into a more active role of 'managing' nature, to maintain natural diversity. Two dates can be seen as symbolically significant in this revaluation of wilderness, and this reconstruction of nature as wilderness: 1872, when President Grant inaugurated the Yellowstone National Park, the world's first sizeable nature reserve; and 1890, when the US Census officially proclaimed that the frontier was no more, making it clear that there was no vast reservoir of wilderness left.[90] What *was* left was the wilderness of myth, to be recuperated later by Hollywood in the Western, the phases of which symbolically recapitulate these changes in attitude to wilderness, from a celebration of conquest through to an elegy for the lost paradise.[91]

Still powerful in our own time, the romanticism of 'nature as wilderness' remains deeply paradoxical. For a start, wilderness is fragile. Once touched, it disintegrates; once entered, it is lost. 'Wilderness' represents the ideal of immediate contact with non-human otherness; but that very contact corrupts the rationale for the contact in the first place. Your very presence in the wilderness is a barrier to what you seek; and as others come after, the corruption spreads. The effect of standing where no one has stood before is rather lost if you find a cigarette end at your feet. And as for 'preserving' nature, in the national parks, MacCannell writes, of the American experience:

> The great parks are not nature in any original sense. They are marked-off, interpreted, museumized nature. The park is supposed to be a reminder of what nature would be like if nature still existed. . . . By restricting 'authentic' or 'historic' nature to parks, we assert our right to destroy everything that is not protected by the Park Act.[92]

And Rodman argues that the idea of 'conserving' wilderness is in practice bound to be self-defeating:

> Either what is preserved is so successfully segregated from the impact of human civilization that it cannot be experienced in a participatory way, or else it is transformed by the impact of human overuse due to its very scarcity, or else human use is methodically rationed as part of a deliberate plan of 'wilderness management' that eliminates much of the quality of the authentic wilderness experience.[93]

If you *have* preserved wilderness, you cannot *know* that you have; if you know enough to wonder whether you have, you know enough to know that you haven't. As long as nature is thought of as 'other', separated from a humanity that relates to it externally through domination or propitiation, this paradox is unavoidable. When McKibben mourns what he calls the 'end of nature', nature as 'the separate and wild province, the world apart from man to which he adapted, under whose rules he was born and died', he argues that this is because 'We have deprived nature of its independence, and that is fatal to its meaning . . . without it there is nothing but us.'[94] Yet this very view, in its nostalgia for a lost other, is very much a modern product, a result of the dualism between the observing, consuming self, inevitably immersed in a 'nature' from which it is nevertheless deeply separated.

What is clear is that present dilemmas result from a deep-seated historical process. Increasingly, as Giddens suggests, 'the natural world has become in large part a "created environment"'.[95] This has resulted from the modern orientation towards both exploiting and shaping nature; from this point of view, the Romantic emphasis on the transforming power of imaginative subjectivity is not necessarily so far from the technological emphasis on manipulation and control. And Nash observes that 'As a rule the nations that have wilderness do not want it, and those that want it do not have it.' Or, in slightly different terms, 'the civilizing process which imperils wild nature is precisely that which creates the need for it';[96] as civilization destroys nature in practice, so its beauty and spiritual value are increasingly celebrated, thus propelling us further towards the 're-creation' of nature to which Giddens refers. Modernity has provided us with a construction of nature as an exploitable resource – an aspect of modernity as project – but by that very fact has also made possible the search for an experience of nature as sublime, as a source of reinvigoration, even as a basis for a critique of modernity itself. Hence the environmentalism that goes back deep into the history of modern attitudes to nature.[97] And the twofold modern paradox of nature is that our proclaimed transcendence of nature goes hand in hand with a powerful sense of nature as 'the natural', as a grounding, a bedrock, a legitimation for whatever is taken to be the 'natural order' of social and gender relations; while this very search to control nature, or to experience 'real' nature, leads increasingly to its recreation as 'unreal', as simulation.[98]

Notes

1   R. Nelson, *Make Prayers to the Raven: A Koyukon View of the Northern Forest* (Chicago University Press, 1983), p. 14.
2   P. Duerr, *Dreamtime* (Blackwell, 1985), p. 90.
3   C. Manes, 'Nature and Silence', *Environmental Ethics* (1993), 15:1, p. 349.
4   Cited in B. Devall and G. Sessions (eds.) *Deep Ecology* (Peregrine Smith, 1985), p. 110.
5   A. Naess, *Inquiry* (1979), 22:1–2.
6   A. Leopold, *Sand County Almanac* (Oxford University Press, 1968).
7   T. Todorov, *The Conquest of America* (Harper, 1985), pp. 97, 251.
8   E. Evans, *The Criminal Prosecution and Capital Punishment of Animals* (Faber and Faber, 1987), pp. 10–11, 49.

9   J. Berger, 'Animal World', *New Society* (25 November 1971), p. 1042. See also W. B. Ashworth Jr, 'Emblematic Natural History of the Renaissance', in N. Jardine et al. (eds.) *Cultures of Natural History* (Cambridge University Press, 1996).

10 K. Thomas, *Man and the Natural World* (Penguin, 1984), pp. 98, 35.

11 H. Ritvo, *The Animal Estate: The English and Other Creatures in the Victorian Age* (Penguin, 1987), p. 2.

12 K. Tester, *Animals and Society* (Routledge, 1991), p. 63.

13 E. Leach, 'Anthropological Aspects of Language: Animal Categories and Verbal Abuse', in E. Lenneberg (ed.) *New Directions in the Study of Language* (MIT Press, 1966).

14 R. Willis, *Man and Beast* (Paladin, 1975), p. 9. See also R. Williams, *The Country and the City* (Hogarth, 1985), ch. 3.

15 W. Connolly, *Political Theory and Modernity* (Blackwell, 1989), p. 2.

16 On the contemporary revival of some of these ideas, see R. Coward, *The Whole Truth* (Faber and Faber, 1990) and V. Plumwood, *Feminism and the Mastery of Nature* (Routledge, 1993).

17 C. Merchant, *The Death of Nature: Women, Ecology and the Scientific Revolution* (Wildwood, 1980), p. 3.

18 J. E. Lovelock, *Gaia* (Oxford University Press, 1982).

19 Merchant, *Death of Nature*, p. 9.

20 L. Schiebinger, 'Feminine Icons: The Face of Early Modern Science', *Critical Inquiry* (1988), 14, pp. 663, 675, 686.

21 L. Jordanova, *Sexual Visions: Images of Gender in Science and Medicine* (Harvester Wheatsheaf, 1989), p. 94.

22 B. Turner, *Medical Power and Social Knowledge* (Sage, 1987), p. 35.

23 Cited in M. Foucault, *The Birth of the Clinic* (Tavistock, 1973), p. 146.

24 Cited in F. Capra, *The Turning Point: Science, Society and the Rising Culture* (Fontana, 1983), p. 95.

25 F. Jacob, *The Logic of Living Systems: A History of Heredity* (Allen Lane, 1970), pp. 28, 34, 83, 85. See also D. Outram, 'New Spaces in Natural History', in Jardine, *Cultures*, p. 249, and C. Lawrence, 'Disciplining Disease', in D. P. Miller and P. H. Reill (eds.) *Visions of Empire: Voyages, Botany and Representations of Nature* (Cambridge University Press, 1996), p. 81.

26 M. Foucault, *The Order of Things* (Tavistock, 1970), p. 273.

27 Jacob, *Living Systems*, p. 91.

28 P. Slack, *The Impact of Plague in Tudor and Stuart England* (Routledge, 1985), pp. 28–9; and B. Turner, *The Body and Society* (Blackwell, 1984), p. 83.

29 S. Osherson and L. Amarasingham, 'The Machine Metaphor in Medicine', in E. Mishler et al., *Social Contexts of Health, Illness and Patient Care* (Cambridge University Press, 1981), pp. 224, 225.

30 G. L. Engel, 'The Need for a New Medical Model', *Science* (1977), 196. See also Capra, *Turning Point*, chs. 2, 4.

31 G. Barker-Benfield, 'The Spermatic Economy: a Nineteenth-Century View of Sexuality', in M. Gordon (ed.) *The American Family in Social-Historical Perspective* (St Martin's Press, 1978), p. 380.

32 Merchant, *Death of Nature*, p. 214.

33 S. Clark, 'The Scientific Status of Demonology', in B. Vickers (ed.) *Occult and Scientific Mentalities in the Renaissance* (Cambridge University Press, 1984), pp. 355, 360, 356, and passim.

34 R. Rorty, *Philosophy and the Mirror of Nature* (Blackwell, 1980), p. 248.

35 Merchant, *Death of Nature*, p. 214.

36 B. Easlea, *Science and Sexual Oppression* (Weidenfeld and Nicolson, 1981), p. 72.

37 Merchant, *Death of Nature*, p. 193.

38 Cited in ibid., p. 171.

39 J. Starobinski, *The Invention of Liberty* (Rizzoli, 1987), pp. 115, 116.

40 C. Taylor, *Sources of the Self* (Cambridge University Press, 1992), p. 149.

41 K. Eder, 'The Cultural Code of Modernity and the Problem of Nature: A Critique of the Naturalistic Notion of Progress', in J. Alexander and P. Sztompka (eds.) *Rethinking Progress* (Unwin Hyman, 1990), pp. 67–8.

42 E. F. Schumacher, *Small is Beautiful* (Abacus, 1974), pp. 10–11.

43 Thomas, *Natural World*, pp. 257, 258.

44 J. Passmore, *Man's Responsibility for Nature* (Duckworth, 1980), p. 36; and M. Hoyles, *The Story of Gardening* (Journeyman, 1991), p. 32.

45 C. Mukerji, 'Reading and Writing with Nature: Social Claims and the French Formal Garden', *Theory and Society* (1990), 19, p. 653.

46 A. Bermingham, *Landscape and Ideology: The English Rustic Tradition 1740–1860* (Thames and Hudson, 1987), pp. 11–12.

47 M. L. Pratt, *Imperial Eyes: Travel Writing and Transculturation* (Routledge, 1992), pp. 52, 51–2, 38. See also B. Latour, *Science in Action: How to Follow Scientists and Engineers through Society* (Open University Press, 1987), pp. 215–57, and D. Arnold, *The Problem of Nature: Environment, Culture and European Expansion* (Blackwell, 1996), ch. 8.

48 D. Haraway, *Primate Visions* (Routledge, 1989), p. 9.

49 Cited in Starobinski, *Invention*, p. 116.

50 Thomas, *Natural World*, p. 226.

51 Hoyles, *Gardening*, pp. 95, 151.

52 Bermingham, *Landscape*, p. 1. See also M. and J. Bloch, 'Women and the Dialectics of Nature in 18th Century French Thought', in C. MacCormack and M. Strathern (eds.) *Nature, Culture and Gender* (Cambridge University Press, 1980).

53 Starobinski, *Invention*, p. 195.

54 Passmore, *Man's Responsibility*, pp. 36, 212.

55 Williams, *Country and City*, p. 127.

56 Mukerji, 'Reading and Writing', p. 670.

57 S. Pugh, *Garden–Nature–Language* (Manchester University Press, 1988), pp. 102, 4, 1, 4, 125.

58 Bermingham, *Landscape*, p. 9.

59 Starobinski, *Invention*, pp. 195, 196.

60 C. Thacker, *The History of Gardens* (Croom Helm, 1979), p. 201.

61 Starobinski, *Invention*, p. 180.

62 Thacker, *History*, p. 191.

63 Pugh, *Garden*, p. 58.

64 Bermingham, *Landscape*, pp. 13–14, 14.

65 Pugh, *Garden*, pp. 34, 6, based on Williams, *Country and City*, p. 120.

66 Pugh, *Garden*, p. 127.

67 J. D. Hunt, *Gardens and the Picturesque* (MIT Press, 1992), p. 263.

68 J. Williamson, *Decoding Advertisements* (Marion Boyars, 1978), ch. 5; and, on gender aspects, N. Fiddes, *Meat: A Natural Symbol* (Routledge, 1991), pp. 152–62; and Coward, *Whole Truth*, chs. 1, 6.

69 Bermingham, *Landscape*, p. 171.

70 Hunt, *Gardens*, pp. 286–7.

71 Thomas, *Natural World*, p. 266.

72 N. Green, *The Spectacle of Nature: Landscape and Bourgeois Culture in 19th Century France* (Routledge, 1989), pp. 83, 87.

73 Hunt, *Gardens*, p. 287.

74 M. Andrews, *The Search for the Picturesque* (Scolar Press, 1989), p. 45.

75 Starobinski, *Invention*, p. 160.

76 Thomas, *Natural World*, p. 260.

77 R. Nash, *Wilderness and the American Mind* (Yale University Press, 1982), p. 4.

78 Cited in P. Marshall, *Nature's Web* (Simon and Schuster, 1992), p. 273.

79 Taylor, *Sources*, p. 297. See also the discussion of the sublime in my *Exploring the Modern: Patterns of Western Culture and Civilization* (Blackwell, 1998), ch. 7.

80 Starobinski, *Invention*, p. 147.

81 Cited in Marshall, *Nature's Web*, p. 270.

82 S. Hampshire, *Two Theories of Morality* (Oxford University Press, 1977), pp. 92–3.

83 Taylor, *Sources*, p. 300.

84 Cited in Marshall, *Nature's Web*, p. 268.

85 Cited in Taylor, *Sources*, p. 301. See also C. Thacker, *The Wildness Pleases: The Origins of Romanticism* (St Martin's Press, 1983).

86 Coward, *Whole Truth*, pp. 16, 39.

87 Green, *Spectacle of Nature*, pp. 138, 133, 71, 95.

88 Nash, *Wilderness*, p. xi, passim, and p. 342.

89 J. M. MacKenzie, *The Empire of Nature: Hunting, Conservation and British Imperialism* (Manchester University Press, 1988), pp. 20, 26.

90 Nash, *Wilderness*, p. 270, and passim.

91 J. R. Short, *Imagined Country* (Routledge, 1991), p. 194.

92 D. MacCannell, *Empty Meeting Grounds: The Tourist Papers* (Routledge, 1992), p. 115.

93 J. Rodman, 'The Liberation of Nature?', *Inquiry* (1977), 20:1, p. 111.

94 B. McKibben, *The End of Nature* (Penguin, 1990), pp. 44, 54.

95 A. Giddens, *Modernity and Self-Identity* (Polity, 1991), p. 144. See also K. Eder, *The Social Construction of Nature* (Sage, 1996), for a general account.

96 Nash, *Wilderness*, p. 343.

97 R. H. Grove, *Green Imperialism: Colonial Expansion, Tropical Island Edens and the Origins of Environmentalism, 1600–1860* (Cambridge University Press, 1995), pp. 1–3, 475.

98 See the further discussion of the implications of this in my *Exploring the Modern*, ch. 12.

7 Forbidden Desires:

Taboo, Transgression and Sexuality

The Delights of Defilement

In his *London Labour*, published in the 1860s, Henry Mayhew reveals a deep, ambivalent fascination with the world of rats, and with the professional rat-catchers who plied their trade not only in tenements and sewers, but in 'respectable' homes, where rats were particularly feared. While unpleasant and dangerous – both carriers and symbols of pollution – rats clearly cast their spell over this chronicler of the times. Mayhew describes rat-baiting rituals, involving dogs and bets, and tells, in awed tones, of an old man who gets down on all fours and kills rats with his teeth, inspiring both admiration and dread in his audience. Rat-handlers would pluck out 'the big 'uns' from a seething mass of wild sewer rats, or remove their clothes to detach half a dozen that were attached to their legs. All this was performed as a spectacle for the amusement of the public; and the horror, it seems, was integral to the pleasure. Finally, we are presented with the figure of Jack Black, 'the Queen's Ratcatcher', easily recognized as he trundled around London, going about his business, and providing entertainment for the public. In addition to his distinctive 'vestments',

> He had a cart . . . with rats painted on the panels, and at the tailboard, where he stood lecturing, he had a kind of stage rigged up, on which were cages filled with rats, and pills, and poison packages. . . . In front of his array of painted rat icons, Black holds up the fiercest varieties of wild sewer rats in his bare hands, then puts them to death with poison before transfixed crowds of spectators.[1]

Something of a sexual frisson is suggested at times: 'I should faint . . . if a rat was to run up my breeches', says an old rat fancier,[2] and the salacious danger of such an event was made to seem all the more likely by the widespread assumption that rats were indeed highly libidinal creatures, driven by sex, consumed by rat passion. We are in the same world that could produce Freud's celebrated 'rat man', the patient tormented by a dream about the punishment supposedly meted out to 'a criminal in the East', in which rats had to escape from a container by gnawing through the prisoner's buttocks; and this dream was recounted, according to Freud, with an expression on the patient's face that revealed *'horror at pleasure of his own of which he himself was unaware'*.[3]

What is important is what these rats tell us about purity and dirt, and the attractions of defilement. Pointing to the social and cultural context, Stallybrass and White suggest that the rat 'furtively emerged from the city's underground conscience as the demonized Other'. But as it transgressed the boundaries that separated the city from the sewer, above from below, 'it was a source of fascination as well as horror'.[4] Herbert adds that 'Victorian uncleanness is at heart a *moral* category, and one of central importance in modern life'. In addition, filth carries power; dirt *contaminates*, it is not just distasteful. Thus 'dirt takes on its characteristically Victorian field force of moral evil and hysterical anxiety'; it 'seethes with life, radiating dangerous effluvia'.[5] But always there is the fascination that reveals attraction. . . .

Let us pursue this through a further exploration of the links between dirt and sexuality, hinted at above. Heath has referred to 'the peculiarly Victorian development of an investment of sexual pleasure in the *sensation* of class difference'.[6] This 'sensation' was a tabooed experience of proximity and distance, in which the very difference of status becomes the attraction; and that difference is inseparable from the interaction of purity and defilement, cleanliness and dirt. This is most familiar to us in the combination of risk and attraction that draws the 'respectable' middle-class man to the working-class woman, even the prostitute, in a love transaction in which defilement becomes the very engine of sexual desire itself.

Evidence of these sexual quadrilles is legion in the diaries, novels, even official reports, of the period. In one of the latter, from 1842, the lawyer Symons writes of the labouring conditions of pit girls:

> One of the most disgusting sights I have ever seen was that of young females, dressed like boys in trowsers, crawling on all fours, with belts round their waists, and chains passing between their legs . . . the chain . . . passing high up between the legs . . . had worn large holes in their trowsers, and any sight more disgustingly indecent or revolting can scarcely be imagined than these girls at work.

And he concludes, revealingly: 'No brothel can beat it.'[7] Referring to this, and other examples, Mort comments that 'this discourse eroticized the cultural distance between observer and observed. . . . Here was male sexuality constructed through the erotic mechanism of a voyeuristic gaze and the fetishization of cultural difference.'[8] The celebrated diaries of the 'respectable' Arthur Munby, detailing his relationship with Hannah Cullwick, a maidservant, suggest that Munby equated female dirt and degradation with female strength, eroticism and sexuality, so that an exaggeration of their status difference was crucial to the attraction; and it must be added that Hannah seems to have played her full part in these games, finding a variety of ways to emphasize her 'lowliness'. Davidoff comments on how a fascination with the 'alien, often forbidden but exciting' world of the servants is a commonplace of the time. In Hermann Hesse's *Demian* (1913), we are told of the attractions of working-class life to a middle-class boy, and the way this class contrast is coded in terms of light and dark, the light being 'the bourgeois world of parents, sisters, law and order', while the dark world, 'the world of his awakening sexual desires', inextricably draws him to the maid-servant.[9] Freud commented on this fateful separation of love and sexual desire, whereby the pure middle-class wife can become the object of her husband's love but it is the 'dirty' servant girl who is more likely to turn him on: 'where they love they do not desire and where they desire they cannot love'.[10]

It would be too easy to assume that these are just passing peculiarities of the Victorian sexual imagination, for the erotic power of dirt retains significance as a feature of the modern construction of the transgressive. Dirt represents pollution, the threat that one's boundaries will be defiled and hence violated, and that one will be corrupted or 'unclean' as a result; in all these respects, it could be said to represent both a threat to the 'civilizing process', and a manifestation of it. From this point of view, 'civilization' could be described as a mechanism for the production and proscription of increasing amounts of dirt, and this is particularly so in the home, the sacred arena of domesticity.

Housework itself is above all about the management and control of dirt, a process in which further dirt is produced and reproduced; in short, a ritual through which order and disorder feed off one another endlessly. Dirt represents a deadly threat at the heart of domesticity, and the figure who serves both to combat the threat and to symbolize it, constantly re-creating it, with all the ambiguous power of the role, has of course been the housewife. In her person she combines the contradictory attributes of matriarch and maidservant, purifier and polluter, menial because of her association with dirt, yet also powerful because of her role in vanquishing it and maintaining 'order'.

The gamut of possibilities opened up by all this is explored by Bernice Martin, who writes that

> Woman *is* the mistress of the household; she enshrines female dominance. Yet, at the same time, she is humiliated by having all the dirtiest, meanest and most degrading chores heaped upon her, and not even being paid for it. She *is* both power and pollution. . . . Woman habitually humiliates her menfolk by being in control of domestic order, but is, in turn, humiliated by the nature of the work that entails. Yet, that same work is one of the crucial sources of her power.[11]

Power, gender, humiliation: a potent mix. Humiliation, it should be remembered, was a theme of carnival, where it signified renewal through contact with the earth, the lowly. Cowan reminds us that 'Humiliation, then, is a process of decay and decomposition, of matter's feeling rotten. That which is dark and soiled in us, which decomposes and causes us to lose our composure, becomes fertilizing material, life-giving, vital.'[12] Humiliation can come through loss of power, but can also be a source of power; either way, it involves proximity to dirt. And Martin argues that while feminists are right to quarrel with inequalities in the public sphere, they have not explored the full implications of women's domestic power, embedded as it is not only in domestic gender politics but in the reproduction of gender roles and sexual identities. If dirt implies power, the woman who controls it also possesses, and symbolizes, that power; the man, in turn, may want to escape this power, control it, or submit to it. Here, the shift along the spectrum from 'normal' to 'transgressive' sexuality can be made very easily, with the woman's humiliating power being transformed into the humiliating gratification of the sexual masochist. What Freud described as the 'tendency to debase sex objects'[13] can as easily be debasement of self as of other, and either way becomes central to sadomasochist ritual. Martin refers to the activities of the clients of Cynthia Payne ('Madam Cyn') at her establishment in Streatham, giving us the singularly appropriate example of the 'slave' who derived satisfaction from being pelted with the contents of the vacuum cleaner. . . .

Summarizing these themes, Stallybrass and White write:

> The bourgeois subject continuously defined and redefined itself through the exclusion of what it marked out as 'low'. . . . Yet that very act of exclusion was constitutive of its identity. The low was internalized under the sign of negation and disgust. But disgust always bears the imprint of desire. These low domains, apparently expelled as 'Other', return as the object of nostalgia, longing and fascination.[14]

This reminds us of Julia Kristeva's discussion of 'abjection', of how this 'low other' can never really be lost from the self: the abject is 'something rejected from which one does not part'.[15] From rats to vacuum cleaners, dirt thus emerges as symbolically powerful, a resource for the transgressive imagination, linked to desire. We begin to see what the Marquis de Sade might have meant in claiming that 'the greatest pleasures are born of conquered repugnancies',[16] though the dimensions of this clearly require further exploration.

Sexuality and the Temptations of the Self

Rosalind Coward suggests, in her book *Female Desire*, that sexual excitement in our culture does seem to have very close links with transgression, with 'enjoying hidden sensations, bringing an underground stream to the surface'.[17] Indeed, it can be suggested that the links are so close that transgression enters into 'normal' sexuality itself, that it makes no sense to conceive of sexuality without this dimension. Although *ideologically* the category of the forbidden and prohibited is seen as totally separate, and sharply contrasted with the 'normal', actually there is an essential continuity. Taking up Foucault's claim that 'sexuality' is a distinctively modern mode of experiencing 'the sexual', and Bataille's work on the link between erotic pleasure and the breaking of taboos, I will argue that sexuality is distinctive in that it involves *violation*: violation of the boundaries of the body, of self and other.[18] This violation involves the transgression of important taken-for-granted assumptions of modern Western culture: of the body as a 'possession' of the individual; of self as 'master' of the body; of individual experience as autonomous and private. But, as we have seen, violation can also involve other boundaries between what are normally kept separate; boundaries of class, for example. Jessica Benjamin suggests that the modern obsession with body regulation and rational autonomy makes it difficult to achieve intimacy with others; the emphasis on boundaries promotes 'a sense of isolation and unreality', hence fantasies of violation represent an attempt to break out of this 'numbing encasement'.[19] Sex as violation testifies to the ultimate artificiality and impossibility of the boundaries so carefully erected between individuals, around bodies and selves, and promises delicious, albeit dangerous, delights in the very possibility of their subversion.

In the perspective of modernity, sex itself becomes quite centrally transgressive. After all, sex represents the *opposite* of mastery of the body: an irrational subordination *to* the body, an engulfment *by* the body. At one extreme, this, coupled with the traditional Christian distrust of the body as the seat of sin and temptation, can lead to a sense of sex itself as being the tabooed, the unspeakable, reaching its apogee in Victorian puritanism. Yet the opposite move is also opened up as a possibility: precisely *because* of this censorship, sex can be romanticized, seen as liberating; hence 'permissiveness'. Both of these are moves in the sexuality game, produced by the very construction of 'sexuality' as an autonomous domain of modern experience. In the one case, self-fulfilment is equated with self-control, the body a recalcitrant challenge to be mastered; in the other, fulfilment requires abdication of self-control in mastery *by* the body.

The early modern history of sex and transgression is useful for showing how the emergence of 'sexuality' involves a radical reconstruction of body/self experiences and the categories through which they are defined. In the case of 'homosexuality', Weeks and Dollimore have drawn our attention to the sense in which the distinctive conjunction of sexual, gender and personal attributes that constitute the connotations of the term 'homosexual', and make it a master signifier for a 'type of person', is a specific historical product.[20] The early modern category of 'sodomy' is in no sense a simple antecedent. Dollimore claims that

> Sodomy was associated with witches, demons, werewolves, basilisks, foreigners, and (of course) papists; and it apparently signified a wide range of practices including prostitution, under-age sex, coitus interruptus, and female transvestism. . . . Imaged in such terms, the sodomite indeed became the supreme instance of the demonized other. . . . Sodomy was not thought to originate in a pathological subjectivity (the modern pervert); rather, the sexual deviant was the vehicle of a confusion never only sexual. . . . As such the deviant was the point of entry into civilization for the unnatural, the aberrant, and the abhorrent, the wilderness of disorder which beleaguered all civilization.[21]

'Sodomy' was hence an umbrella category, representing the possibility of an undifferentiated deviance, not even primarily or exclusively sexual; it is only by the nineteenth century, with the construction of the distinct domain of 'sexuality', that a niche opens up for the 'homosexual' in the modern sense. As sexuality emerges on to the public stage, becoming constructed as an arena of public and political regulation, so we find the development of what Foucault calls 'discourses of sexuality', whereby a whole range of sexual practices – homosexuality, fetishism, and so on – become simultaneously *defined* and *proscribed*. Sexuality, hedged around with prohibitions that are also temptations, comes to occupy its position as the troubled and troubling 'truth of our being', as Foucault puts it, a crucial testing ground for our precarious sense of self; and if, as he adds, 'it is in the area of sex that we must search for the most secret and profound truths about the individual',[22] then we must expect these 'truths' to be frequently in conflict both with self-image and with the prescribed patterns of sexual and gender identities.

This can be elaborated by pointing out that modern attempts to found sexuality on gender and gender on (biological) sex, so that these domains become consistent and give each individual one subject position, are forever problematical. The 'truth' of the individual is not to be captured in some single homogeneous sexuality, for sexuality necessarily raises the question of fantasy and its role in the construction of the modern self; fantasy opens up desires and possibilities that reveal the inherently transgressive structure of modern individuality. Fantasy is crucial in the construction of the 'interior world' of emotion and desire, and sexuality – as the mode of pleasure-seeking that involves the violation of the boundaries of body, self and other – necessarily explores that world and the imaginative resources it opens up. Hence the instability of sexuality in the subject positions it offers for self-fulfilment, and its significance as a site of conflict and tension. The bedroom is not, after all, immune from panoptic surveillance,[23] and, through its own capacity for self-regulation, the self intermittently attempts to put its own house in order: guilt and insecurity can ensue if what goes on in the head and what goes on in the bed diverge too far, even though the very constitution of modern selfhood ensures that there is no necessary consistency between them at all.

The sources of modern sexuality are therefore threefold: the 'civilizing process', producing a sense of 'body' and 'self' as polarized and related through control; the 'panoptic gaze' and the construction of sexuality through regulation; and the 'interior world' of emotion and fantasy, with its potential for gratification through the exploration of the gaps opened up by the first dimension, and through evading, escaping or parodying the controls of the first and second. Out of this matrix, the possibilities and pleasures of modern transgression are born, centred on the destruction of the boundaries that separate, the exploration of an otherness that comes into being with our sense of self but by that very fact exists as promise, temptation and challenge. The further reaches of sexuality, though proscribed, thereby come to exercise a fascination for the modern mind: sexuality conceived as 'beyond good and evil, beyond love, beyond sanity; as a resource for ordeal and for breaking through the limits', as Susan Sontag puts it. This is clearly not the cosy liberal view of sex, in which sex, like freshly baked bread, is inherently wholesome and good for you, any problems simply being due to the silly guilt feelings and hangups that we get about it. She concludes with the reflection that

> Tamed as it may be, sexuality remains one of the demonic forces in human consciousness – pushing us at intervals close to taboo and dangerous desires, which range from the impulse to commit sudden arbitrary violence upon another person to the voluptuous yearning for the extinction of one's consciousness, for death itself. . . . Everyone has felt (at least in fantasy) the erotic glamour of physical cruelty and an erotic lure in things that are vile and repulsive.[24]

No doubt the boundaries that constitute forms of sexuality as particularly unacceptable have shifted over the modern period, and the picture is further complicated by the relation between proscription and visibility: some implicit taboos can be so strong that the object of the taboo disappears from social consciousness altogether. But two examples seem appropriate, at this point. First, sex reminds us of our irreducible baseness, our 'uncivilized' roots in nature, so it is all the more important that it be controlled, so as to distance ourselves from nature; and bestiality emerges as the unspeakable otherness that transgresses this boundary. We know animals have sex, we know we are animals, we know we have sex; but animal/human sex becomes unthinkably awful, 'dirty'. . . . And second, we see the process whereby our ambivalence about 'civilization', and a nostalgia for lost innocence, are projected on to children, so that the contemporary revival of the pre-Freudian myth of childhood purity, going hand in hand with continuous, repetitive media representations of sexualized under-age girls (and boys), increases both the potential for paedophilia and the guaranteed intensity of its denunciation. Thus do we frantically seek to protect children from the 'corruption' we simultaneously produce.

Censored Texts, Transgressive Images: The Pornographic Imagination

In practice, these issues have been most widely raised in the debates over pornography. In considering these, it helps to focus on pornography as a cultural and historical product, intimately associated with modernity. From this point of view, it can be said that pornography emerges as the always controversial and unacceptable face of the novel, partaking of the same privatization of experience that makes the novel possible. Indeed, from the beginnings of modern pornography in the mid-eighteenth century, through to the mid-nineteenth century, when it was becoming a major cultural industry, it would be reasonable to say that the novel's legitimacy rested in part on the projection of what were seen as inherent dangers and temptations of the novel on to pornography itself. Indeed, the modern category of 'pornography' emerges out of attempts to regulate and prescribe the reading of the 'lower classes', and of women; what might be given a limited tolerance, in private, among the elite, as 'erotica', was denounced as 'pornography' elsewhere.[25] It also emerges in a significant relationship with the camera. As early as 1859, Baudelaire observed that 'pornography is the major function of the new art of photography'.[26]

Pornography can thus be seen to present a challenge at several levels. It is positioned on an awkward boundary between reality and representation. So, suggests Falk, 'in terms of (sexual) conduct pornography is not real enough while in terms of representation it is too real'. It has an 'anti-representational logic',[27] violating the aesthetic norm of distance: it couples arousal on screen or in text with arousal in the spectator or reader, attempting to obliterate the gap between them, thereby scandalously subverting the canons of pure representation. The object 'forces' itself on us, insisting we surrender to it, transforming representation into stimulus, and hence it can as easily precipitate disgust. What forces us to turn on also turns us off. And one can observe here that right across the spectrum of sexuality one object, in particular, has largely retained its status as conventionally unrepresentable: the erect penis. Hence this becomes the key element in proscribed films or novels ('hard-core'). Here, erection and ejaculation are central, as the key signifiers of pleasure: and not just male pleasure, but female, too, since the latter always presents the risk of fakery, a serious problem when, after all, the whole appeal lies in immediacy, presence, the claim to unmediated authenticity. But if the erect penis carries the message of masculine power and status, even standing in for female pleasure, it also subverts this mystique of masculinity, its identification with purposeful self-control, reducing it to the unpredictable fallibilities of mere flesh; the taboo on its representation is therefore heavily over-determined.[28]

These representational challenges imply social challenges also. Since reading pornography is even more private and solitary than reading the novel, and since pornography represents the fantasy of obliterating the distinction between depicting and doing, to read is to be sexually aroused; hence the public existence of pornography (books, pictures, films), as discourse and depiction geared to arousal, violates norms of decorum and public order. Pornography threatens the body-centred rules of shame and modesty so central to the modern civilization of selfhood, and implicitly challenges the public/private distinction itself. This has enforced what has been, right from the start, the intimate and constitutive relationship between pornography and censorship. By driving a wedge into the continuum, by proscribing some texts and images as threatening perversions, thereby instituting the 'normal' and the 'tabooed' as a dichotomy, the censor both constitutes pornography as a social category and guarantees that the category is invested with all the exotic fascination of the forbidden. The censor becomes the pornographer's best friend.

In summarizing the implications of this in the nineteenth century, Marcus also gives us clues to the content of pornography:

> For every warning against masturbation issued by the official voice of culture, another work of pornography was published; for every cautionary statement against

the harmful effects of sexual excess uttered by medical men, pornography represented copulation *in excelsis*, endless orgies, infinite daisy chains of inexhaustibility ... for every effort made by the official culture to minimize the importance of sexuality, pornography cried out – or whispered – that it was the only thing in the world of any importance at all.[29]

The central fantasy of pornography is that of the absolute power of sex, sex as a force that overcomes all constraints and boundaries. Ann Snitow claims that

> Like a lot of far more respectable twentieth-century art, pornography is not about personality but about the explosion of the boundaries of the self. It is a fantasy of an extreme state in which all social constraints are overwhelmed by a flood of sexual energy. . . . Class, age, custom – all are deliciously sacrificed, dissolved by sex.[30]

Everything in pornography is either sexualized, or reduced to the status of a context in which such sexualization occurs; and sex is presented as a remorseless drive that overcomes all taboos, partly because they *are* taboos, and also as a mode of exploring aspects of consciousness and experience that are normally out of bounds. Pornography points to the lawless in sex, the fascination with prohibition and with boundary-crossing as such. Snitow adds:

> In pornography, the joys of passivity, of helpless abandon, of response without responsibility are all endlessly repeated, savored, minutely described. Again this is a fantasy often dismissed with the pejorative 'masochistic' as if passivity were in no way a pleasant or a natural condition.[31]

Really, this is perfectly continuous with the common everyday view of sex as a powerful force that can sweep all before it; and this in turn reflects the modern construction of 'the sexual' as an autonomous dimension that embodies the power of alienated nature in and over our lives. But if this engulfment by the body represents transgression, this threat can be experienced as fearful, producing a response of anger or loathing, as well as being alluring or tempting; and doubtless these responses are not mutually exclusive.

The sense in which the conventional and the pornographic can shade into one another also comes out in discussions of women's romantic fiction; Snitow goes so far as to characterize it as 'pornography for women'. Certainly there are themes in this fiction that are clearly transgressive. The Black Lace imprint – erotic fiction 'by women for women' – sold 400,000 copies of the initial titles in 1993, and there is an explicit focus in many of these on sadomasochistic fantasy. The best-selling blockbuster romances of the 1970s and 1980s often included violence, and sexual violence, in the formula. Heather, the heroine of *The Flame and the Flower*, the first big seller of this kind, is raped, very early on in the story; beatings and enforced prostitution follow. This clearly raises the whole difficult issue of the place of rape and sexual violence in fantasy, representation and life.

It is crucial to remember that fantasy is an imaginative transformation of reality; it derives its power from its very deviation from reality, its transgressive potential, its ability to envisage and image the tabooed. As Soble puts it, 'that which repeats reality leave little room for the fantasizing that generates sexual arousal'.[32] This is how fantasy serves desire. A first point that can be made about rape fantasies, then, is that it is *not* the case that women necessarily identify with the victim, the passive position, in rape fantasies; they can identify with the active role as well, or with elements of both at once. Nor, of course, is it only women who have such fantasies; it is clear that men do, too, and as *victims*, either of women or of other men.

Anyone who identifies with the victim position in a rape fantasy can set up the scene as he or she wants it, even though the fantasy itself points to the delights of *lack* of control, of being 'taken', of not having to be responsible. It is 'designer rape', as it were. (The reality, of course, would be totally different.) The way rape fantasies embody this element of unreality can be seen from Helen Hazen's candid description of her own rape fantasy in her book *Rape, Romance and the Feminine Imagination*; in her case, the despicable act in question is carried out by a marquis. . . . But if it is a sexist travesty to say that a woman who fantasizes rape straightforwardly wants to be raped, it is also true that, as Hazen argues,

> The world of imagination is a different matter, and there is plentiful evidence that both rape and a broader spectrum of seemingly unpleasant impositions are forced onto women by themselves for the sheer sake of enjoyment. . . . Rape occurs in the woman's world of illusion; it is a ritual of love that exists in fantasy: a man says to a woman that she is so desirable that he will defy all the rules of honor and decency in order to have her.[33]

This seems to be consistent with Radway's finding that violence was only acceptable to readers of romantic fiction when traced to the passion or jealousy of the hero: if he is 'mad with desire', rape reflects *her* power over *him*.[34] And Hazen points to another element here:

> That there is a desire in everyone for adversity, so that the conquest may be sweeter, is an idea easy to grasp. . . . Men continue to read stories of courage in the adversity of overcoming evil, and women continue to read about courage in the adversity of overcoming men. . . . Everyone knows that men yearn for trouble, but no one is quite so ready to admit that women do exactly the same, that they hope for their own adversity and its eventual destruction with as much energy as do their partners.[35]

If the contemplation of danger can be significant in sex, Kate Ellis adds that, in a more explicitly pornographic context, the very *detachment* of the images can facilitate that contemplation. The symbols that make danger erotic can, in their normal context, be very repellent (e.g. instruments of torture); yet there can be a wish to 'encounter these terrifying realities at as close a range as possible under highly controlled circumstances'.[36] It is partly on these grounds that some feminists, while critical of the sexist bias of most mass-produced pornography, nevertheless want to argue that in principle pornography can have something to offer both sexes. Thus Snitow comments that pornography 'can depict thrilling (as opposed to threatening) danger. Though some of its manic quality comes from women-hating, some seems propelled by fear and joy about breaking the always uncertain boundaries of flesh and personality.'[37] And Paula Webster adds that 'Whatever its limitations, pornography does demystify a number of sexual practices that have been taboo for women.'[38]

Feminist critics of pornography have of course been right to draw attention to a widespread anger and hostility in pornographic images themselves, frequently directed against women, but the interpretation of this is controversial. For a start, Ellis points to an element of mutuality in this configuration:

> If men project, in fantasy, a culturally tabooed part of themselves onto women in order to simultaneously indulge and control it, why should we assume that women do not project onto men the aggression that is as culturally taboo for women as is the feminine side of men . . . perhaps men act *for* them as well as against them when they convert anger into domination.[39]

It is as though if men can demonstrate anger, women can only do so vicariously, through men. In this cultural configuration, aggressors and victims are both yoked together, in mutual dependence. But how does one account for the significance of this 'revenge motif', anyway? Whether or not there are any transhistorical elements present, one must surely point to the way 'virtue', civility and the restraint of the body have been central to the development of the modern self, and the fateful conjunction of these with gender stereotypes, as explored in a previous chapter. Pornography therefore involves fantasy revenge against the carriers of virtue, the triumph of the body over its controllers, and thereby reveals the deep structure of mind, body and gender in the organization of the self. Connolly argues that

> If the libertine was one who affirmed sins of the flesh over the call of spirituality, the pornographer invokes reason and power to degrade women who accept their terms of existence as social bearers of virtue and responsibility. The tightening and intensification of the affirmative standards of reason, order, virtue and responsibility creates a subordinate space within which pornography attacks this entire network of ordering concepts. Pornography is the perverse revenge bodies take against the modern terms of their spiritual organization. . . . Pornography comes into its own when this new regime of bodily regulation is challenged by textual acts of revenge against these standards of reason, virtue, interests and health.[40]

This passage occurs in a discussion of the work of the Marquis de Sade – the 'old monster', as Angela Carter dubs him, not without affection – and it seems appropriate to consider him here, since his two heroines, Justine and Juliette, exemplify the two pole positions just elaborated. Justine is dedicated to virtue, so she is doomed to a life of suffering; everyone she turns to betrays her, tortures her, degrades her. Yet she has persuaded herself that so long as she protests her innocence, and, above all, derives no pleasure from the violations perpetrated on her body, then her virtue remains intact. Indeed, one feels she protests too much; she clearly *needs* the degradations she suffers. How else can she prove her virtue? She is, as Carter delightfully puts it, 'the persecuted maiden whose virginity is perpetually refreshed by rape'.[41]

Very different is Justine's wicked sister, Juliette. She learns of the uselessness of virtue very early on. For her, the law is corrupt, and reason teaches not the upholding of the law, but its subversion; not morality, but self-interest. A pleasure shared is a pleasure halved; one achieves selfhood not through masochistic subordination, but through the domination and exploitation of others. So Juliette uses her body as a source of power; her orgies and the violation of her victims become ways in which she can assert her own autonomy, shore up the boundaries of her selfhood.

Actually, it is Mother who is the ultimate figure of revenge in Sadeian fantasy. It is she, after all, who teaches us civilization (and its discontents); as Nancy Friday writes, she is 'the source of love, but also of inhibition, constraint and guilt'.[42] Connolly points out that for Sade, it is she who

> representing nurturance, moral restraint and the acceptance of authority, is a bearer of arbitrary power concealed under the cloak of objective virtue. . . . Pornography emerges as pleasurable acts of degradation and cruelty perpetrated upon those who willingly or innocently embody standards which degrade themselves.[43]

Mother's embodiment of power and virtue is her undoing for Sade, just as we saw that for the masochist – male or female – it is the source of her superiority. For the former, she has to be made into dirt; for the latter, she presides as the conqueror of dirt. It is all part of the imaginative universe of the modern self, twin extremes of desire.

Pleasure, Pain and Paradox

In further pursuing the dynamics of transgressive sexuality, it is necessary to explore the links between pleasure and gratification, and between emotion and sensation. It soon becomes apparent that there are paradoxes here: how and why is it that pleasure can apparently be derived from the deferment of gratification, or indeed from what appears to be the opposite of pleasure, namely pain? This is doubtless more evident in the wilder shores of sex, for example in the so-called 'suspense factor' in masochism, the endless repetition of sexual ritual that defers release, postpones gratification into the indefinite distance; but Marcus also sees this as a feature of pornography, since 'although pornography is obsessed with the idea of pleasure, of infinite pleasure, the idea of gratification, of an end to pleasure (pleasure being here an endless experience of retentiveness, without release) cannot develop'.[44] As we have seen, however, these issues are also raised in an everyday context: adversity can have its attractions, and daydreams and romantic fiction alike can testify to the pleasures of deferment and the pleasures in 'unpleasure'.

To develop this, we need to draw on Campbell's analysis of the links between pleasure, imagination and emotion in the development of modern hedonism, as discussed elsewhere.[45] 'Pleasure' emerges as a feeling, an attitude, capable of cultivation, under the control of the self. Campbell refers to this as a crucial 'shift of primary concern from sensations to emotions', for it is 'only through the medium of the latter that powerful and prolonged stimulation can be combined with any significant degree of autonomous control, something which arises directly from the fact that an emotion links mental images with physical stimuli'.[46] Emotions could thereby emerge as pleasurable in themselves; and right from the early phase of this development, in the seventeenth and eighteenth centuries, it is clear that this can be true, in principle, of *any* emotion. Sadness and pain, for example, could be cultivated as pleasurable; the enjoyment of suffering, a kind of 'emotional masochism', became almost a recommended perversion of puritanism. The grief felt at loss or adversity could be indulged as an exquisite reminder of one's sensitivity and refinement. And this can lead us to the insight that the anticipation, or even deferment, of pleasure, could itself come to be experienced as pleasurable, and cultivated as such:

> in addition to the pleasures derived from the anticipatory drama of fulfilment, there are those associated with the present, deprivation-induced, 'suffering' which create the enjoyable discomforts of desire. The intimate association between pleasure and pain, which is so characteristic of modern hedonism, derives in large measure from this source.[47]

Gratification becomes a distraction from pleasure; it is the 'suffering' of desire that is really the pleasurable state. And indeed, 'since the so-called "negative" emotions often evoke stronger feelings than the others, they actually provide a greater potential for pleasure'. Such emotions can provoke physiological changes that provide *greater* pleasure than can be derived from 'mere sensory stimuli' alone. A crucial amendment is needed here: that the two *together*, the emotion and the sensory stimuli, can provide an even greater potential for pleasure. This move is suggested by Campbell's own observation that the hedonist seeks stimulating experiences and 'pain itself can be an extremely effective means of providing just such pleasurable excitation'.[48] It is surely this conjunction of emotion and sensation, the cultivation of self in and through the engulfment of the body, that marks the shift from pre-modern sex to modern sexuality, with all the potential that the latter opens up for the paradoxes and tensions of the pursuit of pleasure.

We can make sense of that characteristic figure of the early modern imagination, the libertine, as a point of transition between old and new, traditional and modern hedonism. For him, living at a time when the body has been invested with all the attractions of taboo, vice becomes the royal road to pleasure; but happiness is defined as exclusively a matter of the senses. As Simone de Beauvoir puts it:

> Sensation is the only measure of reality, and if virtue arouses no sensations, it is because it has no real basis. . . . Virtue, chimerical and imaginary, encloses us in a

world of appearances; whereas vice's intimate link with the flesh guarantees its genuineness.[49]

But ultimately, the libertine's own pleasures are chimerical: defined purely in sensory terms, the pleasures pall; the act of vice is devoid of feeling and emotion, and excitement gives way to a strained and strange detachment, even as one engages in it. In this sense, Sade is the last of the libertines as much as the first of the modern transgressives; yet he is the latter as well, since the link between sensation on the one hand, and self-involvement through the emotions on the other, is strongly hinted at in his work. Thus, Simone de Beauvoir points out that, in Sade, 'What the torturer demands is that, alternating between refusal and sub-mission, whether rebelling or consenting, the victim recognize, in any case, that his destiny is the freedom of the tyrant.'[50] This dialectic of recognition and control is inherently a mutual involvement, making possible the systematic linkage between emotions (fear, anger, joy), sensations, and sense of self. With Sade (and Hegel) we are, in this sense, into the universe of the modern self and modern sexuality, wherein sex becomes both sensation and symbol, action and self-revelation.

The outcome is that if pleasure can be invested in, and derived from, antici-pation and deferment, this can easily become pleasure from struggle, overcoming obstacles, breaking taboos. Desire may desire itself, seek to enjoy the experience of the gap between itself and the object of desire. The pursuit becomes more pleasurable than the goal, and the latter may be more pleasurable in the anticipa-tion than in the achievement. One could even say that non-pleasure can be pleasurable, if one takes this as a definition of 'pain', either in the literal sense or in the sense of struggle to overcome adversity. If pain is non-pleasure, it provides all the greater potential for pleasure, since the extra investment of effort and energy involved in overcoming our normal fear of it means that even greater plea-sure can be attained if the process succeeds. Conversely, if pleasure is non-pain, it generates a potential for pain; the pleasure of gratification can decrease the appeal of such gratification in the future, fuelling a search for new partners, new activities.

Self-discipline and release, taboo and transgression, again can be seen to feed off each other. Tabooed physical sensations or experiences can provoke horror or disgust; yet we know that these reactions are not 'natural', they are the acquired inheritance of the 'civilization' of the body. This process produces the taboos which in turn become a source of fascination; after all, if the taboo can be over-come, then, as already stated, the activity might be all the more pleasurable. If, *because* of the taboo, the experience becomes tempting, then the pleasure of the experience can have the thrill of breaking the taboo added to it. The taboo can thus become essential to the gratification. Thus Bataille:

> If we observe the taboo, if we submit to it, we are no longer conscious of it. But in the act of violating it we feel the anguish of mind without which the taboo could not exist: that is the experience of sin. That experience leads to the completed trans-

gression . . . which, in maintaining the prohibition, maintains it in order to benefit by it.[51]

Let us see whether further insight can be gained by considering that most challenging of sexual scenarios, namely sadomasochism.

The Erotics of Power

Freud himself described sadism and masochism as 'the most common and most significant of all the perversions';[52] and Jessica Benjamin brings this nearer home by referring to 'the strange union of rationality and violence that is made in the secret heart of our culture', as a result of which 'the fantasy of erotic domination permeates all sexual imagery'.[53] If sex is indeed 'the truth of our being', then the suggestion is that perhaps sadomasochism is 'the truth of our sex'. I will firstly summarize this thesis, and then consider various aspects in more depth.

The everyday assumption is that sadomasochism (S/M) is basically about the infliction and suffering of pain, but this element can be overemphasized; Pat Califia remarks that 'the basic dynamic of sexual S/M is an eroticised, consensual exchange of power – not violence or pain'.[54] The claim is that this is essentially an extension of the power dynamic present in any sexual relationship: Alice Echols argues that 'We should acknowledge that power inheres in sexuality rather than assume that power simply withers away in egalitarian relationships.'[55] Modern sexuality does, after all, involve engulfment by the body, or mastery of it: it implies masochistic subordination to a power that can only be propitiated through being indulged. If sexual desire is projected on to the other, we can see how the subordination to sex can be subordination to the other; and an attempt to deny or control this subordination can become desire for power over the other. Furthermore, given the 'civilizing process', the power of the body is experienced as *shameful*, and this experience can be sexualized and harnessed through being 'acted out'. As Ashcroft remarks, 'The fantasy of surrender allows that space for "uncivilised" yet essential energies to burn.'[56] And in abdicating self-mastery, masochism also reinforces the links between pain and pleasure discussed previously, as Lyn Cowan explains:

> Masochism is a fantasy of being struck, not stroked, of pleasure in feeling bad, of abdicating control. Masochism acknowledges other gods, gods with radically different perspectives on suffering. . . . Pain and pleasure go inextricably together, defying logic, rationality, reasonableness – all those things we equate with sanity.[57]

It is the body itself, that source of power and taboo, that carries the symbolism through which release is sought. 'Give me a way to be so in my body that I don't have to think', writes one practitioner; or, 'I am my body, nothing more.'[58] But of course the body carries a crucial emotional charge. A participant writes that 'In S/M sex each seeks to open as much as possible, to push past the limits, to turn each other on so intensely that there is no possibility but full satisfaction, not just physically but emotionally as well.'[59] To *be* one's body is deeply humiliating, in a world where control of the body is fundamental; the body becomes the carrier not just of powerlessness, but of degradation, the intense emotion of shame. And this shame is experienced as a fundamental flaw in identity, powerfully reinforced by the sense of inadequacy of the self to the burdens of aspiration laid on it by the culture of modern individualism. Cowan explains that such shame 'implies the non-existence of antidote, the permanence of deficiency, the impossibility of rectification (and also of justification). It is the sense of permanent lack, insufficiency, inadequacy which cannot be made right or corrected by any activity of the ego.'[60] Shame is the cost of the autonomy of the self, exacted by the other; a reinforcement of its inadequacy, even a celebration of it, through its eroticization.

But along with shame, there is also guilt, the transgression of the Law; masochism as eternal punishment. The crime is never so serious that it is a capital offence, but neither is it so minor that it can ever be expiated: 'Souls that are not good enough for heaven and not bad enough for hell must keep riding till doomsday.'[61] In this Kafkaesque world, 'The Law . . . defines a realm of transgression where one is already guilty',[62] as Deleuze puts it; and the masochist knows how to turn this to good effect, while subtly ridiculing the Law that has been transgressed:

> the masochist . . . stands guilt on its head by making punishment into a condition that makes possible the forbidden pleasure. . . . The essence of masochistic humor lies in this, that the very law which forbids the satisfaction of a desire under threat of subsequent punishment is converted into one which demands the punishment first and then orders that the satisfaction of the desire should necessarily follow upon the punishment.[63]

If submission to the Law is a condition of freedom, then masochism could be said both to celebrate this, and to parody it. And Anne McClintock points out that these inversions are also present when S/M practitioners are on trial in a law court: 'If the sex trial isolates "deviant" sexual *pleasure* for *punishment*, commercial S/M is the dialectical twin of the trial, organising the *punishment* of sexual deviance for *pleasure*.'[64]

And the embodiment of the Law, the figure of the dominant other? Sadomasochism is an extreme form of the dialectic of self and other put into place by the modern revolution of selfhood, wherein the internalization of the panoptic gaze results in a split in the self, an oscillation in the subject, simultaneously self and other: the masochist becomes 'Both the victim and the executioner; the spectator thrilled at his own execution', in Brown's words.[65] The 'other' thus constructed embodies the vicarious sense of difference, and this can easily encompass gender, as Cowan points out:

> That which is unknown and 'other' exerts a strong pull. It is not surprising that one should seek dominance in the opposite sex, precisely because it is opposite. As the

Other, the Unknown, the opposite cannot be readily identified with; thus to experience it, one must reach a place of submission to it.[66]

Distance plus inversion can be particularly potent; given that masculinity is conventionally coded as 'dominant', the male masochist submitting to a woman can thereby eroticize this sense of maximum difference. Kaja Silverman writes that the male masochist

> acts out in an insistent and exaggerated way the basic conditions of cultural subjectivity, conditions that are normally disavowed; he loudly proclaims that his meaning comes to him from the Other, prostrates himself before the Gaze even as he solicits it, exhibits his castration for all to see, and revels in the sacrificial basis of the social contract. The male masochist magnifies the losses and divisions upon which cultural identity is based, refusing to be . . . recompensed.[67]

Once again, we see that sexual fantasy and its enactment frequently do *not* conform to orthodox gender roles and expectations. When interviewed, prostitutes invariably say that many more of their clients want to enact scenarios of female domination than the reverse.[68] If the poet Sylvia Plath tells us that 'every woman adores a Fascist', Elizabeth Wilson replies that, for her part, she does not 'drool at the word "discipline" or melt at the sight of a jackboot'.[69] These issues became highly controversial within the feminist movement in the 1980s, with the emergence, in both the USA and the UK, of a lively and flourishing lesbian sadomasochist subculture, with women playing both dominant and submissive roles.[70] The controversy is hardly surprising: if feminism, from this point of view, can be seen as a critique of modern sexuality as male-dominated and oppressive, then lesbian sadomasochism emerges as its mocking face, the feminist carnivalesque, incorporating the language and ritual of domination and submission into its own practices, thereby becoming both a parody of the critique, and of its target. . . .

As a summary and exemplification of these themes, let us consider Pauline Réage's celebrated pornographic novel *The Story of O*. O's search for self-transcendence through suffering is presented as a pilgrimage, a quest with semi-religious undertones. Here, sexual fulfilment goes hand in hand with self-destruction; the self must be totally subordinated to the will of another, and this subordination is both symbolized, and furthered, by ever-intensified degradation. The self seeks the extinction, the dissolution, of its own boundaries, total engulfment by the other. O welcomes pain because it is precisely a violation of her separateness, her autonomy. On this, Benjamin claims that the body stands for 'discontinuity, individuality and life', and that consequently 'the violation of the body in erotic violation breaks the taboo between life and death and breaks through our discontinuity from the other'.[71]

Benjamin's insightful discussion builds on Bataille's ideas in suggesting that eroticism is above all the exploration of taboo, and that the ultimate taboo is that separating life and death: in Bataille's words, eroticism is 'assenting to life up to

the point of death'.[72] Life means discontinuity, autonomy; eroticism is the attempt
to break out of this separation and isolation, a drive towards unity and continuity that must ultimately mean death, though it represents also the promise of liberation and transcendence through sexual fusion. This is, after all, the poet's idea
of sexual ecstasy as '*le petit mort*'. Masochistic guilt thus emerges as the price paid
by the separate, individualized, 'rational' self. The latent violence is emphasized
in Christian's claim that, for Bataille, eroticism 'exorcises death by ritual sacrifice,
by acting it out. . . . Erotic activity does not so much transform as unmask the
murder behind.'[73]

O is indeed frequently subjected to whipping, and more can now be said on
the significance of pain in these rituals. Pain permits a transcendence of self and
body, simultaneously mental, emotional and physical, yet in paradoxical ways. The
transcendence of body occurs through an intensified experience of embodiment;
and the escape from self is simultaneously a mode of self-inscription and self-
constitution. Through pain, body and self are assimilated; indeed, self becomes
body, becomes object, subject to the other's control. Self as body and as object
becomes *merely* object. Simone de Beauvoir suggests that

> The world of the masochist is a magical one, and that is why he is almost always a
> fetishist. Objects, such as shoes, furs and whips, are charged with emanations which
> have the power to change him into a thing, and that is precisely what he wants.[74]

The pain itself operates as a mediation between the surface of the body and its
interiority, its role in constructing the subject. The surface of the body can be
marked through the lacerations of the whip, and these marks constitute a kind of
language, a discourse of servitude; one is reminded of the torture machine in
Kafka's story *In the Penal Settlement*, where the sentence of the court is inscribed
on the victim's body through the 'writing' of the needles on the harrow of the
machine. . . . Silverman observes that

> The whipping of O serves a very precise and important signifying function (more
> so, it should be noted, than penetration, which leaves behind only temporary traces):
> it constitutes her body as 'readable' through a system of writing. . . . It is no exag-
> geration to say that her body is constituted through the regimen to which it is sub-
> jected – that it is the consequence of a specific discursive operation.[75]

When O is told that she is to be whipped every day, it is pointed out that 'this is
less for our pleasure than for your enlightenment';[76] we are still in the universe of
rational education and the panoptic gaze. Silverman spells out the consequences:

> It is in fact by means of the constant violation of her body that O comes to have
> whatever interiority she ever enjoys. . . . O's 'soul' is nothing other than a psychic
> registration of the power relations by means of which her body has been mapped
> and defined. . . . The 'case' of O shows as clearly as the Panopticon that the subject
> can be made to oppress herself by internalizing the external structure within which
> her body is organized, and that this oppression can have a terrifying relentlessness.[77]

With her 'soul' is created O's sense of herself as 'guilty'. The masochist must always be worthy of his or her punishment (and always is); guilt must be constantly produced and reproduced. 'New levels of resistance must be found, so that she can be vanquished anew.'[78] It is as though O has to retrace, through the inscription of pain on her body and the simultaneously emergent sense of self, the whole 'hidden history' of modernity, whereby the internalized cruelty of 'self-discipline' and what Miller calls 'the paradoxical convergence of pleasure and pain that characterizes it' contribute to understanding 'the pleasure that many men have clearly learned to feel in taking pains to rule themselves'.[79] With O, however, the self-discipline is projected outward, and we find a distinctively sacrificial aspect of modern transgression: the person in control, the bringer of 'enlightenment', necessarily maintains his or her boundaries – thereby upholding the sovereignty of reason and control for both – by accepting limits to violence even as it is perpetrated; and it is the victim who carries – again, for both of them – the risks of the confrontation with death.

In effect, we once again encounter *Homo clausus*,[80] and Benjamin's attempt to trace out the implications of the sense of separateness and unreality provide an appropriate conclusion:

> The Western rational world view emphasizes . . . boundaries over continuity, polarity and opposition over mutuality and interdependence. . . . If the sense of boundary is established by physical, bodily separation, then sexual and physical violence (if not in reality, then in fantasy) are experienced as ways of breaking the boundary. The fantasy, as well as the playing out of rational violence, does offer a controlled form of transcendence, the promise of the real thing.[81]

If we ask what the expression 'acting out' means here, we will find that this, too, turns out to have significant wider implications.

Enacting Fantasy, Transgressing Reality

Susan Farr claims that 'while the essence of punishment play is eroticism, the structure of it is pure theater'.[82] This claim is expanded by Susan Sontag as follows:

> To be involved in sadomasochism is to take part in a sexual theater, a staging of sexuality. Regulars of sadomasochistic sex are expert costumers and choreographers as well as performers, in a drama that is all the more exciting because it is forbidden to ordinary people.

As enacted fantasy, it is 'the rehearsal of enslavement'.[83] The stage props, the uniform, convey a sense that power is being not just eroticized, but aestheticized as well. And the raw material of these enacted fantasies frequently draws on a very real twentieth-century horror, which again gives a clue to the affront that all this gives to the conventional liberal viewpoint, namely Fascism. The aesthetics and politics of Fascism are grist to the mills of the sadomasochist imagination. For Sontag, 'Fascist art glorifies surrender, it exalts mindlessness, it glamorizes death', and she reminds us that Hitler regarded leadership as a kind of sexual mastery of the masses, whereby 'the leader makes the crowd come'. Translated into sexual fantasy and its ritual enactment, this is powerful imagery: domination and enslavement become a form of theatre, 'a form of gratification that is both violent and indirect, very mental'.[84] And as McClintock graphically puts it, S/M is 'the theatrical organization of *social risk*'.[85]

In effect, then, this is a masque, and the participants are masked; the mask, literal or metaphorical, both protects identity and shapes it all the more intensely, allowing for powerful emotional investment, although only after overcoming an initial blocking. This blocking effect, preventing release, builds up the emotional pressure, thereby ensuring, through prolonging the agony of tension, that the release will be all the greater. As pointed out elsewhere, in a discussion of theatricality,[86] there may be a sense in which the eighteenth-century capacity to 'lose' the self in what may strike us as highly artificial, stylized clothes and behaviour, might actually have enhanced the capacity to experience one's feelings, through projecting them and crystallizing them in public, ritual form. In this latter-day theatricality, in which the modern potential for emotional intensity is coupled with the eighteenth-century creation of identity as role-play, all in the context of a private and tabooed world, we find the creation of a powerful 'ritual space':

> What is clear is that by 'acting out' the participants create a highly charged and highly personal alter-identity, that is neither themselves nor not-themselves. . . . It is a direct communion between two 'Others'. . . . It is a private, hermetic world. . . . A world where nothing is quite what it seems, where the boundary between dreams and reality flickers momentarily out of focus and allows a new per-spective to take form.[87]

'Neither themselves nor not-themselves': in putting one's identity on the line, as it were, one puts it on the boundary. This again reveals identity as enactment, mediating between polar opposites: not just self and other, but also 'reality' and 'fantasy', as these categories have been constructed in modernity. The realm of 'enacted fantasy' thereby interrogates any rigid reality/illusion dichotomy, while asserting the claims of theatricality as a powerful mode of being in the world.

This enables us to return to the issue of desire and consent, raised briefly in connection with rape fantasies. We can now see that when it is said that the person who occupies the submissive position in a rape fantasy does not 'really' want to be raped, and that masochistic submission is 'unreal', since in each case it is the 'victim' who writes the script and runs the show, these claims are both true, in a crucial sense, yet false as well. In the case of masochistic submission, the claim that the 'unreality' of the scene is necessary to its being pleasurable is criticized by Cowan as follows:

The fallacy in this idea is that if there is only an illusion of force, there is only an illusion of humiliation. In short, humiliation is regarded as unreal because fantasy is regarded as unreal. This attitude could only occur in a culture in which people say, 'It's only a fantasy.' It fails to understand the vitality and importance of fantasy in human life. It also misses the important fact that most masochists suffer humiliation at having masochistic fantasies at all. . . . The shame *at* masochism is the shame *of* masochism; the feeling of having it forced upon one, being subject to it, having little control over its forms, and none at all over its visitation. It is the same sort of shame one feels in being subject to uncontrollable instinctual needs and physiological responses. . . . The need for humiliation, the primary *necessity to experience primal shame*, is itself a humiliating recognition of need.[88]

So although it is correct to stress the *consensual* element in these fantasy enactments, there is also a sense in which the notion of consent is *subverted*. After all, if the turn on is surrender to power, or its exercise, then an emphasis on the consensual element would negate the fantasy. Hence the appeal of 'going to the limit', the point at which consent threatens to turn into its opposite. Enacted fantasy is on a knife-edge between fantasy and reality, and subverts the clarity of the distinction between them: enacted fantasy has – or is – its own 'reality', after all.

This theatre, then, exists on the borderlines between consent and non-consent, in which the former is pushed up to the point of the latter, and the latter is experienced *in* the former. And there is, after all, another sense in which 'consent' is subverted: we can recall here the repetitive, compulsive aspect of S/M. Acting is acting out; resolution is endlessly deferred; we are reminded again of the fetishistic compulsiveness of many of our other rituals, including the most apparently 'rational' aspects of work, housework, everyday routine. . . .[89] All in all, sado-masochistic sex becomes transgressive at all levels: consent and non-consent, fantasy and reality, self and other, autonomy and dependence, masculine and feminine. Overall, argues McClintock, in her insightful account:

> The outrage of consensual S/M is multiple. It publicly exposes the possibility that manhood is not *naturally* synonymous with mastery, nor femininity with passivity. Social identity becomes commutable, and the boundaries of gender and class open to invention and transfiguration. . . .
>
> S/M publicly performs the failure of the Enlightenment idea of individual autonomy, staging the dynamics of power and interdependency for personal pleasure.[90]

Thus S/M 'plays social power backward, visibly and outrageously staging hierarchy, difference and power, the irrationality, ecstasy, or alienation of the body, placing these ideas at the center of Western reason'.[91] And, as we have seen, it is transgression with humour: it not only transgresses the categories, it ridicules them; and it reminds us, in its very extremism, of the way sexuality itself both exemplifies and questions these taken-for-granted assumptions of modern life. Most fundamentally, transgressive sexuality is an offence against the 'real', the modern structure of reality and illusion; it is an ontological 'crime', before it is a moral one.

Notes

1   Cited in C. Herbert, 'Rat Worship and Taboo in Mayhew's London', *Representations* (1988), 23, p. 21.
2   Cited in ibid., p. 18.
3   S. Freud, *Case Histories II* (Penguin, 1979), p. 48 (original emphasis).
4   P. Stallybrass and A. White, *The Politics and Poetics of Transgression* (Methuen, 1986), p. 144.
5   Herbert, 'Rat Worship', pp. 10, 8, 10.
6   S. Heath, *The Sexual Fix* (Macmillan, 1982), p. 12.
7   Cited in F. Mort, *Dangerous Sexualities: Medico-moral Politics in England Since 1830* (Routledge, 1987), p. 49.
8   Mort, *Dangerous Sexualities*, p. 49.
9   L. Davidoff, 'Class and Gender in Victorian England', in J. Newton (ed.) *Sex and Class in Women's History* (Routledge, 1983), p. 26. See also the extended discussion in A. McClintock, *Imperial Leather: Race, Gender and Sexuality in the Imperial Contest* (Routledge, 1995), ch. 3.
10 S. Freud, *On Sexuality* (Penguin, 1977), p. 251.
11 B. Martin, '"Mother Wouldn't Like It!": Housework as Magic', *Theory, Culture and Society* (1984), 2:2, p. 33. See also A. McClintock, 'Maid to Order: Commercial S/M and Gender Power', in P. C. and R. Gibson (eds.) *Dirty Looks: Women, Pornography, Power* (British Film Institute, 1993), pp. 212–17.
12 L. Cowan, *Masochism* (Spring Publications, 1982), p. 36.
13 Freud, *On Sexuality*, pp. 247–60.
14 Stallybrass and White, *Politics and Poetics*, p. 191.
15 J. Kristeva, *Powers of Horror: An Essay on Abjection* (California University Press, 1982), p. 4.
16 Cited in Cowan, *Masochism*, p. 47.
17 R. Coward, *Female Desire* (Paladin, 1984), p. 97.
18 See M. Foucault, *History of Sexuality*, Vol. 1, *Introduction* (Penguin, 1979) and G. Bataille, *Eroticism* (Marion Boyars, 1987).
19 J. Benjamin, 'Master and Slave: The Fantasy of Erotic Domination', in A. Snitow (ed.) *Desire: The Politics of Sexuality* (Virago, 1984), p. 293.
20 See J. Weeks, *Sex, Politics and Society* (Longman, 1981), ch. 6, and J. Dollimore, *Sexual Dissidence* (Oxford University Press, 1991).
21 Dollimore, *Sexual Dissidence*, pp. 238–9.
22 M. Foucault, Preface to *Herculine Barbin* (Harvester, 1980), p. x.
23 On panopticism as a form of social control mapped on to self-control through the development of surveillance systems in the prison, school, and so on, see M. Foucault, *Discipline and Punish* (Peregrine, 1979), and my *Exploring the Modern: Patterns of Western Culture and Civilization* (Blackwell, 1998), ch. 2.
24 S. Sontag, 'The Pornographic Imagination', in *A Susan Sontag Reader* (Penguin, 1982), pp. 221–2.
25 L. Hunt, 'Obscenity and the Origins of Modernity', in L. Hunt (ed.) *The Invention of Pornography* (Zone Books, 1994) and W. Kendrick, *The Secret Museum: Pornography in Modern Culture* (Viking, 1987).
26 Cited in P. Falk, 'The Representation of Presence: Outlining the Anti-Aesthetics of Pornography', *Theory, Culture and Society* (1993), 10:2, p. 20.

27 Falk, 'Representation', pp. 1, 2.

28 Falk, 'Representation', pp. 17–19, 33–4. See also M. Simpson, *Male Impersonators* (Cassell, 1994), p. 187.

29 S. Marcus, *The Other Victorians* (Basic Books, 1964), pp. 283–4.

30 A. Snitow, 'Mass Market Romance', in Snitow, *Desire*, p. 269.

31 Ibid., pp. 268–9.

32 A. Soble, *Pornography* (Yale University Press, 1986), p. 88.

33 H. Hazen, *Endless Rapture: Rape, Romance and the Female Imagination* (Scribner's, 1983), pp. 17, 8. See also B. Sichtermann, *Femininity: The Politics of the Personal* (Polity, 1986), ch. 3.

34 J. Radway, *Reading the Romance* (Verso, 1987), pp. 75, 141–4. And see H. Taylor, *Scarlett's Women* (Virago, 1989), suggesting that some *Gone With the Wind* fans found the rape scene erotic.

35 Hazen, *Endless Rapture*, pp. 86, 18, 20.

36 K. Ellis, in *Caught Looking: Feminism, Pornography and Censorship* (Real Comet Press, Seattle, 1988), p. 46.

37 A. Snitow, in *Caught Looking*, p. 14.

38 P. Webster, 'Pornography and Pleasure', in *Caught Looking*, p. 35.

39 Ellis, in *Caught Looking*, p. 42. On women and dominance, see also McClintock, 'Maid to Order', p. 227, and C. Siegel, *Male Masochism* (Indiana University Press, 1995), ch. 4.

40 W. Connolly, *Political Theory and Modernity* (Blackwell, 1988), pp. 83–4.

41 A. Carter, *The Sadeian Woman* (Virago, 1979), p. 49.

42 N. Friday, *Men in Love* (Arrow, 1980), p. 8.

43 Connolly, *Political Theory*, pp. 80, 84.

44 Marcus, *Other Victorians*, p. 279.

45 See my *Exploring the Modern*, ch. 4.

46 C. Campbell, *The Romantic Ethic and the Spirit of Modern Consumerism* (Blackwell, 1987), p. 69.

47 Ibid., p. 88. See also pp. 214–15.

48 Ibid., pp. 70, 69, 64.

49 S. de Beauvoir, 'Must We Burn Sade?', in her *Marquis de Sade* (Calder, 1962), p. 69.

50 Ibid., p. 78.

51 Bataille, *Eroticism*, pp. 38–9.

52 Freud, *On Sexuality*, p. 70.

53 Benjamin, 'Master and Slave', p. 292.

54 P. Califia, cited in K. Harriss, *What Is This Big Fuss About Sadomasochism?* (Women's Studies Occasional Papers, University of Kent, 1988), p. 13. See also B. Thompson, *Sadomasochism* (Cassell, 1994), for extensive discussion.

55 A. Echols, cited in S. Jeffreys, *Anticlimax* (Women's Press, 1990), p. 285.

56 C. Ashcroft, 'Idols of Perversity', *Skin Two* (n.d.), 9, p. 60.

57 Cowan, *Masochism*, pp. 31, 48.

58 Cited in Harriss, *What Is This Big Fuss*, pp. 14, 15.

59 Juicy Lucy, in Samois, *Coming to Power* (Alyson, 1982), p. 31.

60 Cowan, *Masochism*, p. 82.

61 N. O. Brown, *Love's Body* (Vintage, 1966), p. 71.

62 G. Deleuze, 'Coldness and Cruelty', from G. Deleuze and L. von Sacher-Masoch, *Masochism* (Zone Books, 1989), pp. 83–4.

63 Ibid., pp. 89, 88.

64   McClintock, 'Maid to Order', p. 221.
65   Brown, *Love's Body*, p. 70.
66   Cowan, *Masochism*, p. 112.
67   K. Silverman, 'Masochism and Male Subjectivity', in *Camera Obscura* (1988), 17, p. 51.
68   McClintock, 'Maid to Order', p. 211.
69   S. Plath, 'Daddy', in *Ariel* (Faber, 1968), p. 55, and E. Wilson, 'A New Romanticism?', in E. Phillips (ed.) *The Left and the Erotic* (Lawrence and Wishart, 1983), p. 37.
70   See Samois, *Coming to Power*; Harriss, *What Is This Big Fuss*; *Caught Looking*; C. Vance (ed.) *Pleasure and Danger* (Routledge, 1984); and, for a hostile account, Jeffreys, *Anticlimax*.
71   Benjamin, 'Master and Slave', p. 296.
72   Bataille, *Eroticism*, p. 11.
73   D. Christian, 'Inversion and the Erotic: The Case of William Blake', in B. Babcock (ed.) *The Reversible World* (Cornell University Press, 1975), p. 123.
74   De Beauvoir, *Sade*, p. 38.
75   K. Silverman, '*Histoire d'O*: The Construction of a Female Subject', in Vance, *Pleasure and Danger*, pp. 337, 332.
76   Cited in Benjamin, 'Master and Slave', p. 298.
77   Silverman, '*Histoire d'O*', pp. 332, 339–40.
78   Benjamin, 'Master and Slave', p. 300.
79   J. Miller, 'Carnivals of Atrocity', *Political Theory* (1990), 18:3, p. 475.
80   See chapter 2, above, and references to Elias therein.
81   Benjamin, 'Master and Slave', pp. 306–7.
82   S. Farr, 'The Art of Discipline: Creating Erotic Dramas of Play and Power', in Samois, *Coming to Power*, p. 185. The theatricality also comes out in contributions to M. Thompson, *Leatherfolk* (Alyson, 1992).
83   S. Sontag, 'Fascinating Fascism', in *A Susan Sontag Reader*, pp. 324, 325.
84   Ibid., pp. 316, 323, 325.
85   McClintock, *Imperial Leather*, p. 148.
86   See my *Exploring the Modern*, ch. 1.
87   Introduction to T. Sellers, *The Correct Sadist* (Temple, 1990), p. v.
88   Cowan, *Masochism*, pp. 54–5. See also Kristeva, *Powers*, ch. 1.
89   McClintock, *Imperial Leather*, pp. 147, 169–73.
90   McClintock, 'Maid to Order', pp. 222, 224.
91   McClintock, *Imperial Leather*, p. 143.

Part III

Continuities, Challenges, Transformations

8 Blacks, Whites and Hybrids

'The Other' has traversed this book just as it has traversed modernity; but, for all that, it has remained crucially mute and undifferentiated. There is a risk that we could end up with a subtle apologia for the modern, reinforcing an ultimately unanalysed notion of a unitary other that is itself a product of the modern. And it could well be argued, against this, that we do have an experience of otherness that in fact breaks down this structure of opposites; or indeed that 'experience' is precisely this, the experience of an otherness that is subverted even as it is constituted, testifying to the ultimate impossibility of the modern strategy of self-coherence, the 'project of the self' and other aspects of the project of modernity, resting on this dualist logic of exclusion. Experience emerges as the terrain on which this structure breaks down – or, rather, reveals its tensions and incoherences. Identity is dynamic, ongoing, never reducible to stereotypes, however all-encompassing it may purport to be in its very existence *as* stereotype.

Although this has always been true, it may be that it is with the period of 'modernism' in the arts, and in culture generally, from the late nineteenth century through the first couple of decades of the twentieth, that it emerges most clearly – partly because it is a central theme, and challenge, of modernism itself. It is in the zone of representation, then, that the political, aesthetic and subjective correlates of these experiential dynamics are played out most dramatically. As was suggested in the earlier discussion of modernism and primitivism,[1] a sense that the 'other' escapes representational capture and closure, and, for this very reason, becomes a challenge that must be engaged with, is central to modernist exploration, and this is as true of 'popular culture' and cultural experience generally as it is of 'high art' – indeed, more true in some ways, as popular culture itself comes to play something of the role of 'other' to 'high art'.[2] And in exploring this, we will find that we have slipped imperceptibly on to the terrain of what is often characterized as 'postmodern', since it can usefully be viewed in the light of recent 'postcolonial' debates and the emergent 'discourse of hybridity' that seem to point beyond the dualist structure of modernity and otherness.

It is time to develop an example. Let us take Josephine Baker, dancer extraordinary, the poor girl from the slums of St Louis who took Europe by storm in the late 1920s, and who ultimately became, along with Coco Chanel and the great Hollywood stars, one of the popular female culture icons of the century. She remains difficult to 'place': she has been an inspiration to successive generations of African-Americans, yet – perhaps appropriately, as we shall see – she was herself only half-black, and can easily be presented as victim to the stereotypes that undoubtedly shaped and influenced her, and indeed her reception – by audiences that were, after all, mainly white – can hardly have been independent of existing primitivist and gender stereotypes, and may in some ways have reinforced them.

Dancing the Other: Josephine Baker in Paris

On 2 October 1925, at 8.30 in the evening, *La Revue Nègre* opened at the *Théâtre des Champs-Elysées* in Paris. Expectations were high: this was the era of 'negrophilia' in Paris, when 'black' was fashionable, jazz was all the rage, and the perceived vitality and dynamism of black culture were being assimilated into, and reinforcing, the impact of 'primitive' African and Polynesian artefacts on the modernist consciousness.[3] 'All Paris' was there: the artists Picabia and Léger, the dramatist Cocteau, the music-hall star Mistinguett, the composer Milhaud. The stage set, the backdrop, and the show itself, presented the myth of the Deep South, with other 'primitivist' imagery thrown in for good measure: 'black mammies', bales of cotton, steamboats, Harlem, the jungle. . . . But it was Baker who set the show alight. For one set, she entered on all fours, bottom raised, with her mouth painted in the old, exaggerated minstrel style, in tattered shirt and sawn-off pants, and danced as Paris had never seen before, using her whole body, strutting, jerking, gyrating, 'legs this way and that, eyes crossing, buttocks quivering, face grimacing'.[4] Later came versions of her *danse sauvage*: wearing only pink feathers in strategic places, accompanied by a black male dancer in a loincloth, she threw herself around, prowled, was lifted and embraced, in a parody of ballet; and she appeared in a jungle set, walking backwards on all fours, then slithering along and down the limb of a felled tree, this time doing her *danse sauvage* in the famous 'banana skirt' – the 'primitive' huntress with her girdle of phallic trophies (see plate 7). The 'wildness' of the act met an equally wild audience response; stardom was virtually instantaneous. By 1927 she was sitting for Picasso, was being dressed by the leading couturiers, the show was touring Europe, and a film was in the offing.

Dance itself has a problematical history in modernity. Subject to the discipline of the civilizing process, transformed from a rowdy, spontaneous folk culture into the more refined, rationalized and stylized spectacle of the middle classes, it had retained, through its inevitable reminder of our embodiment, a potent capacity to disturb.[5] Indeed, music and dance had long been associated both with 'primitive' peoples and with the primitiveness of carnival itself.[6] After all, dance, however disciplined, can hardly avoid reminding us of the disciplined otherness of the body itself; and with modernist dance, the discipline may have become less apparent than the celebration of that embodied otherness. And this body, as alien, becomes a site for the exploration of other aspects of the alien, above all the otherness of the primitive itself. Thus Burt can argue that 'alien bodies . . . were a central subject of modernist dance', thereby making dance performance and the dancing body into areas of contest within the culture. Baker's dancing body could, after all, be profoundly disturbing, yet 'uncannily familiar because of the extent to which individuals were themselves alienated by modernity', so that, overall, 'the alien dancing bodies of modernity embodied this uncanny strangeness that is inscribed within'.[7] Through Baker, the disruptions, dislocations and repressions of modernity could be danced through, or away; through her, the audience could be reminded of what it had always known, but had powerfully disavowed: the knowledge of carnal embodiment, the language of spontaneity and excess, the transgressive power of sexuality. Her dancing was decadent and dangerous, writes Kear, 'saturated with intoxication, frenzy, delirium and unbridled sensuality'.[8]

Part of her dangerous fascination was indeed this way in which the stereotypes of otherness were subtly displaced and superimposed. Like the South Sea islanders who so puzzled Bougainville and Cook, she was both innocence and depravity, nature before and after the Fall, the body as nature and the body as culture, as representation; actively sexual, hence masculine, yet intensely feminine. Nineteenth-century theories linking race and sex invariably racialized the sexual woman and sexualized the black woman, and both became coded as deviant, as threat.[9] Hence, as Andrea Stuart argues, the iconographies merged: 'Blacks and sexual women – both regarded as outsiders, primitive, lacking in refinement – found themselves irrevocably tainted by what was perceived as their unbridled sexuality.'[10] And by Baker's time, it was the showgirl, the dancer and the actress who had inherited this mantle, carrying it into popular culture itself, where Baker added the vital ingredient of colour, thereby embodying the merger of all these stereotyped iconographies in her own performance.

It is worth examining Baker's role in the context of its production; for 'produced' it certainly was. During rehearsals, the original gospel and blues revue was totally reworked, evolving from blues spirituality to exuberant 'savage' spectacle; precision chorus-line dancing was rejected as 'too European', and gradually the raw, exotic talent of Baker came more and more to the fore. Paul Colin, who designed the famous posters, drawing on the crude minstrel stereotypes of blackness, the fashion designer Paul Poiret, impresarios, publicists, all helped to shape her image, and the Helena Rubinstein make-up accentuated the lips and made her skin ochre-brown.[11] Not surprisingly, one or two critics saw her act as 'inauthentic', designed for a white audience.[12] Again, later photographic studies of her, in her years of fame, have been shown to have been modelled on 'primitive' masks and Gauguin statuettes.[13] So Kear can suggest that 'this relative freedom and opportunity accorded to black artists in Paris was contingent and acquired at the cost of another form of bondage – ambivalently placing themselves in the service of mirroring the projected images that Parisian culture offered them'.[14]

Yet these questions of interpretation remain difficult. Her dancing was undoubtedly rooted in African traditions, and the apparent 'improvization' itself – using rehearsed material – was an important element of these traditional skills.[15] Again, although Gilman has illuminated the bizarre history of the stereotypical (white, male) fantasies constructed around the allegedly protruding African buttocks,[16] it is also true that buttocks have a long history as eroticized objects in black sexual iconography.[17] Where the shaping of Baker's persona to fit the stereotypical expectations of a white audience ends, and the contribution of her own version of 'African culture' begins, is therefore difficult to tell; the 'shaping' may be a bringing-forth of what is already potentially 'there', as much as a reconstruction from outside. (Much the same, indeed, can be said of the production and reception of jazz.)

Nor should we forget the significance of the humour, the parody. For Burt, what we can see in her dance is neither the Charleston nor an 'authentic' African dance – although both are there – but a 'wonderfully inauthentic, misleading and mischievous performance. It is full of irony, multiple meanings and innuendo.'[18] It is concealment and revelation, disguise and display. For Wendy Martin, too, she succeeded by 'deploying conventions of the burlesque to create a *danse sauvage* that played with the paradigm of the black exotic in the context of white colonialism'.[19] And Baker herself comes over as very self-aware, with a clear view of the significance of her performance: 'It represents slavery, discrimination and liberation. All of it is there, in the songs and dances.'[20]

Her own performance nonetheless shifted markedly in the years of her stardom. In the early 1930s, the creature of the jungle had become 'Queen of the *Folies-Bergère*', the home of the choreographed display of the chorus girl and her undressed charms; she also embarked on a career as a sophisticated jazz singer. And again, the issues of interpretation are not straightforward. If she had indeed evolved from a parody savage to parody royalty, it is also true, as Kear points out, that the *Folies-Bergère* produced 'popular culture' for a mixed bourgeois crowd, including tourists; it was popular culture as spectacle. And he adds that, in her 1928 film, she played an innocent girl from the tropics who goes to Paris and is transformed into an elegant woman by means of beautiful clothes, thus becoming an allegory of her own life.[21] Yet this, too, is subtle; although, as Martin suggests, she created a legend in which she was 'the living embodiment of the civilizing process', true also is Martin's apparently contradictory claim, that 'By juxtaposing images of the jungle and the royal court, the carnal and the cerebral, she subverted the trope of cultural evolution and progress.'[22] Her sophisticated 'jungle' clothes, her elegant 'plumage', her pet leopard and pet panther, all operate as a juxtaposition of primitive/civilized that plays with them both, mocks them in their crude mutual exclusion even while acknowledging their historical influence in the shaping of the self-perception of the modern West. So Kear can claim that 'black artists cast as the "other" simultaneously mimed and mocked these differentials, enacting a kind of cleaving of subjectivity, achieving Parisianism through a form of masquerade'.[23] In this hybrid, ambiguous civilizing process, the otherness remains. . . .

So, Josephine Baker could dance and sing her way through, round and over the 'primitiveness' imposed by her cultural milieu; but could she cope so well with gender stereotyping? Martin suggests that she 'effectively deployed feminine artifice to create a stage persona that parodied yet depended on the display of masculine wealth', and her account tends to emphasize the dependence. It is as though the emancipation she achieved elsewhere exacted its price here. The 'plumage' is significant, carrying messages of decoration and the male gaze:

> Although she achieved the highest levels of ornamental femininity, she was a woman dependent on men for her status. . . . On the one hand, this conflation of female sexuality with feathered creatures creates an illusion of tamed eroticism; on the other, the female display of costly feathers confers status on the man who possesses her.[24]

Yet Martin herself refers to this as 'illusion'; in pandering to male fantasies, Baker nevertheless teases, tempts . . . and escapes. Once again, illusion and reality play off each other: the dependency of 'pandering to illusion' nevertheless masks the independence, the ambiguity of the masquerade. And this is, after all, the 1920s, the era of the 'New Woman', of self-conscious emancipation from what were increasingly seen as the repressions and restrictions of Victorian norms of femininity. For the emancipated young women of the age, it was the over-dressed Victorian woman who was the trophy on display, reduced to decorative use-lessness; Josephine Baker, on the other hand, with her daringly displayed, under-dressed body, was an icon of subversive mobility, both physical and social, the very embodiment of the freedoms they craved. For them, suggests Burt, 'the wild energy, disruption and frenzy of Baker's "savage" dances meant progress',[25] and a 'progress' which drew on, rather than distanced itself from, the 'primitive'.

Not that Baker's mobility could take her everywhere. In her films, for example, she could never overcome the miscegenation taboo. Yet even this could be transformed into a kind of triumph. Hybrid herself, she could present this as a virtue, indeed as the way forward: 'I think they must mix blood, otherwise the human race is bound to degenerate. Mixing blood is marvelous.'[26] This gloriously inverts the terms of nineteenth-century racial theory to explosive effect, with implications in both life and theory that are even now still to be fully explored. And it brings her modernism into focus. For Martin, she used 'the modernist concept of self-construction', as well as the modernist interest in primitivism, 'to create a series of dramatic personae that both parodied and challenged notions of essentialism in the areas of race, class, and gender'.[27] But Andrea Stuart can have the last word:

> Written on her delicious cinnamon-dipped body, post-war Paris read the entire history of colonialism, the intricacies of *fin-de-siècle* sexual politics, as well as the

evolution of modern art. She was a map of Africa, a jazz riff in motion, the New Woman all rolled into one. And the highly charged symbols of her nude body, her race, her role as popular performer, her irrepressible sexuality must have seemed to them either like the Second Coming or the advent of a latterday Sodom and Gomorrah: a beacon of the future – or the end of the world.[28]

The Black and White Minstrel Show

The presence of modernist artists in the audience at Josephine Baker's show, and the frequent descriptions of it – and her – as 'modernist', remind us that the music hall, the nightclub, the circus, the variety theatre, exhibitions and Wild West shows, were all a central part of the context and culture of modernism, a major influence on it, and a contribution to the challenge of its subject matter and innovations.[29] This has been obscured at times through a frequently unwitting complicity in high modernism's own self-assessment as a serious, separate, pure revolution in the arts that keeps its distance from the polluting superficialities of popular culture and everyday life. But this view of modernism in the arts has increasingly been undermined: we know that its boundaries are traversed and transgressed, its exclusions return to haunt it, its 'impurities' – social, cultural, aesthetic – are actually essential to its existence, to its vitality then, and its continued relevance now.[30] The decades around the turn of the century were a time when both popular culture and the phenomenon of 'crowds' were of great interest not only to artists and their audience, but to the authorities, precipitating both fear and fascination, a sense that this undisciplined, 'primitive' energy was both a threat, a temptation, and – possibly – a force to tame and use for conservative, nationalistic purposes. The threat to an exhausted civilization could also be the means to its renewal; it was the residue of the 'savage' in the popular that made it modern.[31]

The specific form of 'popular entertainment' that is particularly important for Baker's own background and reception is the tradition of 'blackface' minstrelsy. Elements of blackface – such as the exaggeration of the lips – and aspects of minstrel shows – such as the clowning – were overtly present in her *Revue Nègre* performances; and there are photos of Baker's early American acts, showing her in full blackface. This is itself intriguing: after all, blackface minstrelsy has been generally presented as a white tradition in American popular culture, and one which has been seen as inherently racist, as 'a white imitation of a black imitation of a contented slave',[32] or as in Gilroy's reference to 'the absurd representations of blackness offered by minstrelsy's pantomime dramatisation of white supremacy'.[33] Certainly there is much truth in this, but recent research has made the issue more complex, and more challenging. Lott floats the possibility that one could even present blackface minstrelsy as 'an African-American people's culture', and certainly as 'one of our first popular institutions'.[34] Even Pieterse, whose account is generally hostile, concedes that 'Even so, the entertainment ghetto on the margins of Atlantic culture has at times been refashioned into an avenue of protest, and the song and dance into a vehicle of emancipation.'[35] It can surely be agreed that without minstrelsy we would not have had major anti-racist tracts such as *Uncle Tom's Cabin* (1852) and *The Adventures of Huckleberry Finn* (1884) – not to mention a large proportion of the canon of American popular song, from Stephen Foster through to Irving Berlin, Jerome Kern and the Gershwins – just as, notoriously, these texts can reveal the presence of gratingly intense racial stereotypes. Overall, Lott's summary seems fair: 'At every turn blackface minstrelsy has seemed a form in which transgression and containment coexisted, in which improbably threatening or startlingly sympathetic racial meanings were simultaneously produced and dissolved.'[36]

Blackface minstrelsy has its origins in the maelstrom of ongoing cultural formation, reformation and deformation, the dynamics of class and race fusions, conflicts and controversies that characterized American urban centres, particularly northern cities such as New York, in the 1820s and 1830s, a period that witnessed the gradual emergence of a 'popular culture' based not only on the songs and dances of minstrelsy but also on theatrical melodrama and the 'dime novel', in contrast to an elite culture of opera, concert hall and conventional theatre. Minstrelsy itself was fundamentally eclectic. Rice, who published the 'original' Jim Crow lyrics in the early 1830s, is said to have picked them up from a black heard singing in the street; black lore was undoubtedly present, and so were British folk music and Irish jigs; the banjo itself seems to have had black sources, while the tambourine was Irish. There was something of a common lower-class culture in this period, not fundamentally divided by race, though of course tensions were always potentially present. Indeed, the basis for a common language and experience of exploitation can be seen in the emergence of the phrase 'wage slave': business bosses and plantation owners could thereby be assimilated, as targets. Nevertheless, the ambiguity of blackface minstrelsy was there from the start: it could easily be given a racist slant, and it actually emerged just as areas of black cultural autonomy in the theatre came under attack.[37]

The world of Rice and his audience was one of immediacy, burlesque, the pleasures of indulgence and the body; blackface signalled a 'letting go', articulating a spirit of licence central to working-class entertainment. Thus Lott can suggest that minstrelsy can indeed seem to be 'nothing less than a carnival space devoted precisely to excesses outgrown in the service of workday rationality',[38] a celebration of the physical, the childish, the non-rational, at a time when employers were tightening the screws of the civilizing process to produce a sober, 'moral' workforce. At the end of this book, then, we return to the beginning: for there can be little doubt of the significance of carnival here, and the tensions it both feeds on and engenders. Public masking in militia burlesques and Christmas street festivities, Lords of Misrule, black festivals and pageants, working-class 'Callithumpian' bands (masked in chimney soot and grease), causing revelry and disruption around the New Year, all featured.[39] And as the authorities gradually moved against most of these, minstrelsy emerged as a 'safer' form, resting on an audience/performer split, though often, in the early days, involving disruption: both safety valve and survival strategy, conservative yet harbinger of change, imparting clues as to how to make out in the puzzling diversity of the modern city.

Blackface itself seems to have been present from early on. The Boston Tea Party, that iconic founding event of American independence, featured howling 'Indians' and 'blacks', after all; and Morris dancers, popular in 1830s New York, were often in blackface. (So, in the English context, were the Luddite rioters of 1811–16.) Remembering the lessons of Bakhtin, we could say that, most fundamentally, blackface signals that 'what follows is not to be taken at (white)face value, but at burlesque value', as Cockrell puts it,[40] and the targets of this 'burlesque' could vary and, indeed, be multiple: conventional theatre, elite culture – and, indeed, blacks themselves. As Lott suggests, blackface could thus serve as 'an equivocal emblem of popular resistance'.[41] Blackface represented the force of hybridity, of change, of the new as transformation of the old: 'Pure blood lines mixed with the stuff of the Other, procreating the new', claims Cockrell, adding that masking in blackface was 'making a statement more about what you were not than about race'.[42] This is surely true, and remains a powerful clue to later instances of blackface; but of course minstrelsy is, nonetheless, crucially implicated in the construction of racial identity, a construction that entails what Lott describes as 'a simultaneous drawing up and crossing of racial boundaries', a carnivalizing of race in its very staging, hence making it potentially available for contradictory uses and interpretations, for sympathy, hostility and ambivalence. But always there remains this sense that the minstrel mask incorporates otherness, that self-identity is being exposed through the identity of the other, whatever disavowal or distancing may be involved here. It stands in for the hybridity of identity, the transgression of culture itself.

This staging of race, then, is also a revelation of a complex skein of contradictory emotions, of desire and aversion, envy and insult, fun and fear: 'less a sign of absolute white power and control than of panic, anxiety, terror and pleasure', as Lott puts it, adding that for a long period 'white people were so politically, historically, emotionally and sexually bound up with black culture that they directly mimicked and displayed it for their own enjoyment'.[43] At a more general level, Gilroy makes a claim with ramifications that spread in many directions:

> Nowhere were the masters, mistresses and other beneficiaries of slavery and colonialism sucessful in insulating their own lifeworlds absolutely from the disruptive and contaminating effects produced by those they dominated, but upon whom, perversely, they were dependent. The dominant groups were always themselves transformed by the historically novel conditions of their dominance.[44]

Unsurprisingly, it is in the arena of gender and sexual identification and desire that these tensions were most clearly revealed. Minstrelsy involved 'manly mimicry'[45] in which the blacked-up white man would swagger around in a way that might be bold, ludicrous or threatening, but was certainly 'cocksure', presenting a diversified object of desire or identification; in the former case, desire could be directed at the 'wench', also played by a man. . . . Indeed, it is often the gendered complexity of these productions – and the frequent misogyny – rather than the racism, that is more striking nowadays.

Present in these stagings of gender and race, overlapping with minstrelsy but also constituting an independent structure of feeling, is the strong strand of sentimentalism that is also, of course, an aspect of stereotypical constructs of femininity in the same period. Songs and narratives of sorrow, nostalgia and death are projected on to black victims, often passive, 'feminized' males; even when masquerading as attacks on slavery, one senses that not just sympathy, but aggression, hatred and disavowal can be present in complex ways in these stagings.[46] The tearful 'killing' of the plantation melodies can later slide towards the more obvious sadism of the kind Foster recognizes in some of the primitivist imagery of Picasso, suggesting that modernist identification or desire for the black man 'is also his erasure, and this erasure is crucial to primitivist fantasy'.[47] And sentimentalism is perfectly compatible with real killing, as later in the nineteenth century when 'Jim Crow' becomes part of the culture of lynching. . . .[48]

Yet even here, we must be careful: it can be argued that sentimentalism is an aspect of black culture itself, as well as of its stereotyping by whites; and certainly aspects of the latter are also absorbed, lived, transformed, in the experience of the former. It is through some such fusion that the culture of black spiritualism developed in the nineteenth century. With the 1870s tour of the Fisk University Jubilee Singers to the UK the perception of this spiritualism/sentimentalism nexus as central to black culture spread widely.[49] By 1925, Alain Locke, one of the leading lights of the Harlem Renaissance, could claim that 'The spirituals are really the most characteristic product of the race genius as yet in America';[50] yet this was the very year Josephine Baker, representing the renaissance of the more bawdy and burlesque tradition – coming out in the 'coon' songs of the 1890s – was taking Paris by storm, and whether the reshaping of her act *away* from 'negro spirituals' made it more or less 'authentic' is, as we have seen, difficult to say. . . . Nor can it be denied that aspects of the spiritualism/sentimentalism nexus leave her entirely unaffected: on screen, she was the woman who didn't get her man, condemned to 'success' with sadness.

This returns us to the uncertainties over 'blackface': if this is a staging of race, of black identity, who does the staging, and what (or where) is the identity? If it is undoubtedly the case, as we have seen, that some blacks 'blacked up', then whether this is mimicry or disguise of 'black identity', or mimicry *as* disguise, or whether, as with claims about the 'feminine masquerade', the identity *is* disguise, remains elusive.[51] In the 1840s, the escaped slave, Frederick Douglass, went to see a black troupe, Gavitt's Original Ethiopian Serenaders, and pointed to the 'exaggeration' in their act, indeed finding their 'representation' of blackness inadequate. Indeed, he seems to have been unsure as to their alleged blackness: they are 'said to be' entirely composed of blacks, he writes, adding that 'it may be so'.[52] And indeed, many early observers of (white) blackface thought they were indeed watching blacks: blackface performers were referred to as 'negroes' in the newspapers and song sheets. So the blackness of 'blackface' is a matter of theatricality, but leaves open the whole question of whether racial identity itself exists only in and through the performance of its staging. The famous 'Juba' (William Henry Lane), a black dancer who danced blackface, offered 'imitation' dances of all the leading (white) blackface dancers of the time, culminating in an 'imitation of himself' to show himself to be best of all, an act that deserves to be written out in full, in all its ironic, reflexive complexity: a black imitating a black imitating whites imitating blacks. . . . If this is all, as Lott suggests, the simultaneous production and subjection of blacks, it is also the production of whites, 'racially girding themselves by way of rituals that mirror rather than distance the Other, in which whites are touched by the blacks they would lampoon and are in the process told on, revealed'.[53] Doubling, disguise and disavowal are all present in this cauldron in which identity bubbles forth as relational, projected as theatrical in its essence. Perhaps it is appropriate, after all that, to learn that Douglass escaped slavery by posing as white, 'putting on whiteface', as it were.[54]

The implications of all this for black culture and identity have been explored by scholars working from within this culture, such as Henry Louis Gates, Houston Baker and Paul Gilroy. Since the Enlightenment, reason and writing, rationality and literacy, have been closely assimilated, and what was perceived as an absence of written history among blacks was therefore taken as a crucial index of their inferiority, contributing powerfully to nineteenth-century elaborations of racism. And illiteracy could be reproduced, through force: as early as 1740 a South Carolina statute prescribed punishment for any white who taught literacy to blacks.[55] Clearly this has implications for the forms of black culture, the structuring of black experience. First, we find an emphasis on what Gilroy calls 'expressive culture': 'In contradistinction to the Enlightenment assumption of a fundamental separation between art and life, these expressive forms reiterate the continuity of art and life', and 'art becomes the backbone of the slaves' political cultures and of their cultural history'.[56] This culture emphasizes music, song, dance, an oral culture with a distinctive relationship to the body. Writing and discursive reason are no longer so privileged as expressions of consciousness. But secondly, the challenge of writing and literacy had to be faced, producing a dilemma, for 'how can the black subject posit a full and sufficient self in a language in which blackness is a sign of absence?', as Gates asks. How can one use the language of oppression without further contributing to it? Gates suggests drawing on the black oral, vernacular tradition.[57] For Baker, there can in effect be two interlocking strategies here: a first infuses discursive reason with the distinctive emphases of black expressive culture, and a second attempts to master the language of oppression from within, subverting it through the subtle skills of irony and parody ('mastery of form').[58] In effect, the latter requires the skills of masking; we are in the sphere of blackface again, where mimicry, accommodation and resistance go hand in hand. Both strategies are ambivalent responses to the very modernity of the black experience, drawing on both modern and premodern elements, responses that embody a latent or overt critique of modernity through 'a deep sense of the complicity of racial terror with reason', as Gilroy argues, adding that 'Though they were unspeakable, these terrors were not inexpressible.'[59] And indeed, expressing them, in a distinctive language, is central to what Baker sees as the 'modernism' of the 'Harlem Renaissance' of the 1920s.[60] Finally, Gates has presented a view of the black literary tradition as providing a contestatory, ironic, multilayered 'trickster discourse', with multiple voices set off against each other.[61]

By the 1920s, of course, the minstrel tradition, and its social context, had evolved significantly from the early days. On the one hand, blackface minstrelsy became more slick and streamlined, more a visual spectacle, part of the 'entertainment industry', and had become more overtly patronizing and racist.[62] The decades since the Civil War, after all, had witnessed an intensification of racial division. At the same time, some blacks returned to the stage, and the (re)appropriation of minstrelsy in black culture continued.[63] By the 1890s, major urban centres, notably New York, revealed a thriving, fermenting black culture, in which eclecticism and promiscuity of forms was inherent – minstrelsy providing a key element – in a complexity of culture that would continue to the present day.

Let us now take *Alexander's Ragtime Band*, the Irving Berlin song of 1910, still in many ways the quintessential, and originating, hit song of American popular culture, a song that is itself about blacks, whites and cultural appropriation. In his insightful account, Dawidoff writes:

> The modern popular artist, as a broker in cultural transaction, a half breed, a 'white' black or 'black' white, and the signifier of sophisticated cosmopolitanism, is the subject of American popular songs. . . . That kind of person, the modern kind of person, a creation of American cultural brokerage, is the kind of person you have to be to sing the song. . . .
>
> The lyrics are meant to be 'coon-shouted', and they are clearly about how anyone can africanize him- or herself. . . . The singer is an agent of cultural appropriation, as we say, or hip and cool – a tour guide to the wrong side of town.

Here we encounter, again, the modernist interest in appropriating the 'primitive' so as to enhance one's sophistication, and such cultural appropriation could, of course, go with social exclusion; yet again, the black could be symbolically killed off, the death of appropriation doubled by the death of representation. The song removes the black person, and 'substitutes a presence that acts out a black person that whites can be'.[64] Nevertheless, to be hip, to be cool, requires at least *this* contact with the black; and the songs would not die out when, from the 1930s onwards, blacks would gradually force themselves more decisively into the spotlight, become stars and songwriters themselves; nor did they fail to be reappropriated, transformed, in turn, within the black community. And with the age of pop music, from the 1950s onwards, Gilroy's 'syncretic complexity of black expressive cultures' is also a complexity of white cultures, and an index of the difficulty of drawing clear boundaries anyway, which in turn makes it difficult to use notions of 'authenticity' here. After all, Detroit's Tamla Motown sound of the 1960s to 1980s, a fusion of forms from black and white cultural sources – sources that are themselves already 'contaminated' by each other – was often denounced for 'selling out', but was nonetheless praised by Nelson Mandela for giving solace while he was in prison on Robben Island.[65]

It is important to add that in criticizing the crude dualism of self/other cate-gories, however, and the reifying essentialism implied in their use, we do not need to have recourse to a vague, vapid relativism. If, as Hall suggests, we see 'the end of the innocent notion of the essential black subject',[66] nonetheless blacks *are* con-stituted as subjects – as are whites. Cultures *are* constituted as different, in all their fluidity and change; they are real enough, and decisive, sources of identity; but what matters is that they are never *as* real as they set themselves up to be; that we need to deconstruct their absolutist pretensions, examine the hybridity of their evolution and construction.

So what is it, in the end, to be black and modern, or white and modern? One answer is given by the novelist Toni Morrison, arguing for the crucial importance of slavery: for her, 'modern life begins with slavery', and the 'strategies of sur-vival' needed to accommodate it, while maintaining dignity and autonomy, 'made the truly modern person'.[67] Slavery here becomes the archetypal experience of modern subjection, how to survive in conditions not of our choosing and in which options are circumscribed, how to yet achieve selfhood and a powerful cultural identity. And minstrelsy was part of this: frequently part of the oppression, and one of the resources for coping with it. One of the two key figures of minstrelsy, after all, was 'Jim Crow' (or Sambo), the 'plantation nigger', a figure who might be ridiculed or lampooned but who often had the last laugh, frequently at the expense of 'Zip Coon', the urban, upwardly mobile, black dandy, with his social pretensions and his mimicry of whites.[68] In the long run, of course, the Zip Coons were to triumph, and the figure offers another clue: for Zip Coon is surely the archetypal cosmopolitan, distanced from his roots, no longer at home there – or anywhere, in particular – but at home everywhere, a creature of change, fluidity, essentially hybrid. With Jim Crow and Zip Coon, we swing between the 'primi-tive' and the sophisticated, both suffering and surging on, somehow making it. Josephine Baker's own evolution from Jim Crow to Zip Coon does, after all, trace out the path so many had taken, or were to take: the path, perhaps, we all have to take, in becoming modern. . . .

The Discourse of Hybridity

Clearly the term 'hybrid' needs further discussion. Issues connected with hybridity are indeed coming to the fore during the nineteenth century, and the period of the modernist revolutions. The impact of 'primitivism' was important here. When the British conquered the Edo people of Benin in West Africa, in the last years of the century, they looted bronzes and ivories; and these works, sophis-ticated and oddly familiar, posed a challenge to conventional anthropological histories of art.[69] It duly became apparent that they incorporated Portuguese elements, from Portuguese explorations centuries before, and indeed some had apparently been intended for the Portuguese market. Conversely, carved figures in Western museums that had been 'medieval European' turned out to be African.[70] These objects were themselves characteristically 'hybrid', then, already produced with a market in view, products that implicitly question any simplistic modern/primitive opposition, even though this complexity is ostensibly disavowed so that they can come to be partially constitutive of that very distinction. Miller comments that much 'primitive art' thus turns out to be 'the material result of one people's understanding of what they think another society perceives them to be'.[71]

India furnishes some of the best examples: that India that so troubled Kipling, the site of what he called 'the monstrous hybridism of East and West'.[72] The 'oriental style', found on rich brocades and silks, tapestries and pottery, and collections of chintz, may come from India, but it is a product of the interaction between India and the West, the former fitting in with the latter's preconceptions and subtly strengthening but also influencing these.[73] But now let us take another 'hybrid object', and examine the strange case of the 'flying chapati', documented by Homi Bhabha, which will take us into the theoretical issues in more depth.[74]

Just after the introduction into the sepoy (*sipahi*) regiments of the Enfield rifle, with its notorious 'greased' cartridge – such an affront to the religious beliefs of the populace – and just before the Mutiny itself broke out in May 1857, the historian of the latter tells us of how the Governor-General sensed that a 'great fear' was spreading among the people; and it is in this context that the story of the chapatis emerged. Brought by one messenger and sent onwards by another, from one village to another, was a 'mysterious token', in the shape of a chapati. No one refused to pass it on; all were 'in blind obedience to a necessity felt rather than understood'; but there was no agreement on its meaning. Most likely, records the historian, it was 'a signal of warning and preparation', telling the people that 'something great and portentous was about to happen'; but while 'some saw in it much meaning; some saw none'.[75] This indeterminacy, it seemed, was contagious, as was the associated panic. And if there was escalating confusion and fear among the populace, so we encounter it also among the British colonial officials and officers, and present in their accounts, and those of the historians. These chapatis, observes Bhabha, thus become not only the 'staple fare of Government House', but also the 'totem meal for historians of the Mutiny', who thereby 'bite the greased bullet' and circulate the myth, passing on 'the contagion of rumour and panic into their own serial, sensible narratives that become unsettled in that very act of repetition'.[76]

What we are locating here, then, is 'a new hybrid space of cultural difference in the negotiation of colonial power-relations', a space of undecidability 'in between' colonizer and colonized. Bhabha expands the point as follows:

> The margin of hybridity, where cultural differences 'contingently' and conflictually touch, becomes the moment of panic which reveals the borderline experience. It resists the binary opposition of racial and cultural groups, sipahis and sahibs, as homogeneous polarized political consciousnesses. The political psychosis of panic constitutes the boundary of cultural hybridity across which the Mutiny is fought. The native order of Indian symbols, their indigenous ethnic reference 'inside' are displaced and turned inside-out; they become the circulating signs of an 'English'

panic, disavowed by the official discourse of imperial history, represented in the language of indeterminacy.

And the chapatis, which are in some accounts said to be contaminated with bone-meal, become simultaneously corrupted by, a displacement of, and a defence against, the Enfield rifle: a 'heterogeneous, hybrid sign'.[77] The hybridity of this sign thus operates right across the field here, not just in the indeterminacy of meaning that both produces, and feeds on, the panic, but in agency itself; for both sides in the emerging conflict act in ways that cannot just be fitted to the (and their) pre-existing stereotypes, of tradition versus modernity, or symbol and ritual versus rationality. Yet, in the melodrama of political conflict realized here, this hybridity precisely *polarizes*: the point where the differences 'touch', the troubled confusion of hybrid patterns, becomes the paranoia of otherness in the 'pulling away' of reaffirmed identity. Thus does 'The Mutiny' become the 'defining event' of Indian colonial history.

In effect, what is addressed here, in dramatic fashion, is what is always present: a destabilizing of the clarity of colonial authority. What may be most dramatic at a time of political turmoil is continuous with what is there at the interface of the day-to-day encounter between colonizer and colonized. The colonizer strives to maintain his position of pure authority, unmediated, his position in the grand narrative of history and progress, the charisma of the fount of power; yet every engagement with the necessities of interpreting and applying this, in necessary contact with the colonized other, subverts this clarity. Take translation, for example. It is a constant refrain of nineteenth-century missionaries, on the front line in Indian villages, that no translation of the Bible into local languages is ever 'good enough'; none can guarantee the purity, the uncorruptibility, of the original message. *Every* translation can be reappropriated by the local culture, given an unintended slant: resurrection can slide into reincarnation, for example, and varying the language – to tell people they must be 'born again' – slips into the language of Brahman initiatory rites. Hence, 'in the very practice of domination the language of the master becomes hybrid', as Bhabha puts it. Recourse to 'native' translators merely shifts the problem along; they always have their own cultural agenda, after all. Truth cannot be uncorrupted in 'translation'. And these apparently little local difficulties can have potentially far-reaching implications: this problem of translation threatens a reflexive questioning of the source itself, its charismatic origin. How do *we* possess the word of God, but as translation? Authority must enact a disavowal – always potentially a panic disavowal – of the consequences of its own intervention. And every intervention, every engagement, repeats the problem, multiplies the effects. Authority becomes difference in its acts of repetition; it becomes hybrid, deformed and displaced through its very agency, its very language. The immersion of symbol and stereotype in everyday situations and interventions, the repetitions that carry with them the undecidable discontinuities; this is hybridity, a 'displacement of value from symbol to sign'.[78]

A crucial consequence is that the subject of the colonial gaze becomes a troubling presence in the very constitution of that gaze, and hybridity 'reverses the effects of the colonialist disavowal, so that other "denied" knowledges enter upon the dominant discourse and estrange the basis of its authority', as Bhabha argues, adding that 'The paranoid threat from the hybrid is finally uncontainable because it breaks down the symmetry and duality of self/other, inside/outside.'[79] Authority becomes vulnerable to the subtle threats of mimicry and mockery; we encounter again the ever-present challenge of Conrad's 'mimic man', the 'half-educated' African, a figure both to mock, and to fear, the mockery revenging itself through the fear, mockery of and by the other who is not really – sufficiently – 'other', who is all too close. . . . Mimicry – hybridity in its theatrical mode – answers to the imperative of colonial authority to reproduce itself through a subjection of the other who, as 'reformed', as subject to the civilizing process, must become 'the same', yet never can be, on pain of dissolving that authority itself; hence colonial mimicry produces the other as 'almost the same, but not quite', in Bhabha's intriguing phrase, as both resemblance and menace.[80] For the difference can never disappear: to be 'Westernized' is quite definitely not to be 'Western'. And it is this that makes possible the insubordination of mimicry as mockery.

If Bhabha is particularly concerned with what hybridity and mimicry tell us of colonial identity and its limits, then other authors explore this other side of the colonial divide. Ashis Nandy, for example, shows how there is always resistance, however subtly expressed, by 'Westernized' Indians, and humiliation of the colonialists, just as total rejection of the West is impossible when these influences and patterns of behaviour have become so profoundly introjected and indeed are necessary for survival.[81] And – returning to African-Americans – writers and politicians like Booker T. Washington and W. E. B. DuBois had to confront the hybrid legacy of their own people, so that elements of the mimicry and irony of the minstrel stance recur in their own work.[82] But always we need to remember that the political implications of mimicry and hybridity are not clear-cut. We may recall Burton, slipping in and out of an Indian disguise, using mimicry as a survival strategy in which an interest in 'exploring the other' can readily be compatible with a reflexive recuperation of such knowledge in the furtherance of colonial control; and much the same could be said of Kim, in the eponymous Kipling novel. Anne McClintock warns against essentializing mimicry: 'While crossdressing, drag, passing, camp and voguing are all, generally speaking, forms of mimicry, they also tend to enact very different cultural possibilities.'[83] Similarly, Sakamoto argues that 'The notion of non-essential hybrid identity is neither new nor necessarily liberating', in that 'a hybrid identity may call in another Other to stop the slippage of identity'.[84] He instances the Japanese strategy of resisting the West through hybridizing Japanese identity, incorporating the discourses of 'civilization' and 'modernity' while constructing 'Asia' as the inferior 'other' to the new hybrid Japan.

Whatever the problems with the concept, hybridity must, in itself, represent 'the antidote to essentialist notions of identity and ethnicity', as Pieterse puts it,[85] even if it necessarily remains in some sense parasitic on these notions. It reminds us of the artifice of boundaries, the eclecticism of identities. Bhabha's own use of it contrasts it not just with essentialism but with pluralism as well, suggesting that cultural difference be seen as 'based not on the exoticism of multiculturalism or the *diversity* of cultures, but on the inscription and articulation of culture's *hybridity*'.[86] Discussing this in the context of gender identity, Rita Felski suggests that

> Metaphors of hybridity and the like not only recognize differences within the subject, fracturing and complicating holistic notions of identity, but also address connections between subjects by recognising affiliations, cross-pollinations, echoes, and repetitions, thereby unseating difference from a position of absolute privilege. Instead of endorsing a drift toward an ever greater atomization of identity, such metaphors allow us to conceive of multiple, interconnecting axes of affiliation and differentiation.[87]

Hence, on this argument, hybridity can lead to a path between essentialism and relativism.

The concept has frequently been linked to that of diaspora, which has emerged in post-colonial theory as an attempt to re-think ethnic identity beyond this dualism of essentialism and difference or relativism. Diaspora postulates identity as voyage, testifying to the place of migration in or of identity, and its embeddedness in new challenges and situations, and indeed sets up counter-narratives to imperial history, highlighting the contributions of the subordinate, the dispossessed, and the 'stranger'.[88] Gilroy, who has done much to develop this notion, through his studies of the 'Black Atlantic', tells us that a diaspora is a 'relational network, characteristically produced by forced dispersals and reluctant scattering'; and that diaspora exists in tension both with the nation-state and with the cosmopolitan implications of 'exile', both central to the experience of modernity, destabilizing the former and questioning the universalizing rootlessness of the latter. Diaspora calls our attention to contingency and conflict, and calls for a 'social ecology of cultural identity'.[89] Yet this overlaps with hybridity, rather than being identifiable with it, and neither notion can be reduced to the other. To 'hybridize' the notion of diaspora threatens to subtly dehistoricize it, lose the sense of a 'scattering' from an origin; while to 'diasporize' hybridity threatens to present us with 'origins' as a simplified, homogeneous and nostalgic 'master key' to identity.

Finally, it is important to remember that hybridity is not a new notion: the discourse of hybridity has a history, reaching well back into the nineteenth century. In his account of this, Young points out that the term 'hybrid' emerged in the middle years of the century, when debates over linguistic and biological hybridity were reinforcing fears of degeneration and corruption.[90] In effect, we can distinguish between an apparently less racist position, which depicted hybridity between closely related groups – different but not too different – as a positive force for progress, and a more extreme position, which saw *any* mixture as entailing the threat of degeneracy, and was therefore particularly antagonistic to such proximity. The idea, fashionable in the 1860s, of English culture as a multicultural mix, whereby 'hybridity' became an English virtue (found, for example, in Arnold), rests on a notion of 'proximate' races, and hence is an example of the former; so, at a more sociological and theoretical level, is Spencer's theory of progress through heterogeneity.

In some respects, however, the tension between these two poles can conceal their inseparability. The former, after all, still relies on a distinction between 'acceptable' and 'unacceptable' others, categories which tend to be self-subverting. The 'acceptable' other can be *too* close, losing the link with heterogeneity or difference as a force for progress, so the 'unacceptable' other comes back into focus as a resource for reinvigorating the former; it is a necessary category, for ideological denunciation and purity, but it is always liable to be nibbled away at, in practice, so as to reincorporate the 'difference' needed to fuel progress. The creation, re-creation and subversion of the category go hand in hand. This can also be seen in the context of gender difference, as well as race. In terms of these assumptions, we can see how gender difference is postulated as necessary and unavoidable, but the acute danger of 'degeneracy' will reinforce a politics of close patriarchal regulation of the family and female behaviour. These tensions, indeed, help fuel Victorian homoeroticism, for male–male attraction – the link to one who is indeed the same, but too much so – can seem to be a relatively 'safe' alternative. But this, too, is of course proscribed, as a corruption of manhood and a threat to family life, throwing us back onto the need for difference.[91]

But there is another problem here. According to degenerationist biological theory, the danger was that the offspring of mixed parents would be infertile, or at any rate less fertile. But this seems to make the problem self-limiting, hardly justifying cultural panic. Yet the latter, of course, was prominent, and fears about 'racial vigour' being threatened provided a powerful nexus of concern out of which eugenics developed. Implicity, there seems to have been a fear that actually 'vigour' *could* result, but not *racial* vigour: rather, there is the threat of a possible progress *beyond* race, a subversion of the category of 'race'. And such a threat to essential, constitutive assumptions about racial unity and progress was deeply disturbing; hence the fear of the danger posed by these 'raceless masses'. It is as though hybrids are both sterile *and* fertile, a threat to the possibility of reproduction itself *and* to the purity of the offspring. So Young suggests that these 'raceless masses' thus 'threaten to erase the discriminations of difference: the naming of human mixture as "degeneracy" both asserts the norm and subverts it, undoing its terms of distinction, and opening up the prospect of the evanescence of "race" as such'.[92] Thus do desire and aversion, mixture and separation, circle around one another, depend on one another.

This all gives clues to the discourse of hybridity in our own time; for the nineteenth-century discourse has indeed proved fertile, and its offspring are around today. This contemporary discourse is 'almost, but not quite' the same, and, as always, the 'not quite' is crucial. Beyond the assumptions of biological and racial purity, we now find greater acceptance of fluid and flexible identities, a 'postmodern' interest in mixture and pluralism. But the continuities are there. At a general level, we can find two forms of hybridity involved here: one emphasizes fusion, the production of new forms through intermixing, an 'organic' hybridity of merging, through attraction, desire or convergence; the other emphasizes conflict and contest, separation and subversion, juxtaposition and irony, heterogeneity and discontinuity.[93] Without the latter, the former is impossible; without the former, the latter cannot develop. Young concludes that

> Hybridity is itself an example of hybridity, of a doubleness that both brings together, fuses, but also maintains separation. . . . Hybridization as creolization involves fusion, the creation of a new form, which can then be set against the old form, of which it is partly made up. Hybridization as 'raceless chaos' by contrast, produces no stable new form, but rather something closer to Bhabha's restless, uneasy, interstitial hybridity: a radical heterogeneity, discontinuity, the permanent revolution of forms.[94]

The discourse of hybridity is a dialectic of irresolution, one that defies Hegelian closure; there are no metahistorical vantage points, no inevitabilities. Ultimately, this discourse reminds us of the truth that Josephine Baker lived and danced: that we are, indeed, all bastards, all miscegenated, this and that, same and different, good and bad; it forces us to confront the disavowed, the inescapable otherness, in our lives.

Notes

1   See chapter 3 above.
2   See my *Exploring the Modern: Patterns of Western Culture and Civilization* (Blackwell, 1998), chs. 10, 12, and E. Barkan and R. Bush (eds.) *Prehistories of the Future: The Primitivist Project and the Culture of Modernism* (Stanford University Press, 1995).
3   J. Clifford, 'Negrophilia', in D. Hollier (ed.) *A New History of French Literature* (Harvard University Press, 1989).
4   A. Stuart, 'Looking at Josephine Baker', *Women: A Cultural Review* (1994), 5:2, p. 138.
5   R. Burt, *Alien Bodies: Representations of 'Modernity', Race and Nation in Early Modern Dance* (Routledge 1998).
6   C. B. Steiner, 'Travel Engravings and the Construction of the Primitive', in Barkan and Bush, *Prehistories*, pp. 214–16.
7   Burt, *Alien Bodies*, pp. 6, 17, 194.
8   J. Kear, '*Vénus noire:* Josephine Baker and the Parisian Music-hall', in M. Sheringham (ed.) *Parisian Fields* (Reaktion, 1996), p. 56; see also pp. 54, 62.
9   S. Gilman, *Difference and Pathology: Stereotypes of Sexuality, Race and Madness* (Cornell University Press, 1985).
10 Stuart, 'Looking', p. 141.
11 Kear, '*Vénus noire*', pp. 52, 56, 59; Burt, *Alien Bodies*, p. 73.
12 Burt, *Alien Bodies*, p. 62.
13 Kear, '*Vénus noire*', p. 54.

14 Ibid., p. 70.

15 Burt, *Alien Bodies*, pp. 65–6.

16 S. Gilman, 'Black Bodies, White Bodies: Towards an Iconography of Female Sexuality in Late 19th Century Art, Medicine, and Literature', in J. Donald and A. Rattansi (eds.) *'Race', Culture and Difference* (Open University Press, 1992).

17 Burt, *Alien Bodies*, p. 60.

18 Ibid., p. 68.

19 W. Martin, ' "Remembering the Jungle": Josephine Baker and Modernist Parody', in Barkan and Bush, *Prehistories*.

20 Cited in Stuart, 'Looking', p. 138.

21 Kear, *'Vénus noire'*, pp. 57–8, 56.

22 Martin, ' "Remembering the Jungle" ', pp. 322, 321.

23 Kear, *'Vénus noire'*, p. 70.

24 Martin, ' "Remembering the Jungle" ', pp. 310, 323, 325.

25 Burt, *Alien Bodies*, p. 80; and see my *Exploring the Modern*, ch. 5, on masquerade.

26 Cited in Martin, ' "Remembering the Jungle" ', p. 325.

27 Martin, ' "Remembering the Jungle" ', p. 316.

28 Stuart, 'Looking', p. 143.

29 C. Rhodes, *Primitivism and Modern Art* (Thames and Hudson, 1994), pp. 96–7; and P. Wollen, *Raiding the Icebox: Reflections on Twentieth-Century Culture* (Verso, 1993).

30 See my *Exploring the Modern*, ch. 10.

31 R. Nye, 'Savage Crowds, Modernism and Modern Politics', in Barkan and Bush, *Prehistories*, pp. 43, 49.

32 J. Lynn, cited in J. N. Pieterse, *White on Black: Images of Africa and Blacks in Western Popular Culture* (Yale University Press, 1992), p. 132.

33 P. Gilroy, *The Black Atlantic: Modernity and Double Consciousness* (Verso, 1993), p. 89; but see also his other writings, below, where he recognizes the complexity here.

34 E. Lott, *Love and Theft: Blackface Minstrelsy and the American Working Class* (Oxford University Press, 1993), pp. 16, 64.

35 Pieterse, *White on Black*, p. 148, and ch. 9.

36 Lott, *Love and Theft*, p. 234.

37 In addition to Lott, *Love and Theft*, the main sources here are D. Cockrell, *Demons of Disorder: Early Blackface Minstrels and Their World* (Cambridge University Press, 1997); H. Nathan, *Dan Emmett and the Rise of Early Negro Minstrelsy* (Oklahoma University Press, 1962); and R. C. Toll, *Blacking Up: The Minstrel Show in Nineteenth-Century America* (Oxford University Press, 1974).

38 Lott, *Love and Theft*, p. 145.

39 S. G. Davis, *Parades and Power: Street Theatre in Nineteenth-Century Philadelphia* (California University Press, 1986), pp. 77–111; and S. White, ' "It Was A Proud Day": African Americans, Festivals, and Parades in the North, 1741–1834', *Journal of American History* (1994), 81.

40 Cockrell, *Demons*, pp. 44, 52, 57.

41 Lott, *Love and Theft*, p. 27.

42 Cockrell, *Demons*, pp. 58, 53.

43 Lott, *Love and Theft*, pp. 6, 6, 101.

44 P. Gilroy, ' ". . . To Be Real" The Dissident Forms of Black Expressive Culture', in C. Ugwu (ed.) *Let's Get It On: The Politics of Black Performance* (Institute of Contemporary Arts, 1995), p. 14.

45 Lott, *Love and Theft*, p. 45; see also pp. 25–7, 147, 159–68.

46   Ibid., pp. 187, 189.
47   H. Foster, '"Primitive" Scenes', *Critical Inquiry* (1993), 20:1, p. 99.
48   Pieterse, *White on Black*, ch. 12.
49   Gilroy, *Black Atlantic*, p. 88; see also Toll, *Blacking Up*, and J. Boskin, *Sambo: The Rise and Demise of an American Jester* (Oxford University Press, 1986).
50   Cited in Gilroy, *Black Atlantic*, p. 91.
51   For masquerade, see my *Exploring the Modern*, ch. 5.
52   Cited in Lott, *Love and Theft*, p. 36.
53   Lott, *Love and Theft*, pp. 97–8, 112–15, 4.
54   See the account in A. Bontemps (ed.) *Great Slave Narratives* (Beacon, 1969).
55   H. L. Gates Jr, 'Writing "Race" and the Difference It Makes' in Gates (ed.) *'Race', Writing and Difference* (Chicago University Press, 1986), pp. 11, 9.
56   Gilroy, *Black Atlantic*, p. 57.
57   Gates, 'Writing "Race"', pp. 12, 15.
58   H. A. Baker Jr, *Modernism and the Harlem Renaissance* (Chicago University Press, 1987).
59   Gilroy, *Black Atlantic*, p. 73.
60   Baker, *Modernism*.
61   H. L. Gates Jr, *The Signifying Monkey: A Theory of African-American Literary Criticism* (Oxford University Press, 1989).
62   Cockrell, *Demons*, ch. 5.
63   Lott, *Love and Theft*, p. 104; Toll, *Blacking Up*, pp. 196, 228.
64   R. Dawidoff, 'The Kind of Person You Have to Sound Like to Sing "Alexander's Ragtime Band"', in Barkan and Bush, *Prehistories*, pp. 293, 301, 302.
65   Gilroy, *Black Atlantic*, pp. 101, 96.
66   S. Hall, 'The New Ethnicities', in Donald and Rattansi, *'Race'*, p. 254.
67   Cited in Gilroy, *Black Atlantic*, p. 221.
68   Cockrell, *Demons*, chs. 3, 4.
69   A. Coombes, 'The Recalcitrant Object: Culture Contact and the Question of Hybridity', in F. Barker et al., *Colonial Discourse/Postcolonial Theory* (Manchester University Press, 1994).
70   Barkan and Bush, *Prehistories*, Introduction, p. 1; J. Dorne, 'African Art and the Paris Studios 1905–20', in M. Greenhalgh and V. Megaw (eds.) *Art in Society* (Duckworth, 1978).
71   D. Miller, 'Primitive Art and the Necessity of Primitivism to Art', in S. Hiller (ed.) *The Myth of Primitivism* (Routledge, 1991), p. 61.
72   Cited in R. J. C. Young, *Colonial Desire: Hybridity in Theory, Culture and Race* (Routledge, 1995), p. 3.
73   Miller, 'Primitive Art', p. 60; see also B. Spooner, 'Weavers and Dealers: The Authenticity of an Oriental Carpet', in A. Appadurai (ed.) *The Social Life of Things* (Cambridge University Press, 1986), for another example.
74   H. Bhabha, *The Location of Culture* (Routledge, 1994), ch. 10.
75   J. B. Kaye and G. B. Malleson, *History of the Indian Mutiny of 1857–8* (W. H. Allen & Co., 1888), Vol. I, p. 179.
76   Bhabha, *Location*, pp. 209, 202, 202, 202.
77   Ibid., pp. 204, 207, 207.
78   Ibid., pp. 33, 113, and ch. 6.
79   Ibid., pp. 114, 116.
80   Ibid. (original emphasis).

81 A. Nandy, *The Intimate Enemy: Loss and Recovery of Self under Colonialism* (Oxford University Press, 1983).

82 Baker, *Modernism*.

83 A. McClintock, *Imperial Leather: Race, Gender and Sexuality in the Colonial Context* (Routledge, 1995), p. 68; and see J. N. Pieterse, 'Globalisation as Hybridisation', *International Sociology* (1994), 9:2, p. 172.

84 R. Sakamoto, 'Japan, Hybridity and the Creation of Colonialist Discourse', *Theory, Culture and Society* (1996), 13:3, pp. 114, 122.

85 Pieterse, 'Globalisation', p. 171.

86 Bhabha, *Location*, p. 38.

87 R. Felski, 'The Doxa of Difference', *Signs* (1997), 23:1, p. 12.

88 Pieterse, 'Globalisation', p. 179.

89 P. Gilroy, 'Diaspora and the Detours of Identity', in K. Woodward (ed.) *Identity and Difference* (Sage, 1997), pp. 318, 322. See also K. Mercer, *Welcome to the Jungle: New Positions in Black Cultural Studies* (Routledge, 1994), for applications.

90 Young, *Colonial Desire*, ch. 1.

91 See, for example, C. Lane, *The Ruling Passion: British Colonial Allegory and the Paradox of Homosexual Desire* (Duke University Press, 1995).

92 Young, *Colonial Desire*, p. 19.

93 The latter resembles Bakhtin's 'intentional' hybridity; see M. Bakhtin, *The Dialogic Imagination* (Texas University Press, 1981), pp. 360–1.

94 Young, *Colonial Desire*, pp. 22, 25.

9 Postmodern Possibilities:

Alienating the Modern?

Aliens and Cyborgs

Mulder: 'They're here, aren't they?'
Deep Throat: '*They* have been here for a very long time.'
                                  — *The X-Files*, 2nd programme, 17 September 1993

Indeed they have – since at least 1947, it would seem. That was the year of reported sightings of several objects subsequently christened 'flying saucers' from the descriptions given, and – coming within a few days of this – of the 'Roswell incident', when strange metal debris was found on a ranch in New Mexico, in due course destined to metamorphose into the story of a crashed spacecraft, the recovery of alien bodies (several dead, and one still living), and a massive government cover-up. But 1947 was also the year when the future Cold War president and Watergate conspirator Richard Nixon entered Congress, and the House Un-American Activities Committee (HUAC) began investigating the 'communist conspiracy' in the media. Conspiracies, cover-ups and aliens seem to have been bedfellows ever since, in this strange, nebulous, uncanny realm where popular culture, media melodrama, science fiction and technological innovation, the sociopolitical dynamics of surveillance, and the discourse of the postmodern and the hyperreal, meet in uneasy but fascinating configuration. And this, of course, is the scenario of *The X-Files*, the cult TV series of the mid- to late 1990s that also became a massive popular hit, in which FBI agents Fox Mulder and Dana Scully operate as boundary beings who have to cope with a world in which science fiction, horror, police drama, and special-effects action movie coexist both as genres in unresolved tension and as aspects of a world in which conventional distinctions between real and unreal, appearance and reality, self and other, seem decidedly insecure, unstable, even unknowable.

The word 'alien' has itself evolved, in line with this history. The alien has long been the stranger; and to be 'alienated' is to be estranged, to become 'foreign', either to one's possessions – which can be 'alienated' to another – or psychologically, in terms of feelings or mental states. As we have seen,[1] the nineteenth-century 'alienist' specialized in dealing with the 'mental estrangement' of the psychotic, in which the victim becomes afflicted by an internalization of the self/other distinction, mapped on to the body/mind distinction, thus becoming 'alienated' from, and in, self or body. All these meanings still resonate powerfully today, but with an addition: dictionaries since the 1950s have increasingly included the sense of the alien as a being from another world, and indeed this sense is threatening to become dominant.

In locating the alien in the modern history of otherness, we can notice that this history also carries a geography. In the eighteenth and nineteenth centuries, the other tended to be located in the past, which implied a powerful sense of place: the other as place tended to be the tropics, whether as the site of the noble/ignoble savage, or as an arena in which the exoticism of the Orient held sway; and this 'past' thus remained paradoxically present, available for exploration.[2] As modernity incorporated the future into its cultural schemes and fantasies, this also became mapped, but now as space, as the expansive, ill-defined 'elsewhere' beyond the planet, in due course becoming 'outer' space, the zone where, again, the future is mapped spatially into the here and now, along with the same dualism of positive and negative connotations. Donna Haraway suggests that

> Space and the tropics are both utopian topical figures in western imaginations, and their opposed properties dialectically signify origins and ends for the creature whose mundane life is outside both: civilized man. Space and the tropics are both 'allotropic'; they are 'elsewhere', the place to which the traveler goes to find something dangerous and sacred.[3]

From the tropics to space: a shift from an 'elsewhere' that is located on the surface of the planet, a mysterious past located firmly in a present expanse of place, to an 'elsewhere' that is unspecific, space that is non-place, but always 'beyond', 'out there', and, for that very reason, could be here, too. The tropics are located firmly within Newtonian coordinates, as are their 'primitive' inhabitants; the aliens of space, however, increasingly partake of the mysteries of a post-Newtonian framework, where space and time interpenetrate, lose their boundaries, their fixity and clarity. In this, they resemble the inhabitants of cyberspace, another zone of uncertain ontology where signposts are few, reality becomes virtual, the coordinates of identity become insecure, and lawlessness threatens.[4] In this sense, the H. G. Wells novel *The Time Machine*, for all its futurism, remains transitional; it merely travels backwards and forwards along the arrow of linear time. The only way it disturbs the present is through upsetting our equanimity, our complacency, through listening to the account itself, as narrated by the returning time-traveller.

What has become clear now, though, is that aliens who are 'out there' can be 'in here', too; outer space turns easily into 'inner' space, whether the space of human culture or of 'mind'. A feature of science fiction – and, in 'ufology', of popular culture more generally – that has become clear in recent decades, then, is a sense that the elsewhere is here, among us: the aliens have *already* arrived, they are already screwing us up, perhaps in league with – or having infiltrated – existing centres of power. Now, the boundaries are always under attack, already penetrated; no longer can 'others' be safely located elsewhere. It is an age of conspiracy theories, in which 'they' are always out to get us, an age in which the intersection of risk culture with surveillance and the culture of panopticism engenders a pervasive sense of an other that is ever-watching, that manipulates, and is ever potentially present in the everyday interstices of life, whether in the gaze of the CCTV or in the glare of the media and its attendant melodramas. Victorian fears of miscegenation are not now so banal as to be fears of racial interbreeding, solvable by keeping 'them' firmly apart; the pollution fears have become omnipresent, fears of an unspecific 'enemy within' – and *this* enemy is always already 'within'. Hence its surrogates, those picked out as the victims of media witch-hunts, are constantly shifting, because none can be adequate to the task of carrying, exemplifying, this hyperreal other within.[5] With the HUAC enquiries, with the spectre of cunning Reds penetrating our whole culture, Alison Graham points out that 'As the wagons circled tighter, the wilderness beyond became populated by political phantoms, people who were not then and maybe never had been who they said they were', and she concludes:

> The external enemy had moved inside – and it is still inside. . . . The official enemy was a monstrous projection, and like most projections, it came back to haunt its creators. The horrific Other spawned in the secret chambers of the Pentagon, the CIA and the FBI returned home after tour duty in Russia, Vietnam, and phantom flying saucers. There it waits, having outlived its usefulness – but knowing too much.[6]

Clearly, again, the imaginative universe of *The X-Files*. . . .

This latter-day minotaur, lurking in its secret chambers, seems to require a stream of human sacrifices; but now, they are not consumed, merely genetically modified and released, and the secret chambers tend to be concealed inside a UFO. For here we encounter the 'alien abduction' scenario, much discussed since the first alleged occurrences in the 1950s. These accounts frequently reveal hints of the 'near-death experience', also much reported over the period, together with elements of the sexual abuse scenario – aliens seem to possess a distinct propensity for carrying out sexual and gynaecological experiments on captured females – but all occurring in what appears to be a markedly quasi-medical context.[7] It is as though humans become guinea pigs, undergoing medical experiments that thereby relegate them to animal status, no longer culture but nature, subjects now to 'alien culture'. This is all rather reminiscent of Foucault's picture of the origin of modern medical practice in the corpse on the dissecting table, only now the corpse is still living – just about – and will be regenerated, transformed, through the experiments: death and resurrection on a cold table, under the bright lights and the alien gaze.[8]

When taken together with the conspiracy scenario, the implications of all this implicitly question the twin distinctions of self/other and mind/body. Remembering that the Roswell alien corpse is said to have been subject to an autopsy by government scientists, Linda Badley suggests that 'the autopsied alien is increasingly identified with victims of covert medical, military, and government experiments. . . . The alien abduction and the alien autopsy are reverse mirror images proclaiming the same thing, that aliens R US.' So what is referred to as 'alien' here 'involves a separation of the body from the "self" and imagined as Other'. But this, again, has its roots deep in the modern construction of selfhood and the self/body relation: it reminds us that civility and the civilizing process are also a process of 'alienation' of self from body, which occurs through the technique and cult of self-control, whereby the body becomes subject to 'discipline'. If the fate of the body in *The X-Files*, popular culture generally, and, increasingly, in medicine and technology, is to be 'decomposed, regenerated, transgendered, mutated, hybridized, implanted, cloned or doubled, invaded, possessed, colonized, vanished, vaporized, ensanguinated, cannibalized, dissolved and ingested, zombified, harvested, commodified',[9] then this comes into focus as not just a result of the political economy of modern science, but of the fragmenting, objectifying, reflexive gaze itself, inherently present as a condition of modern selfhood. And if, as Sass suggests, this fragmentation and experimentation is a defining feature of modernism,[10] then we can again see postmodernism as an extension of this into cultural and daily life more generally as much as anything radically new. It is hardly surprising that Badley can conclude that the body – like the alien? – emerges as 'the fantastic space between the empirical and the metaphysical',[11] and Jones can add that the other is neither simply 'out there' or 'in here': 'We have met the enemy and he is *us*, but *we* are not who we are.'[12]

Of course, there is difference, as well as continuity. These bodies are strange, unfamiliar, uncanny, even as we recognize the similarities. This is the realm of the 'posthuman' body,[13] and of the cyborg, defined by its theoretician, Donna Haraway, as 'a hybrid of machine and organism, a creature of social reality as well as a creature of fiction';[14] and indeed, cyborgs seem increasingly prevalent in both spheres, with 10 per cent of the US population claimed to be technically cyborgs (with electronic pacemakers, artificial joints, silicon-chip implants, and so on), and the screens full of Robocops, Terminators, and the Borg, the aliens in *Star Trek* who incorporate organic life forms into their own hybrid system. . . .[15] In her *Cyborg Manifesto*, Haraway situates the cyborg at the intersection of three of the dualisms that have been so basic to modern Western culture – animal/human, organism/machine and fiction/reality – and hence presents it as inherently transgressive, hybrid, crossing (and communicating across) boundaries.[16]

Reshaping the body through technology: such a project triggers deep fears, transgresses sacred taboos. The exotic techno-fetishism of David Cronenberg's 1996 film *Crash*, based on the eponymous J. G. Ballard novel, appropriately illustrates this through introducing sex into the equation, depicting a world in which the intimate man/machine fusion of the car crash – flesh, blood, and gleaming metal – is given an erotic charge, and the car becomes as much an extension of the human body as any other sex aid. Crossing boundaries as they do, cyborgs thus carry with them another set of associations: they become a further manifestation of the discourse, and the experience, of the monstrous. The human body can become monstrous both through alien invasion and through cyborg implantation. And if we recall the discussion of 'woman' as a construct situated on the culture/nature boundary, neither one nor the other, or both together, we can see how these discourses of the feminine and the monstrous can easily be elided, in an uncanny continuation of the nineteenth-century discourse of the 'monstrous/feminine' discussed in a previous chapter.[17]

Embracing this tradition and drawing out its radical potential, Haraway suggests that cyborgs and women indeed become monsters, 'odd boundary creatures . . . that have had a destabilizing place in the Great Western evolutionary, technological and biological narratives'.[18] And while both Mulder and Scully, in *The X-Files*, transgress orthodox gender roles and gender distinctions – indeed, it is generally Scully who is the more 'rational', sceptical, scientific, of the two, with Mulder being more 'intuitive' – it is 'Special Agent' Scully, and her body, that constitute the privileged site of problems. The intersection of masculine science and the female body makes Scully both object and gaze, the body and the doctor, a test site for alien takeover and implantation and the study of its consequences;[19] and, for Linda Parks, Scully's agency is 'special' because 'it incorporates an excess of masculinized power, which is transformed into monstrosity as it engages with the feminine'.[20]

Yet, Haraway can also claim that the cyborg is 'a creature in a post-gender world', and to explore this, we can point to a limitation on the mapping of the feminine on to the cyborg. Such cyborgs, adds Haraway, are 'suspicious of the reproductive';[21] they require regeneration, not rebirth. The cyborg represents the will-to-emancipation of the human from its own origins, the aspiration to being without beginning. The cyborg, then, cannot inhabit the tropics, which is above all a place of origin, a land where the 'primitive', the other that is yet also (to become) us, has its mysterious location. The tropics is the zone of bastard filiation, of troubled parenthood, of the other from whom we are descended but only through our own efforts, through attempting to transcend that very source, and become the charismatic creators of our own being; in short, through purporting to attain a purified self-identity that always rests on a disavowed hybridity. The cyborg is the imaginative embodiment of this dream of fusion without filiation, hybridity without origin – appropriate inhabitant of a postmodern, 'hyperreal' world. Judith Genova suggests that 'To embrace a cyborg future is to relinquish the need for purity, origins, a self/other dualistic consciousness, and the fear of our evolutionary other.' Yet, by implication, its own 'origins' are not so easy to theorize.[22]

I have argued elsewhere[23] that if this term 'postmodern' is to have any useful purchase, it cannot involve any straightforward replacement of the modern by a putative successor, a 'next stage' of history. And a feature of the cyborg that is clearly relevant here is that it cannot be exhaustively described in the terms of just one universe of discourse. The language of machine (design, assembly, disassembly, replacement) and organism (growth, development, death, reproduction) have to be combined and juxtaposed in dynamic incompatibility. New terms of discourse have to be superimposed on older ones, which nevertheless cannot be replaced or die. It is hardly surprising, then, that cyborgs can be seen both as 'the invasion of a deadly alien into the self', and as 'a symbiotic union that results in a new subjectivity', as Katherine Hayles puts it, since both are inherent in the very possibility of cyborg identity. We encounter, again, the two aspects of hybridity. She concludes:

> The cyborg is both a product of this process and a signifier for the process itself. . . . The stories that produce and are produced by cyborg subjectivities are, like the cyborg itself, amalgams of old and new. Cyborg narratives can be understood as stories only by reference to the very life cycle narratives that are no longer sufficient to explain them. The results are narrative patterns that overlay upon the arc of human life a map generated from assembly and disassembly zones. One orientation references the human, the other the posthuman; *one is chronological, the other topological; one assumes growth, the other presupposes production; one represents itself as natural or normal, the other as unnatural or aberrant.*[24]

Both languages are modern, one applied to life, the other to technology; when superimposed, it is as though each becomes refracted through the lens of the other, in a disjunction that reveals the displacement of identity and identity as displacement. Indeed, this refraction is evident in contemporary cybertalk, and can be read back to this tension, between on the one hand the 'Internet hypothesis' that mind can be uploaded directly into cyberspace, becoming a function of the Net, with the body becoming essentially irrelevant, and on the other hand the 'biotech hypothesis', that cyberspace can be downloaded into the body, but a body transformed now so as to incorporate a 'cyber mind' and other implants.[25] Cyborgs themselves become the ultimate hybrids, embodying both of the alternative modes of hybridity, the contestatory and the fusional, their uncertain reproductive status mirroring this undecidable tension present at the heart of their status as possible beings. And this also reveals the hybrid as the embodiment of the possibility of the postmodern as the identity that reflexively incorporates the disavowal, the difference, of modern identity itself, its uncanny other, reminding us, as Sarah Lefanu puts it in her study of science fiction, of 'the effects of the strange, or the alien, or the unconscious, on the familiar and the commonplace' and of 'how the strange and the familiar can inhabit the same terrain'.[26]

This idea that the postmodern exists through being mapped on to the modern – or perhaps, through the modern being mapped on to itself, revealing its necessary otherness to itself – so that they coexist as frames through which we both experience reality and reflexively grasp it, is one way of looking at their relationship. And it can lead us to ask why these issues – of otherness, difference, transgression – have come into prominence now. Where, indeed, is this book written from? Is it because we are already writing from within the postmodern that we can raise these issues at all? In attempting to grasp the modern, are we not thereby 'alienating' it, or ourselves from it, situating it as 'other', yet paradoxically while still inside it? Perhaps this, indeed, is the post-modern predicament, the sense that everything changes yet there is nowhere else to go, or be. . . . We have to reflect from afar, from outside, yet there is no real 'outside'. If 'transgressing the modern' always bears the mark of the reflexive, it is also the move that marks us as indelibly postmodern, our 'otherness' some-thing we have to display on our sleeves, so to speak, as it cannot really be any-where else.

The Same, the Different, and the Fate of Transgression

In this era of the globalization of project, the omnipresent media spectacle, the aspiration to transcontextual, disembodied communication via the Net, in the no-place of cyberspace, we can say that the consequences of project itself, driving towards control, and thereby producing the ability not just to intervene in reality, but to reproduce it and hence replace it, coincide with the consequences of the dynamics of technologies of representation whereby the real can in turn be simu-lated to the point of 'virtual' identity. This is the world theorized by Baudrillard as 'hyperreal',[27] a world of consumerism, of an endless multiplicity of forms that exist as tempting objects of desire, becoming simultaneously sign, reality and simulation. In such a hyperreal world, it would seem that otherness can return only as difference, only in the endless multiplicity of differences that are, by that very fact, also endlessly the same; the differences engineered by the restless ex-pansion of consumerism itself. Mark Taylor thus complains that 'Without alter-ity, experience becomes vacuous, our landscape a desert.'[28] One could of course reply that the desert nonetheless provides for hallucinatory experiences – the shimmering veil of the mirage – but perhaps that is not enough; and one could add that the consumer simulacrum also provides the experience of the formless and the infinite proliferation of forms – the two dimensions of the sublime – but perhaps that is not enough, either.

In a context where otherness becomes inscrutable, dissipated in the prolifera-tion of difference, the aspiration to engage with it, as a condition of the existence of a bounded, cohesive identity, becomes ever more insistent. Both identity and otherness become deeply problematic constructs. The effects of this converge with the effects of our awareness of the limits of knowledge and control: what cannot (so far) be reproduced or simulated becomes increasingly puzzling or threatening. What results are the media witch-hunts and moral panics of our time, melodramas of reinforced identity and denounced otherness; in effect, popular culture – characteristically itself cast in the role of other – has spread everywhere, and its disparate characters, images and stories have become resources drawn on for othering, stereotyping, and victimization. This occurs in a context where the ultimate panic, after all, is over 'reality' itself. If the hyperreal comes to encom-pass everything, so that otherness appears to be lost in the multiplicity of identi-cal differences, the shadow of the real remains; or perhaps the shadow remains as the absence that can be converted into presence only through being made concrete as the 'other' that must be destroyed yet cannot be, as it alone certifies the existence of the hyperreal as the 'really real'.[29]

The consequences of all this for the possibility of transgression are profound but by no means straightforward. The consumerist multiplicity of difference, the glamour of pervasive sexuality in the media, the ethos of individualism and the attraction of 'getting one's kicks', the ready publicity always available in a society subject to the 'panoptic gaze', all tend in turn to multiply both the temptations and opportunities for transgression, while at the same time apparently trivializing them: when everything becomes slightly transgressive, transgression again disappears into the minor differences of consumerism, all endlessly different and endlessly the same. Yet the significance of transgression in our lives is not necessarily so minor, in that the very mechanisms that diminish it also serve to strengthen it. Thus the forms of surveillance and social control subtly reinforce transgression by the increased potential for creating victims who are simultaneously stars as well – both denounced, yet also subtly publicized, rendered into role models. In advertising, after all, negative branding is still branding. And if part of the appeal of deviance is that it can be known as such, it also becomes subject to the vagaries of fashion; once it is known, it duly becomes unfashionable, and the transgressive impulse moves elsewhere. What threatens to tame transgression also serves to encourage it. Once again we encounter the sense of identity as melodrama, as exaggeration, the frenetic reinforcement of the differences that, although minor, become major in our sense of ourselves as distinctive, unique individuals.

There is nonetheless a problem here, which comes into clearer focus if we remember that transgression depends on taboo; without the prohibited boundary, there is nothing to transgress. With Sade, it is the sense of boundary that is unwittingly subverted, in the sexual arena, by making everything possible, breaking through all limits. And if everything becomes pleasure, and there is no limit to pleasure, pleasure itself is anaesthetized. Without limits, there can be no excess. Absolute transgression slides into terminal exhaustion. With the 'death of God' theorists, from Nietzsche through Bataille to Foucault, there is more emphasis on the prohibition: after God there can be no real transgression as there are no absolutes, no rules so vital that to break them would be to enter the zone of the sacred; nor can we even recognize the significance of the death itself, occurring as it does as the culmination of a Christian tradition that has tried to exile transgression, deny it its space as partially constitutive of the sacred, a tradition that is, in turn, perpetuated in the secular ideologies and social practices of modernity. The limit, and the prohibition, both become problematical; if reality has gone the way of God, what place can there be for transgression in the hyperreal? And perhaps these theorists can be recast as critics of the modern, defining a task: how to make possible, re-enact, an experience of transgression that would thereby reconnect us to the real.[30]

'Re-enact' is the key phrase here, perhaps. If there is no ultimate 'outside', no absolute grounding or 'other' – if there is nothing to set limits – then these limits will be engendered internally, as it were, in the practices of constitution and dissolution wherein individuals and groups have their tentative, precarious being. Boundaries exist through the mechanisms that identify and distinguish them, and these mechanisms are those of enactment. They will exist as vicarious, absolute only in their enacted immediacy; and this corresponds to the moment of hybridity as contest, as polarity or dissonance, not hybridity as fusion. There does, of course, seem to be something deeply paradoxical about this: the idea of *enacting* a limit seems to imply a degree of intention or artifice, rather contradicting the absolute character of such a limit, its status as what is, precisely, *not* created, but is simply, awesomely, *there*. But this is not so different from what anthropologists and historians tell us about 'invented traditions', namely that the purported fixity and timelessness of the tradition – and these can, after all, be 'real enough' for the practitioners – are always in some degree spurious, involving a kind of collective amnesia.[31] And this in turn suggests that the 'postmodern' may be more a kind of reflexive move in the modern – this time, perhaps entailing a simultaneous recovery of a disavowed 'pre-modern' – than anything totally new.

If the idea of enactment is crucial to this sense of the possibility of the transgressive – reminding us, for example, of the scenarios discussed in the chapter on sexuality – then another aspect or potential is suggested by this reference to the reflexive. As the attempt to stand outside while yet remaining inside, reflexivity both rests on, and engenders, an inside/outside boundary, which only exists through this very enactment. And in this context, the paradox of the move – the attempt to stand outside a totality to which one inherently belongs – is reflected in the peculiar status of the reflexive act itself, in which transgression is 'carried', symbolized, as implicit commentary. We can remember Josephine Baker here.[32] She was caught, restrained, within a tradition she did not invent and could not directly confront; no longer the trapped slave, but still heir to the burden of that history. Yet, the transgressive potential is there. She did not, could not, 'state' her distance, comment on her role as she performed it; the irony, the parody, could only be *shown*, in *how* she carried it off. Irony and parody are not present on the written page, as it were; they require a context, and an audience; they are only present in their unpredictable effects. These transgressive qualities are situational; the reflexivity is carried on the sleeve, and can only be understood by those 'in the know'. It is hardly surprising, then, that homosexuals and homosexual communities, who know everything about secrets and closets and decoding signs, should be experts in these arts; nonetheless, this corresponds to something inescapable. This (postmodern?) reflexivity carries a message of allusion, indirectness, of the contextual, the local, the sense of belonging that can be embedded, or embodied, but not stated as such; the sense in which we are all in the closet, and cannot really 'come out', for in the end there is no 'outside'. This transgression, then, is performed rather than discursively stated, even if it is performed *as* utterance; and this reminds us once again of the significance of theatricality for the exploration of otherness in the modern period, embodying the transgressive potential of vicarious experience.

Difference and the Fate of Otherness

At the most abstract level, the modern project aspires to reduce the temporal framework of tradition and repetition to the linear and the progressive; the norms of procedural rationality operate to exclude the unexpected and the affective; in terms of the form and variety of experience, diversity and excess are translated into one-dimensional homogeneity; and in terms of the content of experience, the facticity of matter and body are disciplined by the practices of discursive control. These subordinated or excluded dimensions thereby become misrecognized aspects of identity; difference is reconstructed as otherness. And, it might be suggested, this 'otherness' takes its revenge on a modernity that cannot grasp itself with reflexive adequacy, hence sliding into a parody or simulacrum of itself.

It would clearly seem necessary to explore the otherness/difference relation in a bit more depth. Pieterse remarks that 'there is no "*the* other": for "the other" would imply a stable "we"'.[33] Yet this is precisely the point: the modern emphasis on development and change both entail, and render problematical, such a stable 'we'. There is, indeed, no *the* other; yet there also has to be, for this is fundamental to the part it plays. What is disavowed in the modern project, then, is twofold: the heterogeneity of otherness 'in itself', the artifice of its construction, mirroring the artifice of the assimilation of same into self (or 'self-same'), so that self/other and same/different become seamlessly superimposed; and the links that underlie and transgress that distinction, that criss-cross the apparently separate identities of the terms on either side of the dualism. In effect, it is the hybridity that is inescapably present in identity, the difference in and of the same, that is disavowed.

This sense of 'difference', as in Bhabha's discussion, is clearly related to Derrida's notion of *différance*, where 'difference' introduces the idea of a supplement or extension, and, in the temporal sense, of a deferral, thereby adding a transgressive sophistication to the same.[34] And here we can recall Bhabha's warning that 'The problem of the articulation of cultural difference is not the problem of free-wheeling pragmatist pluralism or the "diversity" of the many', nor is it that of 'cultural relativism'.[35] Both of these simply multiply the bounded entities that Pieterse warns us against; they keep intact the idea that the self-same can remain essentially unified, separate, homogeneous, only now there are lots of them. Outlining the background to this since the Enlightenment, Malik argues that

> the belief in universalism became transformed into the concept of the natural or the eternal, while historical specificity became degraded to the idea of particularism or 'difference'. This process gave rise to the biological discourse of race, on the one hand, and the cultural discourse of difference on the other. Both wrenched apart the particular and the universal, and treated each category in isolation. In the absence of any mediation between the particular and the universal, what we had was the eternalisation of difference.[36]

Treating diversity as 'natural' thus tends to deny history and the potential for change, making culture immutable, a homologue for race, whereas the opposite pole, universality, denies difference altogether. In effect, this dichotomy treats difference as particularity, hence setting it against universality; so self/same/universal coalesce, and can be set against other/different/particular. Hence again the homogenizing drive of the project of modernity.

Nevertheless the current interest in pluralism and relativism – widely taken to be a corollary of the collapse of modern Western colonial hegemony and of the self-confident 'grand narratives' – cannot be dismissed so easily. They do, after all, have a place in the discourse of hybridity, for as was seen in the previous chapter, this discourse is itself not uniform: it entails a tension between organic fusion and contestation or critique, between the emergence of new forms and the fission into multiple forms, competing voices. By focusing on just one of these moments, pluralism is not so much wrong as one-dimensional, neglecting the inability of separating forms to achieve final separation at the expense of the *différance* that makes them possible.

All this has resonance in current debates and current cultural politics. Such debates reveal a shift away from the equality ideologies of the 'grand narratives', with their emphasis on access to citizenship, defined in essentially socio-economic terms, towards assertions of a 'right to be different', based rather on the dynamics of what has been called the 'politics of identity',[37] seen in socio-cultural terms. This can, of course, be open to the objections raised by Bhabha and Malik, but can also reveal the interpenetration, the mutual dependence, of identity and difference, in the context of a shift towards 'humble narratives', more sensitive to the local, the contextual, the everyday. In practice, the identity/difference dualism frequently provokes an emphasis on complementarity, particularly in the gender sphere, where the masculine emphasis on an exclusive either/or model of identity and rationality has increasingly been questioned in the name of a more inclusive sense of identity, based on the incorporation of feeling and emotion,[38] and with an emphasis on the reasonable rather than the rational. And Burt is doubtless right in saying that 'On an individual level, to have a rigid definition of the difference between self and Other is unhealthy, just as, at the other extreme, having no sense of difference leads to psychosis.'[39]

Ultimately, the three major themes in these cultural shifts and the discourses they have produced are, first, an emphasis on a notion of 'communication' that is less rationalist, more open to feeling and imagination, than those produced from within the Enlightenment tradition;[40] second, an emphasis on embeddedness, contextuality and embodiment, on the material and the figural rather than the discursive;[41] and third, a rethinking of notions of 'community' to make these more inclusive, less rigidly bounded.[42] All this implies an emphasis on entities as dependent on, and constituted through, relationships, and hence only ever existing as contingent, evolving; and this in turn both implies, and grows out of, a rethinking of what we mean by 'nature' itself: no longer a silent 'other', but rather the set of coexisting and evolving beings, our relationship shifting from one of domination/subordination to one of membership and community. This implies a recognition of the grounding of self in other, in 'forms of life'; the other not as occasion for consolidation of self, but for a movement of dialogue and fluidity. This would fit the case of 'madness', for example, since the very possibility of communication across the boundaries forces a rethinking of the reason/unreason, sanity/madness distinctions, thereby subverting their absolute status and transforming otherness into degrees and variations of difference, on a continuum in which 'normality' is yet another difference. In effect, this reinforces and extends aspects of civility, as emphasized in the humble narratives of modernity, rather than those associated with the grand narratives of progress and the accompanying processes of exclusion. Nor can these tendencies exist in complete immunity from the dynamics of consumer pluralism mentioned earlier; indeed, there is a tension here, as the 'difference' of culture both feeds off, and reacts against, that of market pressures. From this point of view, the postmodern could be seen as a working through of strands always present in the modern: the postmodern as the 'difference' of the modern, perhaps.

Somehow, though, this does not seem to go far enough. Ultimately, the very postulate of otherness, along with the transgressive potential of violating the taboos that separate it, seems to point to something 'beyond', something that escapes being pinned down by either project or representation, but can be made meaningful in experience mediated by the imagination. This does, of course, remain highly problematical; at the very least, the shift in the reality/representation matrix that is implied in the above discussion of aliens and cyborgs is bound to have implications for our very attempt to conceive of otherness. In particular, we confront a sense of the fundamental unclarity of the epistemological distinctions of modernity – reality/appearance, reality/illusion, reality/simulation – together with our own inability to resolve these reflexively, by standing 'outside'.

Several possibilities emerge from this. On the one hand, otherness can be displayed, shown, enacted, as an ongoing reflexive aspect of situations and actions. On the other hand, we may also encounter the exuberant carnivalesque staging of a simultaneous dissolution and affirmation of the categories themselves. Elements of both of these have been shown in the performance and display of the minstrel tradition and its culmination and transformation in Josephine Baker. And if carnival carried the threat of the unlicensed other, it also embodied the undifferentiation out of which modernity gave charismatic birth to itself, through expulsion and disavowal; carnival as the inversion of categories and the confusion of categories, the questioning of the very idea of 'category', the dissolution of boundaries in absolute, impossible transgression, carrying a message of the primacy and potency of the undifferentiated.[43] The would-be birth of the postmodern could hardly be staged more appropriately than as a parodic repeat of this monstrous birth of the modern.

But another range of possibilities emerge here. The 'hyperreal' world of simulation and virtual reality carries its own constitutive tensions, after all. In such a world, 'reality' becomes all the more precious as the ability to assert it or recognize it becomes ever more questionable. Like aura, it becomes a kind of ancestral power, a presence that sustains the world of simulation precisely by asserting its difference, its essential incompatibility with it. Something of this emerges in cyberpunk, in which the exploration of virtual reality serves to render reality itself both strange, yet inescapable as backdrop or resource.[44] 'Real' reality becomes sublime, and we become abject before it, unable to experience it save through this experience of distance itself.[45] And this is true whether it is the external world, or the reality of the self and its own identity, confronting its own inescapable hybridity by rendering it 'other' through the projection whereby the self simultaneously constitutes itself and prostrates itself. The world is thereby rendered sublime, with an aesthetic affirmation of otherness in all its simultaneous proximity and distance, in all the awesome plenitude of its power. Either way, the abjection of the subject of experience, and the sense of the object as sublime, are inseparably twinned in this strange dance of repulsion and desire. Ultimately, it is only through exploring, enacting, this 'otherness' of reality that we can be 'real'; the irony is that the very armour of project, and of consciousness as a defence against experience, becomes what we have to leave behind to experience reality. The experience of otherness is thus grasped in the theatrical relation of the sublime and the abject.

This reverses the usual pattern associated with the project of modernity, whereby the sublime becomes an occasion for the celebration of the power of human reason and a resource for strengthening the self, and it is the other that is rendered abject through domination. Rather, this reminds us of a world that is other before it is self; and what is enacted here is *failure*, the impotence of project, the inadequacy of reason and desire before their object, and the different ways of experiencing and symbolizing that failure; the modern as the vicarious experience of the sentimental pleasure and pain of the otherness of life; ultimately, perhaps, the modern as pathos.

Notes

1 See chapter 4, above.
2 D. Arnold, *The Problem of Nature: Environment, Culture and European Expansion* (Blackwell, 1996), ch. 8.
3 D. Haraway, *Primate Visions: Gender, Race and Nature in the World of Modern Science* (Routledge, 1989), p. 137.
4 Z. Sardar, 'alt.civilizations.faq: Cyberspace as the Darker Side of the West', in Z. Sardar and J. R. Ravetz (eds.) *Cyberfutures* (Pluto, 1996).
5 See my *Exploring the Modern: Patterns of Western Culture and Civilization* (Blackwell, 1998), ch. 12.
6 A. Graham, '"Are You Now or Have You Ever Been?" Conspiracy Theory and the X-Files', in D. Lavery et al., *Deny All Knowledge: Reading The X-Files* (Faber and Faber, 1996), pp. 60, 61.
7 See the account in J. E. Mack, *Abduction: Human Encounters with Aliens* (Scribner's, 1994), and the review in D. Lavery's introduction to *Deny All Knowledge*.
8 L. Badley, 'The Rebirth of the Clinic: The Body as Alien in The X-Files', in Lavery, *Deny All Knowledge*.

9   Ibid., pp. 151, 151, 148.
10 L. Sass, *Madness and Modernism* (Basic Books, 1992), and see chapters 2, 4, above.
11 Badley, 'Rebirth', p. 166.
12 L. Jones, '"Last Week We Had an Omen" The Mythological X-Files', in Lavery, *Deny All Knowledge*, p. 83.
13 J. Halberstam and I. Livingston, *Posthuman Bodies* (Indiana University Press, 1995).
14 D. Haraway, *Simians, Cyborgs and Women: The Reinvention of Nature* (Free Association Books, 1991), p. 149.
15 On cyborgs, see C. H. Gray et al. (eds.) *The Cyborg Handbook* (Routledge, 1995) and C. Penley and A. Ross (eds.) *Technoculture* (Minnesota University Press, 1991).
16 Haraway, *Simians*, pp. 149–52; and see her 'Cyborgs and Symbionts: Living Together in the New World Order', in Gray et al., *Cyborg Handbook*.
17 See references in chapter 5, above, and my *Exploring the Modern*, ch. 8; see also R. Braidotti, *Nomadic Subjects: Embodiment and Sexual Difference in Contemporary Feminist Thought* (Columbia University Press, 1994).
18 Haraway, *Simians*, p. 2.
19 Badley, 'Rebirth', pp. 156, 160.
20 L. Parks, 'Special Agent or Monstrosity: Finding the Feminine in The X-Files', in Lavery, *Deny All Knowledge*. See also A. Balsamo, *Technologies of the Gendered Body: Reading Cyborg Women* (Duke University Press, 1996).
21 Haraway, *Simians*, pp. 150, 223.
22 J. Genova, 'Tiptree and Haraway: The Reinvention of Nature', *Cultural Critique* (1994), 27, p. 18. On technology and reproduction, see also my *Exploring the Modern*, ch. 8.
23 See my *Exploring the Modern*, ch. 12.
24 N. K. Hayles, 'The Life Cycle of Cyborgs: Writing the Posthuman', in Gray, *Cyborg Handbook*, p. 323 (original emphasis).
25 For general discussion, see the 'Cyberspace, Cyberbodies, Cyberpunk: Cultures of Technological Embodiment', special issue of *Body and Society* (1995), 1:3–4.
26 S. Lefanu, *Feminism and Science Fiction* (Indiana University Press, 1989), p. 184.
27 See J. Baudrillard, *Simulations* (Semiotext(e), 1983).
28 M. Taylor, 'Reframing Postmodernisms', in P. Berry and A. Wernick (eds.) *Shadow of Spirit: Postmodernism and Religion* (Routledge, 1992), p. 21.
29 See the comment by J. Baudrillard on Disneyworld and its significance in *Simulations*, p. 25.
30 See my *Exploring the Modern*, chapter 12, on the themes in these last two sections, and chapter 7, for the sacred and the sublime.
31 The main source is E. Hobsbawm and T. Ranger (eds.) *The Invention of Tradition* (Cambridge University Press, 1992).
32 See chapter 8.
33 J. N. Pieterse, *White on Black* (Yale University Press, 1992), p. 233.
34 See J. Derrida, '*Différance*', in his *Margins of Philosophy* (Harvester Press, 1982) and, for Derrida and Bhabha, J. Purdom, 'Mapping Difference', *Third Text* (1995), 32.
35 H. Bhabha, *The Location of Culture* (Routledge, 1994), p. 245.
36 K. Malik, *The Meaning of Race: Race, History and Culture in Western Society* (Macmillan, 1996), p. 267. Malik tends towards a defence of the 'universalist' tradition.
37 See, for example, J. Weeks, *Sexuality and its Discontents* (Routledge, 1985), ch. 8.

38   K. Green, *Woman of Reason* (Polity, 1995), ch. 8. See also C. Gilligan, *In a Different Voice* (Harvard University Press, 1982).

39   R. Burt, *Alien Bodies: Representations of 'Modernity', Race and Nation in Early Modern Dance* (Routledge, 1998), p. 195.

40   The work of Habermas is an example of the latter. See his *The Philosophical Discourse of Modernity* (Polity, 1990), ch. 11.

41   See S. Lash, *The Sociology of Postmodernism* (Routledge, 1990), ch. 7.

42   Of general relevance here is Z. Bauman, *Postmodern Ethics* (Blackwell, 1993). See also S. Connor, *Theory and Cultural Value* (Blackwell, 1992).

43   Foucault's most explicit discussion of transgression tends in this direction: see his 'A Preface to Transgression', in M. Foucault, *Language, Counter-Memory, Practice: Selected Essays and Interviews* (Cornell University Press, 1977).

44   See, for example, B. Sterling (ed.) *Mirrorshades: The Cyberpunk Anthology* (Arbor House, 1985).

45   On the sublime, see my *Exploring the Modern*, ch. 7. On the abject, see, from a different angle, P. Falk 'The Representation of Presence: Outlining the Anti-Aesthetics of Pornography', *Theory, Culture and Society* (1993), 10:2, drawing on Derrida's discussion of Kant in 'Economimesis', *Diacritics* (1981), 11:1. See also J. Kristeva, *Powers of Horror: An Essay on Abjection* (Columbia University Press, 1982), ch. 1.

Key Terms

Some terms – generally in everyday use – have acquired a semi-technical meaning in recent academic discourse, and may in turn have developed a distinctive slant in this book. The following notes – inevitably rather brief and abstract – may be of some help here, as a summary or initial orientation. For 'modernity' itself, see the Introduction, and the entries below (notably **project**, **experience**, **modernism**). What might be regarded as *the* key terms – transgression, otherness – are discussed extensively in the Introduction, and hence are omitted here.

Modernism   A term with two key uses. First, it can refer, rather vaguely, to the general set of attitudes associated with modernity – an interest in the contemporary, a willingness to embrace change, a secular outlook, etc. – suggesting, in effect, a 'modern consciousness'. This could, in turn, be related to both **project** and **experience**. Second, it refers more specifically to the radical movements of renewal in the arts, from the late nineteenth century through the first three decades of the twentieth, which challenged received canons of artistic form and representation; this could be said to develop out of – and be a response to – the experiences pointed at by the first sense of the term.

Postmodernism   Initially, a generalization of the upheavals of modernism (in the second sense) through culture more generally, implicitly questioning the privileged status of art; then, as 'the postmodern', a reflexive, critical take on modernity itself, particularly modernity as **project**, associated with the apparent decline of 'grand narratives' and the accompanying confusion over values. This can also, controversially, be given a more substantive sense: see **hyperreality**, and the last chapter of this book.

Subject   In effect, a fusion of two everyday senses of the term: 'subject' as grammatical subject, a position in language; and 'subject' as subject of power, subject as entailing 'subjection'. The subject is constituted as active, but this capacity for agency depends on networks of discursive and political practices, as embedded in everyday life. Mapped on to the self, such 'subjecthood' gives us a model of the self as subject to self-control: the modern, reflexive self, disciplined yet autonomous.

Narrative   Identity as a story we tell ourselves about ourselves; a story viewed as a reflexively organized property of its own unfolding in linear time. *Grand narratives* are the ideological elaborations of these stories into theories of history, politics, evolution and 'progress' based on increasing emancipation from the constraints of nature and tradition; conversely, *humble narratives* organize the stories of our everyday lives in terms that emphasize the moral embeddedness of our choices, situations and relationships, and can include an exploration of aspects of the repetitive and the cyclical.

Project   Purposeful future-oriented activity, geared to the achievement of practical, secular goals, and capable of elaboration into life-governing values and priorities that can make sense of – and in – individual life narratives. This, in turn, entails the subjection of self and other to norms of instrumental activity; and, when this is expanded into the scientific and technological orientation to the world, treating the latter as a manipulable and divisible resource, organized according to the technical–bureaucratic division of labour, we have the *project of modernity*. Where the emphasis is on the socio-political dimensions, the aspiration to realize a rational, emancipated social order, independent of tradition, religion and imposed hierarchies, this becomes the *Enlightenment project*. The overlap between this and the project of modernity is particularly clear in the shared orientation towards an ethos of control, and in the association with the grand narratives of progress, notably socialism and capitalism, with their divergent implications for patterns of social organization that nevertheless reveal some features in common.

Experience   Important here in that a distinction can be drawn between *modernity as project* (see **project**) and *modernity as experience*. The world of modernity is crucially shaped *by* project, but is not experienced *as* project. Initially shaped by the modern encounter with the city, and the tapestry of accompanying impressions – the bright lights, the shopfronts, the garish advertisements, the constant encounters with strangers and the anonymous mass – modernity as experience refers to this sense of the immediacy of the here and now, the sense of immersion in the flux. And this may, in turn, be coupled with a sense of puzzlement or estrangement, in that the flux may also be experienced as a visual **spectacle**.

Reflexivity   The basic sense is that of self-consciousness and self-reference, fundamental to the modern attitude that self-understanding and self-control are essential in organizing life according to project. This involves bringing into explicit focus what is otherwise only implicit or presupposed, but inevitably this generates elements of paradox: when the drive of the subject to know itself results in positing itself as its own object, a process of alienation or splitting occurs. In practice, then, this reflexive attitude is inseparable from reconstructing the object; self-reflection becomes self-constitution, and is inseparable from it. Reflexivity involves a sense of 'making it up as we go along'; it involves the organization of the self, or the social world, through these very attempts at self-analysis and self-regulation.

Theatricality   Presents identity as a play of masks; through fantasy identifications, projections and roles, the self emerges as multiple, always other to itself. Social interaction becomes an 'acting-out' of identity, an exploration of the artifice at the heart of modern culture. Theatricality is always, in principle, in tension with the world of narrative and project, but, when harnessed to it, permits a degree of controlled flexibility and adaptability in relation to the world of others. In the age of spectacle and the mass media, theatricality becomes an essential component of self-identity through 'personality', the rehearsal of individuality as a distinctive attribute of each person.

Representation   Images, metaphors and descriptions have their own autonomy, their own distinctive attributes; yet they also serve to 'represent' something else, standing in for it, displacing it, while yet referring to it, or even embodying it. This dualism in representation, whereby the representation is both itself and something else, becomes particularly problematical in modernity; the positivist distrust of symbolism reduces it to 'mere' representation while simultaneously making possible the troublesome independence of such signifying systems. This has implications across the whole field of the cultural politics of representation – including the dynamics of political representation itself.

Spectacle   Takes up the everyday sense of the word, referring to a rather extravagant 'visual entertainment'; hence spectacle dramatizes the excess of representation, its ability to replace the world it represents and, in so doing, to position the self as subject to it – simultaneously incorporated in this panorama, yet excluded from real participation. Spectacle thereby also dramatizes and projects the passivity of experience, its dependence on canons of representation through which its meaning is shaped and defined.

Hyperreality   One of a group of words (virtual reality, simulation, cyberspace) introduced in an attempt to grapple with the perceived implications of computing and multimedia technology for our ways of representing, experiencing and manipulating the world of late modernity. (That is not to imply that all those terms are interchangeable, of course.) When the world of representations is sufficiently autonomous and powerful to be independent of reality, so that operations can be carried out on/in this world that have real-enough consequences for our lives, then this can be characterized as 'hyperreality'. But these consequences can also be said to follow from other developments of project in late modernity, such that the world increasingly becomes a world that is a function of our own systems of knowledge and control.

Guide to Further Reading

The most useful sources for each topic will generally be apparent from the notes to each chapter, including the works of key theorists (Bakhtin, Elias, Foucault, Bataille, and so on). However, some books have proved particularly useful in that they range over several areas or help to bring out the underlying themes, and these are listed below. The three shown in bold were particularly thought-provoking.

E. Barkan and R. Bush (eds.) *Prehistories of the Future: The Primitivist Project and the Culture of Modernism* (Stanford University Press, 1995)

H. Bhabha, *The Location of Culture* (Routledge, 1994)

R. Boyne, *Foucault and Derrida: The Other Side of Reason* (Unwin Hyman, 1990)

E. Bronfen, *Over Her Dead Body: Death, Femininity and the Aesthetic* (Manchester University Press, 1992)

N. Green, *The Spectacle of Nature: Landscape and Bourgeois Culture in Nineteenth-Century France* (Routledge, 1989)

L. Jordanova, *Sexual Visions: Images of Gender in Science and Medicine* (Harvester Wheatsheaf, 1989)

A. McClintock, *Imperial Leather: Race, Gender and Sexuality in the Colonial Context* (Routledge, 1995)

R. Nash, *Wilderness and the American Mind* (Yale University Press, 1982)

D. Outram, *The Body and the French Revolution* (Yale University Press, 1989)

V. Plumwood, *Feminism and the Mastery of Nature* (Routledge, 1993)

E. Said, *Orientalism* (Penguin, 1991)

L. Sass, *Madness and Modernism: Insanity in the Light of Modern Art, Literature and Thought* (Basic Books, 1992)

P. Stallybrass and A. White, *The Politics and Poetics of Transgression* (Methuen, 1986)

C. Taylor, *Sources of the Self: The Making of the Modern Identity* (Cambridge University Press, 1990)

T. Todorov, *The Conquest of America* (Harper and Row, 1984)

R. J. C. Young, *Colonial Desire: Hybridity in Theory, Culture and Race* (Routledge, 1995)

Index

References to Key Terms are in bold type